Language, the Learner & the School

Language the Learner & the School

Johanna S. DeStefano
The Ohio State University

JOHN WILEY & SONS

New York • Chichester • Brisbane • Toronto • Singapore

III

Library of Congress Cataloging in Publication Data

DeStefano, Johanna S.
Language, the learner, and the school.

Filmography: p.
Includes bibliographies and index.
1. Language arts.   2. Children—Language.
3. Applied linguistics.   I. Title.

LB1575.8.D48   372.6   77-13511
ISBN 0-471-02378-7

Printed in the United States of America

10 9 8 7

To my Oregon parents, John and Lila,
to my Philadelphia family,
Erminia and Uncle Peter
and to Ralph

Preface

Sitting and watching the waves coming in all the way from Japan to finally break on the coast of Oregon doesn't quite automatically turn one's mind to language, linguistics, learners, and teachers. But even against the powerful perspective of a seacoast surf, language and its effects on people remain an issue crucial to the educational enterprise. Thus, this book contains both up-to-date and comprehensive information on language and its impact on student learning from kindergarten through high school. It is specifically directed toward pre- and in-service teachers in language arts/reading/English education, and generally to others interested in language in education.

The book has two major parts. The first deals with placing language in an educational framework to illuminate its importance in the classroom, then describes the structure of language, the development of language in students, and important types of language variation, which many teachers are confronted by in their classrooms. The second section of the book is devoted to analyzing the role of language in reading, grammar and composition, and spelling—all educational applications of great significance.

It is now being commonly recognized that language is the subject matter—the central knowledge core—of the areas of language arts, reading, and English education. Methods need an "underpinning," which lies in knowledge about the language capabilities and characteristics of the learner, the materials, the teacher her or himself, and how they all interact. How can one decide intelligently on an instructional strategy for improvement if one cannot assess the developmental level of a student? In the curricular areas subsumed under language arts/reading/English education, teacher knowledge about language and various aspects of language provides the basis for intelligent pedagogical planning.

Knowledge about language comes from the related disciplines of linguistics, psycholinguistics, and sociolinguistics. Scholars in these fields have gathered data and proposed theories that have great relevance to pedagogical questions faced by teachers of language arts/reading/English education. The material in this book concentrates on the application of linguistic information and perspectives to educational issues such as those revolving around learning to read, spell, and write. Thus I determined to describe their findings and theories in terms understandable to readers with little or no background in linguistics. Here I would like to thank my many students, both undergraduates and graduates, who have accompanied me through various drafts of this book. The clarity achieved is in large part due to their careful reading and thoughtful comments about their contents.

Thanks go to many colleagues whose comments on the manuscript and inquiry about its progress were both helpful and encouraging. They include Sam Sebasta, whose observations were thoughtful, lucid, and right on; Professor John Broderick and, Professor JoAnn Juncker and Professor Frances Fairchild.

And special thanks to Barbara Fincher whose intelligent typing of the manuscript provided "one of the cleanest copies seen in a long time."

Johanna S. DeStefano
Oregon Coast
July, 1977

Contents

Language, the Learner & the School

1

The Role of Language

What do Jane Austen, Black Elk, Winston Churchill, Martin Luther King, Jr., Emily Dickenson, and Socrates have in common? Well, they are all human beings—or were. But, you say, what else? Generally, each of these people was known as or is known as an effective communicator. Socrates was so effective he was killed for his pains, as many would say was Martin Luther King, Jr. They, along with Black Elk of the Oglala Sioux, were all noted for their speaking ability: one in Ancient Greece, one in modern black America, and one among the dispossessed—the American Indians. Fortunately for us, who do now know the Indian way, Black Elk trusted John G. Neihardt enough to tell him, in Sioux, his life story. As Black Elk began,

> *My friend, I am going to tell you the story of my life, as you wish; and if it were only the story of my life I think I would not tell it; for what is one man that he should make much of his winters, even when they bend him like a heavy snow? So many men have lived and shall live that story, to be grass upon the hills (Neihardt, 1961).*

Winston Churchill was known for both his ability to speak and write. Some of us can remember his BBC radio broadcasts during World War II; then he spoke for us when fear was heaviest and doubt the most rampant. Later he was to write a monumental history of World War II. Parenthetically, he was always considered a poor student in school, one with little talent for much of anything.

And, of course, Jane Austen and Emily Dickenson were and are known for their writing—one for the deceptively quiet tales of manners and morals "danced" in drawing rooms of a disappeared yet curiously familiar society, and the other for the most carefully wrought verse pulling us into an expanded but unpretentious vision of far more than one woman's mind.

Able communicators all—in the spoken and written word. Other than being human, effectiveness in communicating is another common

1

demoninator among them. Communicating effectively is also the common demoninator of this book. Throughout, we will explore various ways of heightening the ability to communicate as well as learn about the communicative process itself.

Communicative Competence

We can think of people as possessing a set of competencies or abilities that enable them to function more or less effectively as part of a social order. For example, an individual develops and possesses a set of social competencies. What sorts of social competencies do we need in the United States? For one, we live in a culturally pluralistic society. Different cultures abound, such as various American Indian cultures, Black, French, Italian, Jewish, Latin American, and Polish. Of almost equal importance is the culture of poverty, which binds together many individuals from diverse cultures. More and more frequently now, these different cultures come into contact with one another; teachers and students are part of this contact situation. We all meet in the classroom. How do we behave in these situations? Our behavior toward others is part of our social competence.

Another set of competencies teachers are frequently concerned with is the ability to think, or cognitive competence. We want students to think "well" and are concerned about their ability to learn to think. And we notice different levels of thinking in students as they progress in school.

A third type of human competence is emotional or affective competence. Probably schools deal little with it, at least in a formal manner, but there is a developmental sequence of emotions in people. Small children have a difficult time feeling empathy, which requires them to step outside of themselves to understand what another person is feeling. Later, empathy is probably the basis of much vicarious experience that adults have, as well as a major component in understanding other people's and other cultures' points of view.

These sets of competencies—social, cognitive, and emotional—all overlap as the individual integrates thoughts and emotions in a social setting in order to make meaning from experiences. Where does communicative competence fit in? One answer is that it is a facilitator of these other competencies, the competence that helps people who are thinking, feeling beings interact with one another socially and in a meaningful way.

Here we define communicative competence essentially as competence in language use or as the language abilities of the speaker and listener (Hymes, 1972). Are you able to vary your speech and gesture to fit the expectations of others in a situation in order to transmit meaning?

Are you able to comprehend what others are communicating, what others mean whether it's spoken or written? The actual language used in the communication is only part of competence. The speaker must also know *how* and *when* to use a language or languages or different varieties of a language, and with *whom* and, of course, when not to. We don't discuss math with our ministers or speak pig Latin in the classroom. Our knowledge of what is appropriate or inappropriate is part of communicative competence and is subject to development as well. Students, as they grow and mature, play a wider role in a society, come into contact with more people, and learn how to interact with them. Gone is the silent six-year-old clinging to mother's skirts the first day of school, looking for all the world like someone who only needs a card saying Displaced Person. Enter the star of Show and Tell or a classroom lawyer able to argue the fine points of recess.

To develop the concept of communicative competence, let me quote Dell Hymes further:

> . . . *Linguistic theory treats of competence in terms of the child's acquisition of the ability to produce, understand, and discriminate any and all of the grammatical sentences of a language. A child from whom any and all of the grammatical sentences of a language might come with equal likelihood would be of course a social monster. Within the social matrix in which it acquires a system of grammar a child acquires also a system of its use, regarding persons, places, purposes, other modes of communications, etc.—all the components of communicative events, together with attitudes and beliefs regarding them. There also develop patterns of the sequential use of language in conversation, address, standard routines, and the like. In such acquisition resides the child's sociolinguistic competence (or, more broadly, communicative competence), its ability to participate in its society as not only a speaking, but also a communicating member . . . (Hymes, 1974, p. 75).*

Communicative Competence in the Language Arts Curriculum

Schools play a powerful role in increasing communicative competence, since schooling includes both instruction designed to increase ability to communicate orally and in writing (speaking and writing) and to help students comprehend others' speech and writing (listening and reading).

The teaching of literacy is a large part of the school's effort to increase a student's ability to communicate in our society.

Giving a functional role to language use as we have done, what might that role be like in the specific language arts curriculum in schools? Many educators feel that language is the major means of learning in school. In other words, much of the learning in the classroom is done verbally, especially in teacher-initiated lessons. Think about testing methods, reading groups, spelling lessons, write-ups of science experiments, and social studies reports. All of these are an important part of the curriculum and all call for verbal ability. Students are expected to speak, read, and write in the schools in our society—and to do it frequently. What does this mean in terms of expanding communicative competence?

In this society, and in our school system, communicative competence means competence in both oral and written modes of expression. Therefore, how can we as teachers help students expand their ability to communicate? First we must know as much as we can about what is considered to be highly developed competence. Then we must learn as much as we can about students' development of that competence and about what factors can facilitate or interfere with that development. Both topics are presented in some detail in Chapters 2 to 4. These chapters, respectively, deal with "mature" competence in the forms of language, with language development in children, and with the attitudinal climate in which this learning takes place and its influence on development.

Some of the components of communicative competence within the context of the language arts curriculum are shown in the following chart.

| | | Process of | |
		Decoding (receptive)	Encoding (productive)
Modes of Communication	Oral language	Listening (hearing)	Speaking
	Written language	Reading (seeing)	Writing

Oral language as a mode comprises listening and speaking in the language arts curriculum. Language is spoken to a hearer by a set of sounds—that is the speaker encodes or "sends." (This sound system will be explained in more detail in Chapter 2.) Sounds are patterned in specific ways to transmit meaning through the spoken language. The listener receives those sounds and is able to make some sense of their sequence —that is, is able to decode. The whole utterance is governed by various other sets of rules—grammatical rules (syntax) and meaning rules (semantics)—which will be described in greater detail in Chapter 2. There are also social rules, which govern utterances (Chapter 4). The student's emerging ability to encode and decode will be discussed in Chapter 3.

In mainstream American culture, we also expect a student to be literate. So the language arts curriculum contains reading and writing—the written mode. Paralleling to some extent the sound system in the oral mode is the spelling system of the written language (see Chapter 6 for greater detail). This system helps to encode meaning in writing and helps the reader decode from the printed page, just as you are doing now. Encoding can be thought of as a producing process—some message must be produced. Decoding can be thought of as more receptive, a kind of figuring out of a message encoded by someone else.

A student learning to write must master not only the spelling system of a language but also the punctuation conventions (see Chapter 7), which only in some ways parallel speech signals by indicating the ends of statements, questions, and pauses (commas) within a sentence.

Thus one should not press the similarities between the oral and written modes too far. Although speech and writing do have features in common and the systems are related in some ways, many people around the world never learn to write, yet speak as fluently as you or I. And there are many languages that have no writing system. So it is not necessarily true that if you speak, you will also write. The same distinctions can be made between listening and reading. Listening is a function of all auditorily capable people (the deaf have to learn other ways to receive messages). But not everyone reads. Also, the process of seeing (visual perception) used in reading differs in certain ways from auditory perception (hearing) used in listening. The same cues are not attended to in deciphering the message. For example, speech sounds "space" themselves differently from marks on a page. They are more continuous, not broken up into silent spaces before and after words. Don't we recognize the sentence "Donchanoit?" is said as one word? Print, on the other hand, does have blank spaces between words, although much Old English writing was done without spaces between words and evidently was not too difficult to read. In speech the ends of sentences are not always clearly signaled, while they are in writing by periods and question marks.

The chart is presented to help you visualize the various language arts curriculum components that enter into developing communicative competence in students. However, we cannot talk about such competence apart from a specific developing individual in a given cultural setting that has attitude sets influencing behavior. The chart shows more *what* is learned than *who* learns it or *what* psychological and social factors are involved.

Consequently, we will also provide information not only on what is learned but also on the nature of the learner involved in heightening his or her communicative competence. Thus, a picture of the complex communicative situations found in this country—including teacher and student in the school—will emerge in the following chapters.

The Study of Language and Communicative Competence

How many of us have heard something like the following? "I know all or just about all I need to know about language. After all, I speak, read, and write it and have for years." This is an interesting set of attitudes because, generally, most people would not presume that because we have a heart beating in our chests, we know all about it. If something is wrong, we rush to the nearest specialist, because we would agree that study is needed for understanding that organ and its function. Yet human language is as complex as the human body. It too bears close study. Linguists are individuals who study language, theorize about it, and describe it. In other words, their work gives us knowledge about language.

Language "sensitization," or knowledge about language that makes us more conscious about it, is central to the language arts curriculum. The data in the succeeding chapters represent a great deal of knowledge about language and help form the core of knowledge for the language arts curriculum.

But first, let's look at how linguists view language. They rather consciously work on the basis of certain premises about the nature of language. These premises can be considered "culture fair" because they are not bound by any particular culture's set of judgments about language. Cultures usually do have a set of language judgments just as they have judgments about other realms of human behavior. Because the judgments are culturally constrained, they must be recognized as being ethnocentric and restricted to a specific culture.

Linguists try to avoid ethnocentric attitudes, and they usually succeed by supplanting a culturally bound set of premises with a set not bound in this manner. However, linguists are not suggesting that "anything goes" as far as language is concerned. They do not promote the use of double negatives or "ain't," although they may describe their use. Instead, it is up to a given culture to decide what "goes" or what "doesn't go." What is considered "proper language" is a cultural decision, varying to some extent from culture to culture. Linguists take another approach regarding language and try to look at it as nonjudgmentally as possible when dealing with various structures in language and with how language functions. A linguist may also describe a given culture's judgments about language.

First Premise:

A major premise of those studying language is that it is patterned. Whatever language or variety of language we care to talk about is a system of patterns. If a language were not patterned and its speakers could speak any way they wanted to, they probably wouldn't be able to understand each other because they could create forms and other patterns as they went along. It's as if I began to say "Milk scat hot like black" instead of "Black cats like hot milk." But in English we have a pattern we follow for making nouns plural. We don't add on the plural form at the beginning of a word as I did above with *scat* (*s* + *cat*). We put the plural form at the end of a word—*cats.* In the writing system we pluralize by adding —*s;* in speaking we pluralize by selecting one of three sounds or sound combinations. (The specifics of pluralizing will be discussed in Chapter 2.)

We probably are not aware consciously of most of the patterns of English, but we certainly "know" them in the sense of using them when we speak or write, listen or read.

Second Premise:

A second premise of many linguists is that every language or variety of a language is as able to communicate what its speakers need to say as is any other language or variety. To the contrary, it was long felt in England that Latin was a language more capable of communicating about such matters as philosophy than English was. People thought that English simply could not convey the subtleties and nuances of thought that Latin could. In fact, the great poet John Milton made a conscious decision to write much of his poetry in English and not in Latin. It is said he did it because of "patriotic feelings" even though he knew far more people could read his work if he had written in Latin. So he cut down on his potential audience and took a bit of a chance with his literary reputation to write *Paradise Lost* in English.

Today, of course, linguists would not agree that English is "deficient" to Latin in communicative power, since each language is felt to be able to cope with the communication needs of its speakers. Taking English again, probably those who spoke only English—namely the uneducated lower classes and most women—had little time, encouragement or education to think about metaphysics and other such niceties of an intellectual, leisured life. But English grew as a language when those who spoke it wanted to talk about metaphysics. The means were there; the attitudes and social climate had not been conducive to it. Now English is widely recognized as a language used in science and philosophy around the world. At one time, of course, no one talked in any language about the concepts that go into the category of, let's say, nuclear physics, but English (with a penchant for borrowing words from other languages) was capable of expanding to include that new area. And all languages can expand, if the speakers feel the need for it. I am definitely *not* saying that English is more suited to scientific discourse than other languages. After all, the Russians got into space before we did—and with Russian!

Third Premise:

A third premise in linguistics is that language change is a matter of fact, not a symptom of decay. Popular feeling generally holds with the latter; Samuel Johnson, the compulsive dictionary writer, bemoaned the fact that *mob* (short for *mobile*) was becoming such a widely used word in his day because it was "imprecise" and also not fit for those of "better standing" to use. In other words, change represented decay. But it is impossible for us to read *Beowulf* in the original, and Chaucer's *Canterbury Tales* is what we euphimistically call "a challenge." Shakespeare's grammar and vocabulary baffle the uninitiated. And if George Washington were to appear now, few of us would believe he would be speaking American English. If he weren't the "Father of our country," we'd probably go into a fit of chuckles about his speech. Languages do change and can change radically over time as Modern English has changed from Old English.

Usage "rules" also change. What was socially acceptable at one time is not necessarily acceptable at another time. In Shakespeare's plays, you'll find double negatives. Elizabeth the First used them, as did Mary, Queen of Scots. *Aks* was a perfectly acceptable, even high-toned pronunciation of *ask;* currently, it is not as acceptable. Certainly now, in the 1970s, *mob* is a perfectly respectable word, rubbing shoulders with such fashionable ones as *heuristic* and *linguistics.* Linguists do not tend to make usage judgments; instead they state descriptively how language changes. What's here today will perhaps be gone in the next century, especially certain types of vocabulary (lexicon), with grammar (syntax) and sounds (phonology) changing more slowly.

In fact, when language change is mandated or decreed to stop, it may mean that a particular language is doomed to become "dead." Evidently

Sanskrit is a case in point. A certain branch of it became the language of Brahman religious ritual and so was decreed by the monks not to be changed. The people, however, went on speaking, and their varieties of Sanskrit changed so much that the average person had to learn the religious Sanskrit as another language.

Language change can also lead to new languages. For example, the Romance languages spoken today are related, all coming originally from Latin. Latin changed, and changed enough over time to evolve into the varieties of French, Italian, Portuguese, Roumanian and Spanish, as well as other less well-known languages such as Sardinian and Dalmation (coast of Yugoslavia), which disappeared as a living language in 1898 when its last speaker stepped on a land mine.

Fourth Premise:

Language is considered an arbitrary system, with its words and other structures having no necessary connection with objects and such things. Our word *dog* is no more "accurate" than the French *chien* or German *hund* to indicate the four-legged, furry "Man's best friend." All indicate well the living animal. We say a dog goes "bow-wow;" the Japanese say a dog goes "tan-tan." So even these so-called sound words or onomatopoetic words do not have that strong a connection to the reality of a dog's bark. They too may vary from language to language; they too are symbols of an event known as a dog barking. We "know" this because we often laugh when children say, "I know why a pig is called a pig. Because it's dirty." In their minds, they think "pig" *is* that dirty animal they can see snuffling about, while we as adults know that "pig" is merely the English symbol set used to designate a rather maligned but intelligent barnyard animal. But even among adults, a bit of "word magic" may cling—meaning the word is the thing itself in some way. This attitude is even reinforced by some phrases and sentences that are in fact actions, such as, "I now pronounce you man and wife." The saying of that phrase by someone properly authorized does, in fact, make two people husband and wife in the eyes of society and under the law. The same thing happens when someone christens a ship. The ship is given an official name through the utterance of a sentence. Generally, however, this use of language is far more rare than its symbolic use. The sequence of sounds making up *sun* is obviously not the same in every language. Different sound sequences stand for the same object in our experience. Thus, the spoken language is a system of symbols.

These four premises undergird the material presented in this book

9

and also form a part of the contribution linguistics has to make to enlarging definitions of what constitutes communicative competence. This process can be effectively assisted by a greater consciousness on the part of the teacher about the nature of language, its structure, and function. This is one of the major contributions linguistics can make to the language arts curriculum—expanding the definition of communicative competence, not to the point of meaninglessness but to the point of making it a meaningful concept for a multicultural society. The following chapters are designed to play a major role in expanding the concept by providing information about language from a variety of viewpoints.

Bibliography

Baugh, Albert. *A History of the English Language.* Second Edition. London: Routledge & Kegan Paul Ltd., 1959.

Hymes, Dell. *Foundations in Sociolinguistics, An Ethnographic Approach.* Philadelphia, Pennsylvania: University of Pennsylvania Press, 1974.

Hymes, Dell. "Introduction" in *Functions of Language in the Classroom,* edited by Courtney Cazden, Vera John, and Dell Hymes. New York: Teachers College Press, 1972.

Labov, William. "The Logic of Nonstandard English" in James E. Alatis, (editor), *Linguistics and the Teaching of Standard English.* Monograph Series on Languages and Linguistics, No. 22, Washington, D.C.: Georgetown University Press, 1969. Also in *Language, Society and Education: A Profile of Black English.* Johanna S. DeStefano, editor. Worthington, Ohio: Charles A. Jones Publishing Co., 1973.

Neihardt, John G. *Black Elk Speaks;* Being the Life Story of a Holy Man of the Oglala Sioux. Lincoln, Nebraska: University of Nebraska Press, 1961.

For Further Reading:

Baugh, Albert. *A History of the English Language.* A very readable book that gives much detail on the origin of English and the changes it's gone through from Anglo-Saxon times to the present. Information on how English was viewed by its speakers throughout its history.

2

The Structure of Language

In this chapter we examine some characteristics of the form of the language we call American English. However, much of the information is applicable to other languages as well because there are certain characteristics that all languages share. This sharing of characteristics is not surprising, since any natural[1] language is as systematic and patterned as any other. And the range of patterns is not unlimited. So, while there is noticeable diversity among languages, there is also much similarity.

Those features shared by languages are called *universals.* One universal noted by linguists is that all languages have a way of turning sentences into questions or commands. So the assertion "You did it" can become, if a speaker wants, "Did you do it?" or "Do it"—all in a very orderly way. Other languages may do the specific changes somewhat differently, but the basic pattern is the same. Another universal is that all languages have two classes of modifiers that behave like adjectives and adverbs. In other words, they pattern with nouns and verbs. And another universal is that all languages have a mechanism to create noun phrases (nominals) from other forms. For example, "a mother works" can become "a working mother," or "Toby left" can become "You know that Toby left." Finally, all languages can make a positive sentence into a negative one (Bolinger, 1968, 18). These basic patterns shared by languages constitute universals and are receiving widespread study at the present time. They are important partly because they can tell us a great deal about where differences actually exist among languages and something about the relative importance of those differences.

The following relatively brief description of the forms of American English can also be seen as a partial description of mature language competence. When I discuss the phonological system, for example, I am essentially presenting a model of "mature" speech to which children, as they develop, get closer and closer. In other words, we are looking at a

---

[1]Natural in this case means not an artificial, "created" language such as pig Latin or Esperanto.

component of communicative competence. In order to communicate to American English speakers, a person must know the forms of the language and how to arrange those forms in peculiarly English ways. The various forms are the "building blocks" of an utterance and a basic part then, of communicative competence. Students need to have a firm grasp of these "blocks" in order to communicate. Some facets of their expanding competence in this area are presented in Chapter 3.

The following description of the forms of American English is also offered to better prepare you to read educational journals and books in which much of the terminology and many of the concepts appear. Because linguistic applications to language arts and reading are central to that curriculum, you will see more and more of these concepts and terms appearing in the material you read. This is because we are now dealing with the subject matter of language arts—*language.*

A Look at Formal Linguistics

The study of form or structure in language may be divided into three areas: *phonology, syntax* and *semantics.* Sometimes the dividing lines among the three areas are quite fuzzy, since semantics, or the meaning component of a language, can be expressed through the sound (phonology) as well as through combinations of words into sentences (syntax). However, you will learn about the various elements included in these areas and something about how these elements pattern in English.

Phonology

Phonological studies have dealt with the systems of sounds in various languages. In a given language, let's say English, there is a group or range of sounds speakers and hearers of English recognize as being English, including both vowel and consonant sounds. For example, an English *r* sound is different from a French *r* sound, which sounds like it's made far down in the throat. In American English we tend not to trill *r*'s as they do in some other languages. Also, Spanish has fewer vowel sounds than English. And French has heavily nasalized vowels (say an *o* with your nasal cavity helping like it does with *m* or *n*), while English has far less nasalized ones, and only in certain sound environments. Hearing these different sounds produced, we either think we are hearing a foreign language or a foreigner speaking English. It strikes our ear as not being quite English.

Sounds also pattern in certain ways, into sequences "permissible" in the English language. Linguists, to illustrate English sound sequences, often use nonsense words because they don't have a meaning attached to them. But some have come to have some meaning. For example, *bik* used to be a nonsense word but, with a change in spelling, it's now the name of a pen line. And it's acceptable because it's a possible English sequence; it rhymes with *kick* and *pick,* both "good" English words. We would also recognize *shrib* as a possible word in English, but not *dzhrulv.* The sequence of sounds in *shrib* fits other English sequences: we have words that begin with *shr* as in *shrink,* and we have words that end with *ib* as in *bib* and *rib. Dzhrulv,* on the other hand, contains few permissible sequences. We do not begin words with *dzhr.* Nor do we even begin words with *zh;* in English it is a medial (middle) sound, as in *azure* or, very uncommonly, a final sound, as in *beige.* So *dzhrulv* sounds foreign, or at least un-English to us.

When we look at actual English sound sequences, we see that words may not begin with more than three consonant sounds. And, if they begin with three, the first sound must be an *s* as in *strip* and *split.* The second sound must be a *p, t,* or *k,* and the third must be an *l, r, w,* or *y.* So in English we can have *spray,* and *squint* where the first sequence is *skw.* But we cannot have such sequences as *ftr-, ktv-,* or *dzhr-,* although other languages may "permit" them (Moulton, 1973). Therefore, not only do we have an English group of sounds but we also have an English set of sound combinations.

Syntax

Another area of language structure is syntax, often called grammar. Before continuing, we should define *grammar* as the term is used here, because there are at least three different meanings often given the word, and one of these is used in a way specific to certain linguistic studies.

One common use of *grammar* is in "grammar book," meaning a volume that contains information about patterns used in a language. We speak of French grammars, Italian grammars, and so on. The term is *not* used in this sense in our discussion of grammar; grammar here does not mean a book written about language.

Nor is a second common definition of *grammar* the one represented in this chapter. *Grammar* is often used to refer to the forms students use in their speech and writing. A student may use "good grammar" or "bad grammar." The term "bad grammar" usually refers to forms such as "she ain't comin," "I don't got none," "Ron gave it to Sue and I," and "It's me." These are what is generally considered "substandard" English, that is, English that isn't quite acceptable to many people, including many teachers. "Good grammar," on the other hand, is what is considered to be "standard English," which is socially accepted usage. "Socially accepted" needs to be stressed in this definition of grammar because it is the key to this definition. What's acceptable is thus a "standard," but what's "good" changes when social decisions change about speech. In Chapter 1 we discussed how, for example, *aks* for *ask* was perfectly acceptable English at one time. But its social acceptance declined over a period of time until now it is considered "bad grammar." This definition of grammar rests on usage that is socially judged, and therefore it is part of a prescriptive set of attitudes toward language. This definition is not the one used here and is one that has little place in linguistic studies.

The definition of *grammar* used here rests on what people do when they speak their language—create sentences that are recognizable as that particular language. This type of grammar is "the knowledge of a language possessed by every native speaker of that language" (Dale, 1976, 65). Grammar is thus seen as an unconsciously held set of rules by which people generate (or create) sentences recognized as, for example, English and by which they decide whether or not a sentence is English. These rules are seen to be acquired early in life as even small children "sound" English or French or Swahili when they speak, depending on their native language. Children are able to generate recognizable sentences at a fairly young age and not to say things such as "A cat black is mine," which would be ungrammatical in English. As native speakers of English, we would also recognize that "Sunlight plants helps green grow" is ungrammatical. Our English rule set (our grammar) doesn't specify such sentences as English. It helps us judge what is an English construction and what is not. We know "Throw mama from the train a kiss" is somehow not completely an English construction; that is, it is not totally generated by a set of rules that generates English sentences. Some linguists attempt to discover these rules which, according to Langacker, are " . . . the principles that specify what strings of words are well-formed sentences of the language, a description of the intrinsic structure of the linguistic system" (Langacker, 1973, 35). So grammars in the book sense may be written to clarify or describe this grammar, which each of us possesses as a native speaker of a language, whether we are young or old, educated or uneducated, lower class or middle class.

The study of grammar, or syntax, traditionally has to do with the patterning of sounds into larger units such as morphemes,[2] phrases, and

---

[2]Morphology is often treated as a separate category, sometimes as phonology, and often as part of syntax. I've chosen the last use in keeping with the distinction often made between sound and meaning.

14

sentences. The sentence is the largest unit often dealt with in much linguistic study. A morpheme is defined as the smallest unit of meaning in a language, largely to distinguish it from sounds that have no meaning in and of themselves and from words that can often be broken down into smaller units of meaning. Take the word *cats.* It means something like "more than one animal which is a four-legged creature, has fur, etc.," and the meaning is coded by the morphemes *cat* and *-s.* The *-s* hooked onto *cat* means, in effect, "more than one." The area of syntax, including morphemes, will be dealt with in more detail below.

Semantics

Finally, a third system within language is semantics, which is the meaning component. Vocabulary, or lexicon, is mostly studied as part of semantics because of emphasis on the meaning of words as opposed to their structure. This is probably the most problematic and least studied area of language, perhaps because it bridges the gap between thought and the structures used to express thought. But it is also a crucial area in language study precisely because of this connection.

These various systems within language can be connected in a meaningful way, thereby specifying a model of the "path" from a thought to its actual utterance. The speaker, beginning with a conceptual structure of some sort, makes a mostly unconscious choice of certain lexical items (or vocabulary) in order to encode the meaning selected from the conceptual structure. The lexicon is then arranged according to the syntactic rules of a given language. That grammatical organization has a set of phonological rules applied to it so that it becomes an actual physical utterance recognizable as English and conveying the conceptual message. At all levels of language there are sets of rules, and the rules are probably applied, in turn, in an unconscious, rule-governed way. In other words, a speaker applies "systematic principles of formation" to an utterance (Lyons, 1970, 21). So the key to language study is *system.* Let us first examine some aspects of the phonological system of American English.

Phonology: Sounds in American English

Sounds of a language (phonetic units) are often described by the location in which the sound is articulated or made by the vocal apparatus, such as tongue and lips (articulatory phonetics), or described by the physical properties of the sound itself (acoustic phonetics). These two approaches are very useful in answering certain questions, especially in speech pathology and audiology. However, most of the questions teachers ask about the sounds in American English in connection with reading, spelling, and usage suggest another way of looking at the sound system by using the concept of *phoneme,* which is not based on articulation or the physical nature of a sound. In fact, a phoneme is actually an abstract unit and not a sound we utter. As Fromkin and Rodman put it, "We do not utter phonemes; we produce *phones,* that is, phonetic segments." (Fromkin and Rodman, 1974, 71).

The sound system is usually divided into two categories: segmentals and suprasegmentals. *Segmentals* are the consonant and vowel sounds we produce with our articulators, including the tongue and lips. These sounds are discrete in that we can tell one from another. We know, for example, that there are three sounds in *kick* and two in *at.* Hence they are segments. *Suprasegmentals* are those elements that overlie but go along with consonants and vowels and are called intonation patterns. Because of intonation, we do not talk in a monotone. They are called *supra-* because they pattern across or over phonemes. Some linguists have referred to suprasegmentals as the "melody" of speech; and certainly each language has its distinctive "melody" as well as its set of vowels and consonants. In fact, the suprasegmentals have a great deal to do with a speaker sounding "native" or "foreign" because of the differences in intonation patterns among languages.

Phonemes in American English

The human voice is capable of making a vast variety of sounds that do not lend themselves neatly to segmentation. In other words, it is difficult to distinguish one from the other, especially on the basis of where in the mouth they are articulated or on the basis of their physical properties. Yet in English we have little trouble distinguishing *chip* from *gyp* if the two are presented as a pair vocally. We know the two words mean different things. And practically the only difference is the voicing of the /ǰ/ in *gyp* and the nonvoicing of the /č/ in chip.[3] Put your fingers over your vocal cords and say *gyp,* holding the *g* sound. Then say *chip,* holding the *ch* sound. Do you notice the vibration in *gyp?* Voiced means simply that the vocal cords vibrate when the sound is produced or do not vibrate if it is unvoiced.

Sets of words such as *gyp* and *chip, tip* and *dip,* with only one noticea-

[3] The / / indicate that the letter or letters inside them stand for phonemes; thus the letters are not like letters of the alphabet, which are used for the written language but not the spoken.

16

ble difference between them, are what are called *minimal pairs*. These pairs are often used in beginning reading instruction to contrast a single difference in sound between two words.

Voicing of a consonant in English, as opposed to being unvoiced, is one of the differences that makes a difference. These distinctive differences effect what we recognize as *phonemes*. A phoneme is a range of sounds that a native speaker recognizes as different from all other ranges; it functions as a different sound. It could also be called a class of sounds, since acoustically and from the standpoint of articulation what we call a phoneme is made up of a group of sounds. Some sounds in this group may be different from the sounds in other phonemes, but are not distinctive differences. In other words, these differences do not make a difference to us; they are not distinctive in helping us distinguish between two pho-

Table 1

	Initial (Beginning) Phoneme in	Medial (Middle) Phoneme in	Final Phoneme in
/b/ (voiced)	bit	fibber	robe
/p/ (voiceless)	pit	supper	rope
/d/ (voiced)	dip	leader	seed
/t/ (voiceless)	tip	butter	seat
/g/ (voiced)	got	beggar	rag
/k/ (voiceless)	cot	pocket	rack
/v/ (voiced)	van	oven	knive
/f/ (voiceless)	fan	gopher	knife
/z/ (voiced)	zing	losing	lies
/s/ (voiceless)	sing	sassing	lice
/ǰ/ (voiced)	gyp	midget	edge
/č/ (voiceless)	chip	pitcher	pitch
/ð/ (voiced)	thy	either	bathe
/θ/ (voiceless)	thigh	ether	bath
/ž/ (voiced)	not an initial phoneme in English	measure	rouge (for some; others may make the same ending sound as in *judge*)
/š/ (voiceless)	shop	mesher	dish

17

nemes. Thus, several or more sounds are classified as a single phoneme because their differences are not important. Think about the difference between the /p/ in *pit* and *tip* used in a sentence. Say "Tip the refuse into the pit" rapidly, listening carefully to the two /p/s. The /p/ in *tip* almost "disappears," while it's quite noticeable in *pit.* They are obviously different sounds, but as English speakers, we do not pay attention to these differences.

In English, phonemes are usually categorized first as to whether they are consonants or vowels. Within the consonant phonemes, a major distinction is between voiced and voiceless. In many languages, voicing is not distinctive; that is, it is not used to distinguish one phoneme from another. But it is distinctive in English. Table 1 presents English consonant phonemes in pairs according to voicing.

There are also the *nasal continuant* consonants, or *nasals.* These phonemes are produced by air escaping through the nose as well as the mouth; contrast *bad* with *mad* (see Table 2).

Table 2

	Initial Phoneme in	Medial Phoneme in	Final Phoneme in
/m/	map	hammer	ram
/n/	nap	panner	ran
/ŋ/	Not an initial phoneme in English	singer	rang

Another category of consonant phonemes is that of the "liquids," which, taken phonetically, are quite complicated sounds and are very similar acoustically. As you are probably aware, Japanese speakers do not make a phonemic difference between /l/ and /r/, and as a result give us fits of giggles over "flied lice." Thus, our distinctive differences between these two sounds are not distinctive for them. Probably when we attempt

Table 3

	Initial Phoneme in	Medial Phoneme in	Final Phoneme in
/l/	lap	caller	reel
/r/	rap	barrel	rear

to speak Japanese we give them fits of giggles about our nondifferentia-
tion between certain of their phonemes (see Table 3).

Finally, in English we have what are sometimes called *glides* because
of their articulatory nature, as illustrated in Table 4. In words they must
be preceded or followed by a vowel (Fromkin and Rodman, 52). To pronounce them, the tongue moves quickly in a gliding manner toward or
away from the neighboring vowel. Since they pattern with certain vowels,
they are also called *semivowels.*

Table 4

	Initial Phoneme in	Medial Phoneme in	Final Phoneme in
/h/	hill	rehash	
/w/	will	mowing	These usually do not occur finally in
/y/	yes	playing	English.

For an analysis of consonant phonemes in English, the minimal pairs
we have presented in the initial phoneme position make fairly clear the
contrasts or differences we pay attention to in English. But the vowel
system is more complicated than the consonant system. For example,
vowels vary much more among various varieties of a language than consonants do. The vowels presented in the chart below represent only one
variety of American English. This is important to note because not all
teachers and students in schools use the same vowel system. A student's
speech may vary systematically from a teacher's. This has important
implications for the teaching of reading and spelling in which sometimes
students are taught to make phoneme-grapheme (sound-letter) relationships different from their own. This is generally now felt to be unneces-
sary. For example, a common pronunciation, found to be widespread in
the South, is /pIn/ for both *pin* and *pen.* In other words, there is no vowel
contrast. So they will read aloud *pin* and *pen* as /pIn/, but they know the
difference in meaning.

The vowel chart presented here (Table 5) is organized according to
the articulation points of the vowels, which are pronounced by placing the
tongue along two planes—high to low in the mouth and front to back in
the mouth. The two planes intersect to produce, for example, high front
vowels. Pronounce a vowel such as /i/ (as in *need*) and feel where your
tongue is. Then pronounce /æ/ (as in *cat*) and feel the difference.

Table 5

| | Part of Tongue Involved | | |
	Front	Central	Back
High	/i/ as in *bead* ("long *e*")		/u/ as in *pool* ("long *u*")
	/I/ as in *bid*		/U/ as in *put, foot*
Mid	/e/ as in *laid* ("long *a*")		/o/ as in *pole* ("long *o*")
	/ɛ/ as in *bet*	/ə/ as in *the* (schwa sound)	/ɔ/ as in *taught*
Low	/æ/ as in *bat*	/ʌ/ as in *but*	/a/ as in *pot*

There are also the common *diphthongs:* /ay/ as in *bite* ("long *i*"); /ɔy/ as in *boil;* and /æw/ as in *round.* A diphthong is a vowel sound and a glide, which function as a single sound in English. To feel how much gliding movement there is, say *bait* and then say *bat,* which contains a "simple" vowel or, more accurately, a *monophthong* to contrast it with a diphthong.

The common terms "long" and "short" are not descriptive of the length of time spent producing a vowel; in English we don't pronounce the vowel in *bat* any more quickly than we do the vowel in *bait,* although one is called "short *a*" and the other "long *a.*" However, there are two subsystems in English vowels that the traditional terms "short" and "long" indicate. The so-called short vowels are produced with relatively little muscular tension in the articulators; these are *lax* vowels. The "long" vowels are *tense* vowels because there is far more muscular tension in their production. Contrast the vowel in *bed* with the vowel in *bead.* The first is *lax* and the second is *tense.*

Again to illustrate differences in vowel systems in a language, note that in some American English varieties there is no difference in the vowel pronunciation in pairs such as *pot—brought, cot—caught,* and *tot—taught.* The /a/ - /ɔ/ distinction is dropped. Also in some varieties, *Mary, merry* and *marry* are all pronounced differently; a person may say /mɛri/ for *merry,* /mæri/ for *marry,* and /meri/ for *Mary.* In my variety, I say /mɛri/ for all three. Such differences are not infrequent in English partly because of the relatively great number of vowel phonemes we have in the language. Spanish, for example, has fewer vowel phonemes and fewer differences among vowel systems in the language's various varieties.

In American English, the schwa phoneme, /ə/, is one of the most common vowels. That is, it appears very frequently in speech and probably offers the greatest spelling problems of any sound because of its occurrence in unstressed syllables. What do we do when we find /ə/ in *janitor?* We could make a case for its appearance twice in the less heavily stressed syllables = /ĵænətər/. Here the /ə/ is spelled with an *i* and an *o*. When stress weakens, the oral language doesn't help clarify which letter is used to spell the /ə/. In fact, virtually all vowel *letters* are used to spell that single vowel sound in American English. (The /ə/ will be discussed in more detail in Chapter 6 on spelling.)

Since a phoneme is an abstraction or convenient construct and not an actual sound, when we do a phonemic analysis of American English we find that there are differences in the pronunciation of a phoneme or in the pronunciation of sounds making up what we call a phoneme. Say *tip* and *sit* quickly in "Tip the bucket over and sit down" and note the difference between the two /t/s. As Bolinger puts it, "Phonemes are indeed affected by the company they keep . . . " (1968, 43), meaning that different places in words and between words affect the pronunciation of a sound. /t/ in one word is not necessarily the same /t/ in another word. In some words /t/ is aspirated—given a burst of air as we often do with /h/ as in *hello* or *help*. Listen carefully when you say "My *toe* is hurt." But it is not aspirated in final position as in "Who broke my *pot?*" Nor is it aspirated in a middle position, as in "Are you coming *later?*" There it is *flapped*. (Say *butter* and *later* in contrast to *toe*.) The /p/ in /pIn/ is also aspirated, but it is not in /spIn/. These differences are quite regular in English, but they are physical differences that are not recognized as creating minimal pairs. Instead they are variations of a phoneme called *allophones* or *phones*. They are the actual produced sounds. However, since these differences are not distinctive, native speakers don't pay much attention to them as they do to phonemic differences. /pIn/ and /bIn/ mean different things, but an aspirated or unaspirated /p/ in /pIn/ would not make a difference in meaning.

Since many of these differences are not distinctive in English, they probably are not as important to teachers as those that are distinctive. However, it is useful to remember that a phoneme stands for a range of actual sounds rather than a single actual sound, even though it is symbolized that way. This difference will become important especially when we learn about children who teach themselves to spell (Chapter 6).

Suprasegmentals in American English

We also have intonation patterns in the English sound system. These patterns have been broken down into at least four distinct categories: *stress, pitch, juncture,* and *terminals*. Sometimes *junctures* and *terminals* are both classed as *pauses*. These are called *suprasegmental* because some overlay as well as pattern with the segmental phonemes of vowels and consonants but cannot occur without some sounds being made. For example, juncture is silence between sounds. The four types also pattern together. In other words, with a certain set of pitches you will have a specific stress pattern as well as a juncture and terminal set. These patterns combine systematically with the segmental phonemes; in fact, some patterns are obligatory in English. In other words, in order to "sound English," you must end a sentence with a certain intonation pattern. So you get a "melody line" that combines stress, pitch, and terminals in specific ways to make you sound like a native speaker. Intonation systems often give away foreign speakers because these systems may vary from language to language, and we usually preserve our native system when we speak another language. Thus my American accent in speaking French is partly due to my use of American English intonation patterns rather than French patterns.

Stress, or the loudness with which a sound is produced relative to other sounds by more or less energy in the air flow from the lungs, is usually described as having four significant degrees in American English:

/ ⁄ /	primary or heavy stress
/ ʌ /	secondary or medium stress
/ ⌵ /	tertiary or light stress
/ ◡ /	unstressed or weak stress

In a physical sense, stress probably occurs along a continuum, but we perceive different, discrete degrees of stress. The four degrees of stress distribute themselves over a series of words in order to help convey the meaning intended by the speaker. To use an example from Wardhaugh (1972, 64), a speaker will say something like:

When talking about a *car*	ă/hót ròd
When talking about a hot *piece* of metal	ă/hôt ród
When talking about a *hot* piece of metal	ă/hôt ród

Notice how the contrasts in meaning are achieved through the contrasts in the stress patterns used.

And we can make intonation jokes with stress placement (Lefevre, 1970, 229):

He always puts the emphásis on the wrong sylláble.

He is a cómič boòk
saîesmăn.   (The books are funny.)

He is a còmič bóok
saîesmăn.   (The salesman is funny.)

Pitch in American English has often been analyzed into three or four levels, beginning with low (or /1/) to normal (/2/) to high (/3/) to extra high (/4/). These levels are relative to each speaker, a man's highest pitch being lower than many women's high pitch. Pitch occurs in a *contour* over a word, phrase, or sentence. Taking the noun and verb *record,* notice the pitch contour differences:

Noun	*Verb*
record	record
3 ⟍	3
2	2 ⌐

That new record is a block buster.	Did you record those figures?

This type of pitch contour is obligatory in American English and not what we could call interpretive. In other words, *record* is marked as a noun by a 3-2 pitch contour and becomes a verb with a 2-3 contour. These contours cannot be changed without changing the class of the word itself.

Pitches pattern intimately with *stress.* Taking the above *record* example, we can also add stress patterns to it to get:

Noun	*Verb*
récord	recórd
3 ⟍	3
2	2 ⌐

The stress is placed differentially in American English to distinguish nouns from verbs as well as compound nouns from adjectives plus nouns, for example. Note the stress differences in:

Compound Noun	*Adjective + Noun*
gréenhouse	green hoúse
bláckbird	black bírd

23

Not only are pitch and stress related, but both are related to *juncture* (/ + /), which means pauses between words. Juncture—or a significant pause—is used to contrast such pairs as:

nitrate and *night* / + / *rate*
ice / + / *cream* and *I* / + / *scream*
great / + / *rain* and *grey* / + / *train*
needed / + / *rain* and *need* / + / *a* / + / *drain*
neat / + / *trick* and *knee* / + / *trick*

Finally, pitch and stress are related to *terminals* or terminal contours, which are used to indicate ends of sentences or other units. The three common terminals noted in American English are / ＼ / falling, / ‖ / rising, and / | / level. We often end both statements and questions in English with a / ＼ / terminal contour.

Say:
Linguists write long sentences. / ＼ /
    and
Do linguists write long sentences? / ＼ /

Notice your voice fades and falls on sentences. Or you may use a level terminal to end a question.

Do linguists write long sentences? / | /

However, if there is no question word such as *how* or question inversion such as *do you*, we end questions with a rising contour.

Say:
Linguists write long sentences? / ‖ /

We also use rising contours when we denote a series as in:

I am buying peaches / ‖ /, pears / ‖ /, apples / ‖ /, and oranges / ＼ /.

Level terminal contours are used in sentences such as direct quotes to indicate the end of the quote.

"She wept bitterly / | /," I said. / ＼ /

They are also used to mark off syntactic units such as noun groups from the verb part of a sentence, particularly if the noun part is rather lengthy.

Say:

The mongoose who lives in our garden / | / loves to kill cobras.
That Picasso painting hanging on the wall / | / is worth $1,000,000.

It is possible to transcribe language into both segmental and suprasegmental phonemes, which then gives a much clearer picture of how our language patterns orally. We have both the distinctive "melody" of English and the distinctive sets of sounds. Such a transcription of a noun phrase could look like:

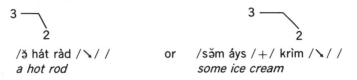

| /ɔ hát ràd /↘/ / | or | /sǎm áys / + / krìm /↘/ / |
| a hot rod | | some ice cream |

A transcription attempts to show what is said by a speaker of a language.

So far I've been describing obligatory intonation patterns—that is the patterns "required" of an English speaker. But we also use intonation in an interpretive way to convey meaning. There's the old saw, "I like what you said but not the way you said it." The words meant one thing but the "tone of voice" meant another. Or take the sentence, "You didn't say that" and place primary stress on each word in turn:

Yóu didn't say that. (Someone else must have.)

You dídn't say that. (You couldn't have said that!)

You didn't sáy that. (Perhaps you *wrote* it instead.)

You didn't say thát. (You said something else.)

Depending on stress placement, that one set of words can have at least four different interpretations. Also think about how many ways you can say *no.* You can be adamant, ashamed, curt, polite, and so forth—all depending on intonation patterns. Or think of how many ways you can say *yes.* Students often take pleasure in such experimentation, which also enters into becoming a skilled oral reader. The oral interpretation of literature is done almost solely through intonation patterns, which are varied to convey different meanings.

As a teacher, you can do a great deal to expand students' vocabulary and knowledge of complex sentence patterns through skillfully reading aloud to them. Students can comprehend orally far more difficult material than they can read, especially in the lower grades. But I found that even high school students comprehended much more from hearing *The Merchant of Venice* read aloud skillfully than from reading it themselves. Again, much of that comprehension rested in what was conveyed through the suprasegmental system of English.

Syntax: The Grammar of American English

Sounds do not carry meaning in and of themselves, but when they are patterned into units such as morphemes, which are then patterned into words, phrases, and sentences, they begin to carry meaning. The syntax of a language is the organization of sounds into meaningful units. That sounds have no meaning becomes clear when you try to say one by itself. What do /t/ or /I/ mean? Nothing much. The next section presents a description of the smallest units of meaning.

Some Morphemes About Morphemes

Traditionally, before the sentence level was analyzed by linguists, the level bridging sound and sentence was described. When we move to this level, we move to the smallest unit of meaning—the *morpheme*. *Word* and *morpheme* are not synonymous, although many people seem to think that words are the most important meaning units of language. They feel that children learn to spell *words* and learn to read *words.* But the patterns *within* words and *of* words into phrases, clauses, and sentences, and beyond, also carry a great deal of the meaning load. For example, even adults don't do well repeating scrambled sentences such as "Floors safes jumping help tall"—essentially a word list. They often can't do it at all when the words are in a certain type of isolation, as they are in the scrambled sentences. But when the sentence is grammatical, when the words are arranged in recognized English patterns, adults can repeat the sentences easily. The patterns in which the words are placed carry a great deal of meaning as do the -*s* on *floors* and the -*ing* on *jumping.*

These elements such as /s/ and /iŋ/ are called *bound morphemes,* which simply means they don't appear alone but always in conjunction with at least one other morpheme. Those that can appear alone are called *free* morphemes. *Floor* in *floors* is an example of a free morpheme, as is *famous* in *infamous.*

The whole *affix* system in English is a set of bound morphemes, which pattern in highly specific ways with free morphemes and with other bound morphemes. For example, -s and *floor* don't pattern into *sfloor,* and *in-* and *famous* don't pattern into *famousin.* The *in* is what we call a *prefix,* meaning it patterns in front of the other morphemes in a word. The *-s* is a *suffix,* meaning it follows the other morphemes, which all pattern to form a word. Some languages *infix,* meaning that, for example, a plural morpheme is inserted within a root. English doesn't do this, but the nearest equivalent would be the shift of *man* to *men,* the *a* to *e* to indicate plurality. Probably what we call word families are essentially free morphemes with a series of affixes—bound morphemes—attached to it. For example:

nation (free morpheme; not the same *-tion* as in *perturbation*)
nation—al (adjective suffix)
nation—al—ize (verb suffix)
nation—al—iz—ation (same as in *perturbation*; used to change verbs to nouns)
nation—al—ity (noun suffix)
nation—al—ism (noun suffix)
nation—al—ist (noun suffix)
nation—al—ist—ic (adjective suffix)
nation—al—ist—ical (adjective suffix)
nation—al—ist—ical—ly (adverb suffix)

In this case, we have a series of suffixes that attach themselves to the root *nation,* but also to bound morpheme, *-al,* to produce another set of nouns, a verb, adjectives, and an adverb. This set of affixes is called *derivational* to distinguish them from *inflectional* affixes such as plurals and tense endings on verbs. An inflectional affix does not change the class the word belongs to—for example, a noun remains a noun as in *cat* and *cat-s*—nor does it change basic meaning as derivational affixes can do. Note what happens to *nationalistic* when the prefix *un-* is added: *unnationalistic.* It means just the opposite, so the basic meaning has been rather radically changed. Also, as you may have noted, some of the suffixes of *nation* changed it from a noun to an adjective or verb or adverb. Derivational affixes can do this—change the class membership of a word. Or they may not, as in *nation* and *nationhood,* where both are nouns. The point is they *can,* while inflectional affixes cannot. Inflectional affixes actually help define a word class: for example, if you can make it plural, it's a noun; if you can add a past tense to it, it's a verb. They do this to a greater degree than derivational affixes, which can also help define a word class. For example, we recognize *-ize* on a word indicates a verb—*nationalize.*

Allomorphs

Allomorphs are to morphemes what allophones are to phonemes. (Remember the differences between the *t*'s in *toe* and *pot*.) They are differences that don't make a difference but do serve to illustrate the highly systematic nature of American English. Essentially they are variations of a single morpheme.

Most of us probably tend to think of English as having one common plural morpheme *-s*. However, in reality the English plural has three distinct, regular allomorphs that occur in specific phonological environments in speech. The allomorphs are /s/, /z/, and /əz/. The same allomorphs are also found for the English possessive *-'s* (*floor's*) and for the third person singular verb inflection *-s* (He *floors* me.)

Allomorphs of Plural, Possessive, and Third Person Singular Verb

1. We say /əz/ after the sibilant consonants /s z š ž č ǰ/: sasses, fizzes, fishes, rouges, pitches, judges.

2. We say /s/ after any other voiceless consonant: pips, Pat's, licks, cliffs, mists, larks.

3. We say /z/ after all others—other voiced consonants and any vowel: fibs, lids, pigs, lives, lathes, pals, pars, hams, pans, signs, boys, cows, shoes, toes.

There are also three allomorphs of the past tense morpheme for verbs.

Past Tense Allomorphs

1. We say /əd/ after /t/ and /d/: parted, subtracted, welded, funded.

2. We say /t/ after any other voiceless consonant: sipped, licked, roughed, sassed, pitched, dished, axed.

3. We say /d/ after any other voiced consonant and after any vowel: fibbed, fogged, lived, fizzed, edged, bathed, rouged, hammed, panned, banged, polled, poured, shoed, toyed, replied, sawed.

Although the rules linguists write to express the phonological regularities in American English are quite different in actual form, the statements about what sound environments the two sets of allomorphs above appear in can give you a clearer idea of the specific rules we as native English speakers follow when we speak. Given a certain phonological environment such as the final consonant /b/, we say /fɪbd/ and not /fɪbt/ or /fɪbəd/. We don't consciously think about such constraints but certainly do apply the "correct" rule in each case. What we do without effort and thinking as native speakers of English, the linguist tries to consciously specify.

Just as the sound system of American English has important implications for teaching the language arts, so does the morphological system. Affixes are an important part of vocabulary development, for example. *Antidisestablishmentarianism* is a series of prefixes and suffixes (bound morphemes) attached to a root (free morpheme in this case.) And words can be analyzed in both reading and spelling along morphemic lines—but only if *word* is not thought of as *the* unit of both those areas. If words are recognized as combinations of morphemes, then another level of analysis can be made available to the student.

The Sentence

The structural linguists, using the methods and techniques established in the anthropological linguistic work of Franz Boaz, Edward Sapir, and Leonard Bloomfield, also investigated American English syntax. The basic premise in structural linguistics was that one worked from the actual speech of a native speaker of the language. These linguists would collect speech from people and then would analyze syntactically this *corpus* or body of speech. They started with actual speech and then abstracted out the various syntactic units. In order to delineate the syntactic categories such as noun parts, verb parts, phrases, and clauses in a language under study, structural linguists make substitutions of one form for another. If these substitutions work, then a category is considered established. For example, taking the sentence "The dog bit her," we can substitute "Monstrous and ravening Alsatian" for "dog," "woman carrying her remaining possessions in a pasteboard suitcase" (a complex nominal) for "her" (a pronoun), and so on. So even though phrases and words don't appear to be similar, if they can appear in the same places and function in a similar manner, they then belong to the same category. The graphic representation of this analysis as diagrammed in the chart below is called *Immediate Constituent* analysis or IC analysis. It is essentially used to show how parts of a sentence pattern together.

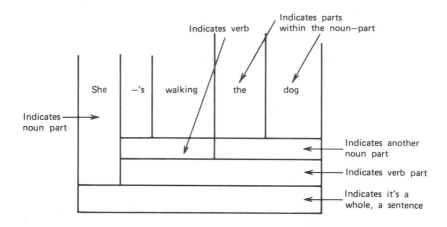

Notice that first the pronoun *she* is separated from the rest of the sentence. This is obviously the "old" *noun-verb* sentence division, *noun* meaning more than one word and *verb* meaning more than one word also. The first split would still occur where it does even if the *noun* were something like "The elderly and eccentric woman who lives in the most expensive apartment in town." As I noted above, if constituents function in the same way and may be substituted one for the other, then they are considered as belonging to a specific category. The next split is between the verb *is walking* and the second noun, which functions as a direct object —*the dog*. The verb is broken into two constituents—*is* and *walking*. And the direct object is analyzed into one article, *the,* and the noun *dog*. Such a diagram makes clear syntactic divisions we intuitively know even though we may not know the terminology.

One major problem of this type of analysis was that it had difficulty explaining how speakers could have two different readings of the same phrase or sentence. This is called *ambiguity*—when we give more than one meaning to the same words. Thus it was difficult to specify the difference between "To fly planes can be dangerous" and "Planes that fly can be dangerous" in "Flying planes can be dangerous" because there was supposed to be only one IC analysis possible for a given syntactic unit. It was even more difficult for IC analysis to explain the differences between:

1. John is easy to please.[4]
2. John is eager to please.

---

[4] This is probably the most famous sentence set in linguistics, one designed by Noam Chomsky for one of his first explanations of the theory of transformational-generative grammar.

All it could do was specify that the two sentences are structurally the same, which is not very satisfactory, because we know those two mean quite different things. The structure, in this case, doesn't help to indicate the meaning differences. Sentence I could be paraphrased: "It is easy for someone to please John," and Sentence 2 could be paraphrased: "John is eager to please someone." So you can see that *John* has quite a different grammatical function in each sentence, which is not at all explained by a immediate constituent analysis of that spoken or written sentence set.

One of the major problems seems to be that structural linguists did not go "below the surface" of language. In other words, we are aware that a sentence is organized in some way other than that the words are strung together from left to right or sequentially in time (the linear organization of a sentence.) It is also organized in some other way than with a "head noun," such as *she,* a verb *'s walking the dog,* and subsequent refinements of the verb (the IC analysis). Although these are important types of organization in language, they don't present a complete picture of how we organize sentences before or while they're being said. When we think about it, we know we don't pick one word such as *the,* then another such as *mongoose,* then finally another such as *garden* to get "*The mongoose is in the garden.*" Instead our sentences are organized hierarchically "below the surface." While IC analysis does show a kind of hierarchy "on the surface"—from noun part to a specific noun word—such analysis cannot explain the following ambiguity. There's *depth* in sentence organization, as you can see from the very different meanings attached to the same structure in an ambiguous sentence such as "It's too hot to eat." One can assign at least four different meanings to that sentence:

The weather is too hot for a person to want to eat in it.
The food is too hot a temperature to eat.
The food is too hotly spiced to eat.
An animal is too hot from exertion to be able to eat.

As mentioned earlier, somehow speakers move from a thought to an actual phonological utterance. The underlying series of structures and processes that result in a string of morphemes to which phonological rules are then applied to arrive at an utterance is called *deep structure.* The *surface structure* of a sentence deals with how the sentence is manifested —how it's *spoken* or *written.* The deep structure of a sentence makes explicit what it means. For example, when you take an ambiguous sentence such as, "Visiting relatives can be boring," you can specify two

31

different deep structures to account for the two meanings of that sentence—"Relatives who visit can be boring," and "To visit relatives can be boring." Also, with sentences (1) and (2)—"John is {eager/easy} to please"—you can specify two different deep structures to account for the same surface structure and for our understanding that the sentences are basically very different.

The theory of syntax that postulates *deep structure* and *surface structure* is called the theory of transformational-generative grammar and is one of the first to propose a set of principles or rules, which—theoretically—can *generate* all the grammatical sentences of a given language or variety. (This definition of rule as a principle is often the one used by linguists.) This obviously has not been achieved, as natural languages are incredibly complex. However, a start has been made on American English. This section on the sentence is done within the transformational-generative framework, which was chosen because it is the most explanatory theory so far of the structure of American English syntax, far more so than either structural or traditional grammar. However, we would stress "so far," since work done up to now has definitely not given us a complete picture of syntax. Also the picture is constantly being modified; it is like giving a set of directions that must be changed as new information comes in.

In transformational-generative grammar, *sentence* is defined as a morpheme string generated by a language's grammer. All strings? We can have what we recognize to be ungrammatical sentences. As native speakers of English, we know something is wrong with:

*Furiously ran path down the.

The * is used to mark a string or sentence as ungrammatical. T-g grammar, as it's commonly called, attempts to indicate the rules that will generate grammatical strings but not ungrammatical ones in order to account for a native speaker's ability to create and understand the grammatical utterances of a language. In other words, what rules will account for our knowledge that "Coming?" is a grammatical English sentence? Below is one t-g "explanation" of these rules. It is presented largely to show the *productive* nature of language: how we can have relatively few rules but produce an infinitely large number of sentences. The actual details and rules are constantly being changed by linguists and therefore are not as important as the principles involved.

Phrase Structure Rules

Base strings in the deep structure (as defined above) are generated by a set of rules that are called *phrase structure rules.* These strings in the deep structure are then changed to surface structures (as defined above) by means of a set of transformational rules—hence the term transformational-generative (or t-g) grammar. Or, as Peter Salus (1969) put it, "A grammar of a language consists of a number of rules which begin with a symbol and replace it with one or more symbols" (p. 18). The phrase-structure rules are very basic ones in the sense that they specify the *constituents* of a sentence such as the noun and verb parts.

A set of phrase-structure rules can be written in the following manner:

PS1[5]　　　　S →　　　　NP + VP

The product of that rule or generative principle is often represented as:

This is called a tree diagram, and it shows the relationship of the S on top or "over" the NP and VP. Remember the IC analysis here. The box diagram also portrays the organization of a sentence. So *sentence* is defined as consisting of a *Noun Phrase* and a *Verb Phrase.* The → means to rewrite the symbol on the left side by the symbols on the right side. The phrase-structure rules 1-9 shown here are *rewrite rules.*

PS2　　　　NP →　　　　NP + (S)
PS3　　　　NP →　　　　D + (Adj) + N

D stands for determiner, which may be an article, such as *a* or *the. Adj.* stands for adjective, and *N* stands for noun. Of course, noun phrases can have other constituents in them, but the structure in PS3 is very common. Since not all nouns have adjectives in front of them, *Adj* is placed in parentheses to indicate that it is optional. The parentheses around S also indicate an optional selection of a sentence in that position.

---

[5] PS1 means Phrase-Structure Rule 1; S means sentence, NP is noun phrase, and VP is verb phrase.

PS4   VP →   (Vt + NP)
                             (be + Adj)

Verb Phrase consists of a transitive verb plus a noun phrase, which has already been given one definition above (PS3). Or it can be rewritten as *be* (linking verb) plus an adjective.

Then in a phrase-structure grammar, the various nouns and verbs are definedby a choice of lexical items, or vocabulary.

PS5   N → $\left\{ \begin{array}{l} \text{cat} \\ \text{milk} \\ \text{linguist} \\ \text{student} \end{array} \right\}$

The brackets mean "any of these" but also indicate an obligatory choice as opposed to the optional choice indicated by the parentheses.

PS6   Vt → $\left\{ \begin{array}{l} \text{like} \\ \text{know} \\ \text{chase} \end{array} \right\}$

PS7   *be* → $\left\{ \begin{array}{l} \text{am} \\ \text{is} \\ \text{are} \\ \text{was} \\ \text{were} \end{array} \right\}$

PS8   Adj. → $\left\{ \begin{array}{l} \text{black} \\ \text{hot} \\ \text{silly} \end{array} \right\}$

PS9   D → $\left\{ \begin{array}{l} \text{a} \\ \text{the} \end{array} \right\}$

Obviously those lexical items within the brackets do not represent the entire set of items possible to specify what *Adj* or what *V* may be rewritten as. But this set of rules serves as an example of a very simple phrase structure for a sentence.

From the rules, we can get a sentence like:

The black cat likes hot milk.

Applying our rewrite rules for the phrase structure, we can get a tree diagram representing the deep structure.

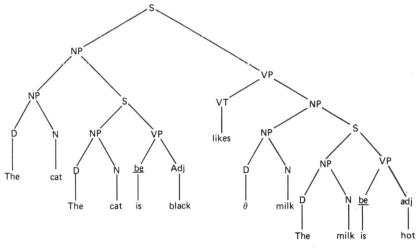

[the cat [the cat is black] likes milk [the milk is hot]]

Note how the strings "the cat is black" and "the milk is hot" are placed within the diagram. Their relationship is specified by the PS2, which is NP → NP + (S). The (S), if present, is an example of what is called recursion; phrase structure grammars have recursive properties. This means an element that has appeared on the left of the rewrite symbol → may also appear on the right of the symbol. These rules permit infinite expansion of the sort seen in this diagram:

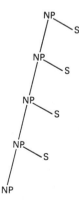

Such a diagram could be used to "explain" the generation of a string like:

the large red square bandana

from [the bandana [the bandana is large] [the bandana is red] [the bandana is square]] or to "explain" the sentence, "This is the dog that worried the cat that killed the rat that ate the malt that lay in the house that Jack built."

Transformations

At this point, we still don't have anything quite like the sentences you and I speak. Only the deep structure has been specified, and somehow we must get to the surface structure—to which the phonological rules are applied to produce an actual spoken sentence. Also the phrase structure does not include an easy rearrangement of various elements *within* or *among* sentences. So transformations have been suggested as a way of explaining how we know, for example, that "Susie socks Waldo" and "Waldo is socked by Susie" are related. The meaning of the two sentences is the same. Since this is the case, they are assigned identical phrase structures:

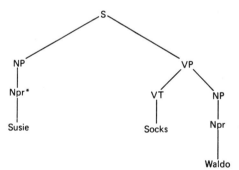

*pr stands for proper, indicating a proper noun instead of other types of nouns.

But the surface structures are different; transformational rules are proposed to link the deep structure to the surface structure, to get from meaning and "basic" syntactic arrangements to what we recognize as spoken sentences. One transformational rule is called the *passive transformation;* that is the one accounting for the surface structure "Waldo is socked by Susie" It operates on "Susie socks Waldo" to create the passive sentence.

How can we derive the string "The black cat likes hot milk," from the cat [the cat is black] likes milk [the milk is hot]]? A series of tranformations have been specified to derive "The black cat likes hot milk." "The cat likes milk" is considered to be generated in the deep structure. "The cat is black" and "The milk is hot" are also considered to be in the deep structure. Then how can we specify possible ways of combining these three strings into the one, "The black cat likes hot milk"?

First we begin with a relative transformation (T relative). It specifies a mechanism for placing elements from one string into another through the dropping or deletion of the element or elements that are the same in both strings. One string is already embedding in the other by the optional (S) in the phrase-structure rules. We have *the* and *cat* the same in both strings. Those two words are dropped and replaced by a *which* or *who*. So we get:

The cat is black.
The cat likes milk.

becoming: The cat which is black likes milk.
There is another optional deletion transformation that allows dropping *which* + *be* verb form to give:

The cat black likes milk.

If this were French, we would leave *black* following the noun. But in English we must have the adjective in front of the noun. So a rearrangement transformation is applied to give:

The black cat likes milk.

We can go through the same process with [. . . milk [the milk is hot]]. An alternative way to showing the transformations may also clarify the movement from deep to surface structure.

[the black cat likes milk [the milk is hot]]

Apply relative transformation
⇓
[the black cat likes milk [which is hot]]

Apply "which be" deletion transformation
⇓
[the black cat likes milk [hot]]

37

Apply adjective movement transformation[6]
⇃⇂
The black cat likes hot milk.

   Through these transformations we have been able to specify the relationship between the strings in the deep structure and the surface form. How we get from meaning to sound has become much more explicit.
   Several types of transformations have been specified by linguists. There are transformations that rearrange elements *within* sentences, for example they give us stylistic variations. Then there are *deletion* transformations—those that drop out elements—such as the *be* deletion transformation; sentence rearranging transformations such as the passive transformation; and addition transformations that put in elements, such as the passive transformation that adds the element *by* as in "The boy was kicked by the horse" This transformation has been symbolized by:

^{T}passive: NP_1 — Vt — NP_2 ⇒

   (The horse)   (kicked)   (the rustler)

NP_2 — be + [en] VT — *by* — NP_1

(The rustler)   (was kicked)   (by)   (the horse)

   The sentence-embedding transformations add greatly to the complexity and creativity of a language. Imagine saying:

The cat is black.
The milk is hot.
The cat likes milk.

   The process of embedding gives us a sentence that we as adults are more likely to say:

The cat which is black likes milk which is hot.

The black cat likes hot milk.   (deletion plus rearrangement transforms)

---

[6] The ⇒ is used to indicate the rewrite rule is for transformations; The → is used for phrase structure rewrite rules.

A classic example of *embedding* (or *subordination,* as it's also called) is the old nursery rhyme "The House that Jack Built."

This is the dog.	This is the dog
The dog worried the cat.	that worried the cat
The cat killed the rat.	that killed the rat
The rat ate the malt.	that ate the malt
The malt lay in the house.	that lay in the house
Jack built the house.	that Jack built.

In other words, elements of various types may be embedded within a sentence. Relative clause transformations are considered embedding transformations and are powerful because they extend the complexity able to be achieved in one sentence.

There are also transformations that *nominalize*—that is, make into NP's elements that are usually found elsewhere. Thus we can get "Painting large oils is my favorite hobby," in which a VP (paint large oils) becomes an NP through a complex series of transformations. English has been identified as a language that uses many nominalizing transformations.

Transformational rules—or simply transformations—can be and are symbolized in a variety of ways by various linguists. And there undoubtedly will be more and more transformations written as linguists work on various aspects of English syntax. But whatever form they take, the idea of transformation once again indicates the systematic and structured nature of language. There is an orderly, rule-governed means of showing the relationship between deep and surface structure. These transformations can also account for the intuitive knowledge we have that certain sentences are related to other ones. For example, remember the previously illustrated passive and active sentence connection. Transformations and phrase-structure rules also specify different deep structures for the same surface structure, as in "He likes entertaining guests," to account for the different meanings we can assign to that sentence:

1. He likes to entertain guests.
2. He likes guests who entertain him.

In other words, these rules deal with ambiguity; sentences with different meanings have different deep structures, even though the surface structure is the same.

Generally, transformations are a powerful construct. They can explain a great deal about language. But one must not think that somehow transformations are actually done in the brain. The theory of transformation-generative grammar attempts to specify the relationships between the elements involved in the progression from meaning to syntax to sound. But it does not and is not intended to specify the way in which we as native speakers and listeners produce and comprehend language.

Semantics: Meaning in American English

Red dreams fall worst in happiness.
Colorless green ideas sleep furiously.[6]

As native speakers, we hear those sentences and know something is wrong. Grammatically they seem to be fine. We can say, using the same syntax:

Blue bicycles may fall heavily in the street.
People sleep well.

Syntactically the first two sentences are American English. Lexically they are also recognizable as American English. We know all those words as relatively common ones in our vocabularies. But there is something wrong in the way the lexical are patterned together. They are anomalous; they don't make sense and have little meaning.

To begin to track down the problem, we realize we don't normally assign a specific color to dreams just as we don't assign a color to items such as *democracy* and *peace*. Color does go, though, with concrete nouns such as *stove* and *sailboat*. We don't speak of dreams *falling*. Again, *ideas* are not colorless or color filled. And they certainly don't *sleep;* only animate things sleep. We wouldn't say, "The rock is sleeping." We also probably think it odd to sleep furiously. We can sleep soundly or poorly or well. But furiously is somehow very odd when applied to sleep.

How can we explain these anomolies, these "nonsense" sequences of words that as English speakers we somehow recognize as strange. One of the currently most powerful explanatory models is that of semantic features (within the transformational-generative theoretical framework).

---

[6] This sentence is probably another of the most famous in linguistics. It was an early illustration for an aspect of the theory of t-g grammar developed by Noam Chomsky.

A lexical item such as *red* or *dream* can be explained as consisting of a set or bundle of features. These feature sets are used to represent the units of meaning we introduce into deep structure, which then are arranged and rearranged according to phrase structure and transformational rules and brought to utterance level by phonological rules.

Feature sets deal with the obvious problem that not all nouns can pattern with all verbs as In "Red dreams fall worst in happiness." Specifying feature sets, we can get:

red	dream
+ adjective	+noun
+concrete	− concrete
+animate	−animate

Notice that red is +concrete and dream is −concrete (or +abstract; often a − is used to keep the feature sets less complicated). Since a plus and a minus for the same feature cannot pattern together in this system, the phrase-structure rules would not generate *red dream*. The feature sets must match in order for lexical items to pattern together.

Obviously, the task of specifying feature sets for lexical items in a language is enormous, as many lexical items are not nearly as "simple" as the ones in the first two sentences. But it also helps to define multiple meanings of words more clearly, including clarifying homonyms such as *bear* and *bare*. This allows us to explain in some fashion anomalies recognized by native speakers. Multiple meanings of a word have sometimes been diagrammed in the following way to show how the features combine to produce different meanings (Salus, 1969, 46):

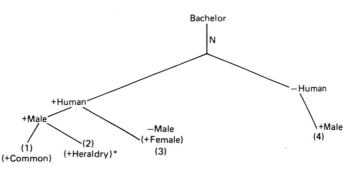

1. A man who has never married.
2. A young knight serving under the standard of another knight.
3. A man or woman who holds the first or lowest academic degree.
4. A young fur seal without a mate during breeding time.
* These terms are not in wide use but merely serve to indicate the tree can branch even further with more features.

41

The idea of a specific feature list being the definition of a lexical item has allowed for some explanation of the meaning component. Even syntactic restrictions can be subsumed under features. For example, *dream* could be defined as:

dream

+noun   (syntactic)
−concrete
−animate
+singular (syntactic)
+definite (syntactic)

The +definite for *dream* would then also specify that any determiner patterning with that lexical item would have to be +definite. Determiners must match nouns on the feature of definiteness. *The* is +definite and *a* is −definite. Thus we would say *the dream* for +definite. If it were −definite, we would say *a dream*. +definite means you're referring to a *specific* dream, while −definite means it may be one of several as in *a dream*.

We could also probably specify distinctive features. To disqualify the "strange" combination *red dream,* we can specify the feature of −concrete for *dream* to have it not pattern with *red,* which is +concrete. The rest of the features for *dream* don't seem to be significant in explaining the anomalousness of the phrase.

However, we must remember that we have been talking about *denotative* meaning rather than *connotative* and *metaphorical* meaning. We use *red* and *dream* in their "usual" senses, a sort of literal meaning. But *red* can connote other meanings as can *green* and *yellow* or *blue:* "green with envy," "he's yellow (cowardly)," "it's a blue day," "she saw red." In the metaphorical sense, perhaps a dream could be red. Certainly a person can be a pig in a metaphorical sense. To allow these combinations, it is proposed that the feature bundles or sets for each lexical item will have to be changed in certain ways. Perhaps now you have an even better idea of the complexity of lexical items alone, and these are not even the entire meaning system.

Finally, there is a question about how the meanings of lexical items add up to the meaning we can derive from a sentence. In other words, lexical items are not simply additive in meaning (remember the word list) as much as they are combinational in communicating meaning. This would follow from what we know about the hierarchical nature of language.

Meaning is somehow "translated" into a string of words, but the combination means more than the sum of the parts. It's the same as that old saying, "The whole is more than the sum of its parts." In other words, the relationships between and among lexical items, as well as the items themselves, carry meaning. This is made quite apparent when you compare a scrambled sentence to a "normal" one:

1. Grow sunlight best plants in green.
2. Green plants grow best in sunlight.

1. carries virtually none of the meaning that 2. does; when the relationship among lexical items is destroyed, much of the meaning of a sentence is also. When word lists such as 1. are used in reading instruction, reading for meaning (an important part of learning to read) is quite effectively destroyed. As teachers we must be aware of the meaning communicated by the relationships among lexical items to be able to help students learn to use that aid as much as possible. Part of this "relationship meaning" is also *syntactic* in nature. N-V-N in and of itself doesn't have that much meaning, but when specific lexical items are used as nouns and verbs the pattern grows in meaning. So "man bites dog" means more than "bites dog man" but is *different* from "dog bites man." And to backtrack a bit, *a mongoose* means something different from *the mongoose*. *Is coming* means something different from *was coming*.

In this chapter, I've described some of the details about the structure of American English. Although the total system is not clear, linguists do know quite a bit about it. Certainly linguistic theory is getting more explanatory, increasing its ability to reveal more and more of the systematic structure of language. These understandings are important for teachers, since they represent a component in the subject matter of language arts/reading: knowledge of the phonological, syntactic, and semantic systems of a language. We must be aware of the systems of a language that our students, as well as we, control. Chapter 3 will discuss in some detail the acquisition of those systems, while Chapters 6 & 7 will draw on your knowledge of the phonology and syntax of American English.

Bibliography

Bolinger, Dwight. *Aspects of Language.* New York: Harcourt, Brace & World, Inc., 1968, and Second Edition, Harcourt, Brace & Jovanovich, 1975.

Dale, Philip S. *Language Development: Structure and Function,*Second Edition. New York: Holt, Rinehart and Winston, 1976.

Fromkin, Victoria, and Robert Rodman. *An Introduction to Language.* New York: Holt, Rinehart and Winston; Second Edition, 1978.

Langacker, Ronald W. *Language and Its Structure.* Second Edition. New York: Harcourt Brace Jovanovich, Inc., 1973.

Lefevre, Carl A. *Linguistics, English and the Language Arts.* Boston: Allyn & Bacon, 1970.

Moulton, William G., "The Nature of Language," in "Language as a Human Problem," *Daedalus, 102,* No. 3 (Summer 1973) 17–35.

Salus, Peter H. *Linguistics.* New York: The Bobbs-Merrill Co., Inc., 1969.

Wardhough, Ronald. *Introduction to Linguistics.* New York: McGraw-Hill, Inc., 1972.

For Further Reading

Fromkin and Rodman's *An Introduction to Language* is one of the clearest and most up-to-date introductions to the subject. Bolinger's *Aspects of Language*, Langacker's *Language and Its Structure*, and Wardhough's *Introduction to Linguistics* can be consulted for further information.

The Development of Language

3

In order to help students expand their communicative competence, as teachers we need to know not only the characteristics of linguistic competence in speaking, listening, reading and writing but also about the patterns of students' emerging communicative abilities. Knowledge of these patterns will better enable us to make plans for increasing our students' competence. In other words, we must know not only *what* we are dealing with—language—but also with *whom* we are dealing—individuals who speak and write. Who are the learners? What are their language abilities? What do their developmental profiles look like?

An important point in defining this *who,* in specifying the characteristics of the learner, is the understanding that individuals develop language systematically. In other words, the *process* of development is as systematic as what is acquired—a language system of many forms and many uses. The process of development can be characterized as a progressive development and revision of sets of rules, based to some degree on input from the language environment surrounding the learner. *Rule* is used in the same sense as it was in Chapter Two. The concept of revision is important, since it enables the learner to "move forward" in development as well as stressing the continuity of development. The nature and extent of the input from the environment is controversial; some of the reasons for that will be discussed below.

It is proposed that the individual's role in this process is one of a hypothesizer. He or she unconsciously formulates a hypothesis about the underlying rule for some linguistic feature such as plurals, tests it through using it to produce and comprehend language, and then may modify the hypothesis—to revise the rules—if it doesn't fit the data. This hypothesizing can be seen in their grammatical "mistakes," which will be discussed below.

Within the process of development, the *sequence* of acquiring various forms has been found to be remarkably stable among children, but the *rate* of development may vary. In other words, children apparently go through the same stages in developing a certain set of forms. The early stages seem to include formulation and use of the most generally applicable rules for a specific part of the language, with the later stages including the ability to consistently use "exceptions" to the rule. So we would expect and actually do find children using the regular past tense morpheme -ed before they consistently use the past tense of the irregular verbs. So we may hear *runned* or *eated.* We also find this for the regular plural morpheme -s; children will say *dogs* and *mouses* and *sheeps.* Then gradually they begin to say *ran, ate, mice,* and *sheep.* And how many times have you heard children say "That's mines" to pattern with *yours, his, hers, ours* and *theirs. Mine* is the single exception, so it's not incomprehensible that a child hypothesizes *mines* to fit the rest of the pattern of English possessive pronouns. This application of a linguistic rule to items it doesn't fit in adult language is called *overgeneralization* or *overregularization* and is probably done by all children. Yet when this is happening in the earlier stages, children will also occasionally produce the mature form—such as *mine, ran,* and *geese.* However, research indicates these forms are probably memorized as separate lexical items and are not part of the developing rule system because they drop out before they appear again after the overgeneralization stage has passed.

Thus there is a predictable sequence of development of various forms, but the rate at which a child goes through a sequence may indeed vary from other children. As a teacher, you may have 6-year-olds who are further developed in some areas than 11-year-olds, or 8-year-olds who say *holded, runned, foots, mines,* that is, who are still overgeneralizing. This is not at all unusual; it's a part of individual differences we have learned to be sensitive to in the classroom. As such, I would say overgeneralization is nothing to be concerned about from an instructional standpoint; as a child's language system develops, these forms will drop out. So you can expect rate differences while finding the same sequence followed.

Overgeneralization allows us to get a look at an even more general process, that of *progressive differentiation.* Say, for example, a child applies a rule to cases it doesn't fit in a language. Gradually we find the child *differentiating* between those cases to which the rule applies and those to which it doesn't. The child somehow gets the idea that this pattern isn't the adult pattern, even though this original pattern is extremely resistant at a certain stage to any intervention by an adult. Try getting a four-year-old to say *held* instead of *holded* (Cazden in DeStefano and Fox, 1974). (A note about this "resistance" to adult input: it is evident that children have their own sets of rules for generating sentences and other forms that they use. If they didn't have their own sets, you could probably get them to imitate and use adult forms. Just try to do it sometime.) You've also probably heard children call men they meet "daddy." I've had my husband referred to as my "daddy" by young children. "Is your daddy coming?" is a familiar question to me. "Daddy" is their word for all men (called a *generic* term in linguistics), which later, as progressive differentiation takes places, becomes applied to only one male.

When children reach school age, they have already developed quite a variety of language skills. They are producing compound-complex sentences and are proficient in making certain social distinctions in their language behavior. It is also contended that children by age six or so have mastered the "basic" syntax and phonology of their language, whatever "basic" is.

This so-called basic competence applies to all children. In other words, no matter what language a child learns, he or she has certain patterns mastered at about the same time that a child speaking another language does. This happens in spite of different environmental inputs; thus we suppose the process of development to be universal in some very real sense. Obviously, then, it is not correct to say that one language is more difficult than another. If that were the case, children would learn Chinese or Japanese more slowly than they would learn English, from our viewpoint at least. But that doesn't happen. Once when in Vaasa, Finland, I remember asking a university student who spoke excellent English, which she found easier—Finnish or English. She replied, "Finnish, of course. It's my mother tongue." And she was referring to a language with 14 noun cases compared to English's 2 cases (singular and plural), and with myriad sets of affixes not existing in English either! Fourteen noun cases boggles our minds while English's relative lack of cases probably appalls Finnish speakers.

Such a universality of development despite the form of the language, as you might expect, has led some researchers and theorists to propose that in some very real way language learning and language itself are biologically based and constrained. Certainly a biological basis would do much to explain this similarity among the earth's children in the process of language acquisition. Eric Lenneberg (1967) is one of the major developers of this biological argument. He has noted, for example, that a child must have an extremely low IQ not to be able to master the basic syntax of a language. Or other rare and extreme events such as complete isolation from speaking humans must happen to a child before he or she will fail to develop language in some "normal" sense. Thus the language environment surrounding the child may merely "trigger" the genetic mechanisms for language learning. But it must be understood that we are talking about some of the "basics" of a language and not about the major part of that system or about the "refinements," which can make the difference between an inarticulate person and a Winston Churchill. Probably this refinement area—carried on through high school as well—is where we as teachers can intervene most successfully.

Given some sort of systematic and universal process of development, what is acquired? Certainly the form of a language is acquired. Children growing up in an English speaking envornment learn to make English sentences. These sentences are lexically, phonologically, and syntactically English. They may not sound always very "adult," but the child is learning to successively approximate their rule set to an adult rule set. Certainly this rule set will generate an infinite number of sentences the same way an adult's does. (Remember the generative nature of language discussed in Chapter 2.)

There is also a cognitive component in this process of development, which probably links up with language in the development of a semantic system. For example, studies by various researchers in child language give us evidence that, across languages even, a relatively small set of meaning relations appear in early speech, which are felt to originate in prior cognitive development (Bloom, 1970; Bloom, Lightbown, and Hood, 1975—American English; Bowerman, 1973—Finnish; Park, 1974—German). These relations have been described as referring to "belief" by the child that objects exist, can stop existing, and can recur as well, that they can be acted upon, are located in space, and may "belong" to certain people. So daddy's shoes come in and out of the child's life, can be played with perhaps, are often found in the closet or on daddy's feet, and belong to him—not mommy, and so on. Or, as Garnica puts it, " . . . consider the case of the two-year-old child who lifts the top of the cookie jar, looks inside, finds it empty and says 'No cookie.' This child is expressing the meaning NONEXISTENCE" (Garnica, 1975, 300). And the child will express much of this in his or her speech.

Importantly, there is also a social component in language that is acquired by the child—and by the student—K-12. A student learns how to talk appropriately to different people, learns that you can't say the same things in the same way to all people. He or she also learns to "take turns" in talking with others, proper forms of address to acknowledge relative social status, to tease and make jokes, when to be silent, and so on. This is sometimes called the acquisition of the rules of discourse.

These last two areas, the sociopsychological as they could be called, deal more with language function and content than with form. In other words, how is language used? For what purposes? What does a child mean? These are the questions we can ask in these areas. As a matter of fact, they are the ones we *must* ask if we are to learn *significant* things about emerging communicative competence. The form of a language doesn't have that much to do with communicative competence beyond the point at which a child either does or doesn't "sound English." True, structures in sentences grow more complex, but that complexity is, in turn, largely dependent on what cognitive and social meaning the student is trying to express.

The stress in this chapter will be on language development in the school-age individual (ages 5-12+), since a teacher's major concern is for that age-group. Development before age 5 will be mentioned in order to help you see the progressive and orderly development of a child's language, whatever variety it may be. Also, these early years will be covered briefly for background purposes to give you a better idea where the student in your classroom comes from linguistically, so to speak.

Finally we will also delve into the development of literacy—reading and writing—because it is a part of the developmental process in a literate society such as ours. But these topics will be discussed in much more detail in Chapters 5, 6, and 7.

Development of the Phonological System

To begin with, we should stress again that the child systematically develops a system—in this case the sound system of American English, one of its varieties, or one of the other languages spoken in the United States. Unfortunately the developmental profile for phonology is not all that clear, especially for school-age children. But we know that we cannot expect all students to be at the same developmental stages while in school, nor can we expect them to develop their sound system in an "adult" way. In other words, they may pay attention to cues such as allophonic differences that are no longer used by adults, so their rule system may be quite different from the adult rule system. We will see some of this in Chapter 7 when we examine the spelling of children who taught themselves to write. Another point to keep in mind is that the perception of sounds and the ability to produce them differ in rate of development, with perception of adultlike phonemes generally coming earlier than production. In other words, children tend to *hear* the phonemes of a language before they can use them in their speech, sometimes long before they can use them in certain combinations such as consonant clusters. This is not surprising because we know children can comprehend quite a bit of speech they cannot produce themselves. In fact, we as adults often do the same thing: we understand the language of a sermon but may not be able to give one ourselves.

Early Phonological Development

In the early stages of phonological acquisition, the infant babbles. The articulators are "played around with" to produce a variety of sounds, many of which drop out when what is called true speech occurs. These sounds cannot be called phonemes because, as Cazden puts it, " . . . a phoneme is a class of sounds that a native speaker considers functionally equivalent and discriminates from other classes of sounds" (1972, p. 57). Infants do not "consider" sounds functionally equivalent and put them into classes; they are not yet at the stage of conveying meaning through speech.

So the infant plays vocally and can be heard to produce sounds that are not in American English and, also, not to produce all the sounds of American English, for example, consonant clusters such as /str/ in *strong* (Clark and Clark, 1977, 390). Listen carefully and you may hear French uvular *r*'s (produced far down in the throat), glottalized sounds used in certain African languages, and nasalized vowels (as in French *non*). It seems as though the infant is trying out its articulators. Another interesting point: it has been noted that some sounds produced easily during the babbling stage are not at all easily producible at the stage in which the child intends them to mean something, that is during production of true speech. As the Danish linguist Jesperson puts it:

> *It is strange that among an infant's sounds one can often detect sounds—for instance k, g, h, and uvular r- which the child will find difficulty in producing afterward when they occur in real words . . . The explanation lies probably in the difference between doing a thing in play or without a plan—when it is immaterial which movement (sound) is made—and doing the same thing in fixed intention when this sound, and this sound only, is required . . . (Jesperson, 1925, p. 106).*

It seems as though the earlier production, then, has little or nothing to do with the production of true speech. Sometimes there is even a period of silence between babbling and speech. It's like the generalization presented at the beginning of this chapter: first occasional "correct" or adultlike production (babbling), which drops out in favor of a more general rule (child's own system), then finally is replaced by an approximation of the adult usage (adult system).

However, whereas segmentals (those sounds we consider to cluster as phonemes) don't seem to develop during babbling, some of the suprasegmentals (intonation patterns) do. This is why many people think that a baby sounds as though he or she is talking a foreign *language*. The phonemes are not English, but you can almost make out sentences; the fading and falling /\/ pattern is there. It's been found that this contour appears as early as the second month, whereas the fading and rising / || / pattern may appear between six to eight months. Recognizable sentence intonation patterns also begin to appear. For example, a "command" contour, which is a sharp rise in the voice and then a fall (say, "Get out"), may appear before the child is a year old (Menyuk, 1971). It should not be presumed, however, that the infant is using these intonation patterns as an adult or older child does—to help convey meaning. This is not the case. But it seems that the infant perceives these patterns early, and that they are used to distinguish between human speech and other sounds in the child's environment. According to Kaplan (1969), this discrimination develops sometime between three to eight months of age.

Let us consider again the development of phonemes. In babbling, we find the infant tending to drop out uvular *r*'s and nasalized vowels, thereby narrowing his or her range in the direction of what we consider English sounds. First words may appear around age one, "word" meaning a meaningful unit, not just a collection of sounds. It is considered meaningful if the baby uses a group of sounds to consistently refer to the same thing —such as "mama" for its mother or for certain women.

It has been suggested by Roman Jakobsen and some other phonologists that there is a type of universal first set of phonemes consisting of almost maximally contrasted sounds as far as articulation is concerned. This first set usually consists of a front consonant such as /m/ or /p/ and a back vowel, usually /a/. Say "mama" and feel how your mouth closes to say /m/ (*front* sound) and opens far in the back to say /a/. In articulation, the front-back contrast is one of the greatest we can make. You can probably see this set is going to give rise to "mama" and "papa"—which it often does. And around the world, in many different languages, the "baby" words for *mother* and *father* consist of a set of front consonants and back vowels. These first constrasts, one of them being vocalic— consonantal, give way developmentally to finer and finer contrasts.

Again, production and perception do not necessarily move together. Perception of phonemes in different positions in words (remember the differences between the /p/ in *tip* and *pit*) and across different speakers must be learned, as well as phonemic production. The child has to learn to pick out what is *invariant* across all the sounds that we class as /p/, for example. There is some indication that by the time they reach kindergarten, children may still be perceiving *phones,* or the actual speech sounds, not phonemes. Some children have been found to perceive the initial sounds of *truck* and *chair* to be the same. They don't chunk phones, the separate, discriminable sounds, together into the bundles of sounds we treat as being functionally the same—phonemes. Obviously these children have not yet developed the adult phonological system—at least perceptually. Think for a moment what this can mean in beginning reading instruction where many teachers work with minimal pairs based on adult phoneme contrasts. *Tick* and *chick* may not be perceived as two different words by some children.

When is the productive phonemic system mastered? Or to put it another way, when is the adult rule system acquired? Some linguists will say by about age four or five. But we probably all know children who still say *cwack* at age seven or eight; the /r/ and /l/ may present problems of production later than many other phonemes, especially if they are in a cluster such as *crack* or *clack.* In an initial position, /w/ is often substituted for /r/ by school-age children. Or if it's /r/ in a word-final position, it may be omitted altogether. Other phonemes as well appear later in the developmental process, especially in certain environments. /ŋ/ frequently becomes /n/ in a *verb + ing* construction: /swImIn/. But it will appear in words like *swing* /swIŋ/ or *pink*/pIŋk/. /θ/ appearing in the medial or middle position in a word as in *birthday* may present problems that aren't present when it appears initially, as in *thumb,* or finally, as in *mouth. Birthday* is frequently pronounced "birfday," and *toothbrush* as "toofbrush."

Unfortunately we know relatively little about phonemic development in school-age children. If most children do master the sound system of American English by age four or five, or at least a large part of it, we as teachers are not intimately concerned with the details of that development. But we also know that children vary in rate of linguistic system development. So you may have children who do not have an adult perception and production system of rules for the sounds of American English. There are data to indicate that for some six-year-olds, not only do /l/ and /r/ present production problems, but also the final /ǰ/, as in *siege.* A six-year-old may also have trouble producing /č/, /š/, /v/, /z/, /ð/, /θ/, and /ž/ in various positions (Menyuk, 1971, p. 76). You may hear a school-age child say *dat* instead of *that* or *dem* instead of *them;* the /ð/ has not been acquired yet in that position.

An important teaching perspective is that these differences need not be considered mistakes but, instead, can be put in a developmental context. The pattern for the ability to produce phonemes seems to be a hierarchy of different distinctions made among sounds by the child. The first one is the consonant-vowel distinction, followed by distinctions between various consonants such as nasal (/m/, /n/, and /ŋ/) and stop consonants (/b/, /p/, etc.) and finally by distinctions within those sets to make the difference between /m/, /n/, and /ŋ/, for example. Again, it's apparently a process of progressive differentiation from the most general contrasts to finer and finer ones. Or, as Clark and Clark (1977, 391) put it, children may work on an hypothesis-testing theory in that they try different hypotheses "about how to produce the right sound." When they get some, they then work out others. "In the course of doing this [building up a set of "articulatory programs"], they work out which contrasts between segments are systematic in the language being acquired." (Clark & Clark, 1977, 391).

As teachers you may also notice differences in the phonemic system acquired by a student based on social and geographical differences. Again, the student is developing a rule-governed system, but it may be different from yours. For example, a black inner-city student of eight or nine may say "Rufe" (sounds like *roof*) instead of "Ruth." That is not delayed development but part of the phonological system used by adults around the child. Or a student from the South may make no vowel distinction between *pen* and *pin,* both being pronounced *pin.* Again, that lack of distinction in that set is part of the adult system in a given geographical area.

As teachers we must ask about the implications of phonological development in school students for the learning of literacy. As I see it, one important consideration when we teach phoneme-grapheme[1] correspondences as we do in reading and spelling lessons, is to realize a student's phonemic set may not match an adult's, which is what we are using. Students may and often do develop their own set of phoneme-grapheme correspondences based on their own rule system. This should probably be encouraged because such children are more aware of their own systems, and being more aware they can more easily perceive the distinctions made in the adult system. You can play on the fact that it's systematic behavior; contrast their system with your adult system. However, you may notice again that there are differences between the student's ability to perceive and produce. For example, how many times have you heard children being teased by someone imitating their speech to which they respond, "That's not right." " . . . a child asked if he could come along on a trip to the "mewwy-go-wound." An older child, teasing him, said, "David wants to go to the "mewwy-go-wound." "No, said David firmly, "You didn't say it wight" (Maccoby and Bee in Dale, 1976). Thus, it's important for you to know if a child is able to perceive differences, but

---

[1] Grapheme refers to the letter or letters in the written system that represent (or symbolize) a phoneme in the spoken language. More about them in Chapters 5 and 7.

just not produce them, or if he or she actually can't perceive the differences.

Development of the Syntactic System

As with the phonological system, much of this system has been acquired by the time children come to school. As we are primarily interested in the school-age child, we will only very briefly sketch some of the earlier stages of syntactic development. If you wish to delve further into details and aspects of this system development, you can find extended and readable discussions in the volumes listed at the end of this chapter under *"For Further Reading."*

Initial Stages in Syntactic Development

The child's first utterances, at around age one, are called *holophrases* or *holophrastic utterances* and are characterized as one word. It may be in the lexicon (i.e., be a word we recognize), or it may be peculiar to the child, such as "gago" for *sister.* But they don't seem to be used in the same way the adult lexical item is, even if it sounds as though they are. A baby may say *cookie* and mean "I want a cookie" or "Mama has a cookie." This comment on something in the nonverbal world, often an action the child is doing or wants others to do, usually has to be heard in the context in which it is uttered in order for us to understand what the child means. Some researchers characterize holophrases as topic-comment constructions with the topic omitted or a fusion of topic and comment. *Topic* is defined as the psychological subject and the *comment* as the psychological predicate. In other words, they're not *form* designations but psychological ones instead. The comment is considered new information about the topic; for example:

The girl	*caught the cat.*
topic	comment

But in early speech there is not the distinction evident between topic and comment. However, intonation patterns accompany these single words, thus providing different meaning. *Shoe* with a fading, falling terminal may mean, "That's my shoe," but said with a rising terminal may mean, "Where's my shoe?" However, the final decision as to what the child means rests on the listener's familiarity with the child in the given situation. We will discuss this in more detail later in this chapter. This early stage tends to be very context bound, the nonverbal environment transmitting a large part of the meaning.

Later, the two-word utterances appear in the child's speech. These are considered to have "true" syntax because they are systematically structured. At this point, the child is beginning to be able to create an infinite set of utterances by means of a limited set of combination mechanisms, which is the same process adults go through. At whatever age this happens, we are still talking about a stable sequence of development with differences in rate.

The next stage commonly identified is one in which both the topic and the comment are present in a child's utterance. At this stage it is common for *function words,* as well as others, to be omitted, but some children will do so more than others. (Again, individual differences.) Function words are usually defined as those having little or no meaning but performing a syntactic function. Examples are articles such as *a, the,* and the verb *to be* in environments such as "The cat *is* pretty," and prepositions such as *in* and *to.* These are also called *structure words.* You'll hear utterances like "Cat pretty," "Want go home," and "Put box," for "Put it in the box."

At this stage it is evident that the child is concentrating on conveying meaning rather than on "getting structure straight;" many of the "niceties" of adult grammar simply aren't present, such as the inflection of pronouns and inflection for possession and plurality. You can hear small children say "me sock" or "that me sock," in which the pronoun is not inflected. Or you can hear "want shoe?" (with a rising final inflection) that probably means "Do you want my (or a) shoe?" The ability of an adult to interpret many of these two-word utterances depends on his or her knowing the context of the child's speech, thus serving to highlight how tied to context most of the early utterances are. In fact, many of us doing research in this area are convinced that this is how, as M.A.K. Halliday puts it, children "learn how to mean" (Halliday, 1975). They "work" in context, meaning arising from what they do and from what is done to them, as well as from their cognitive development.

As language develops, it can become far less contextually bound to the point at which a reader can understand a passage on a topic with which he or she is not directly familiar. Textbooks are a good case in point of this increasing ability for language not to be bound to here-and-now, shared experience. It does not have to be tied to simultaneous action, whereas many early utterances of a child accompany an action. Taking the "want shoe?" example, the child may hold the shoe out toward the adult while speaking.

Continuing research by scholars such as Roger Brown, Paula Menyuk, and Lois Bloom (cited earlier) indicates that these early utterances can be categorized semantically to indicate how they *function*. Function can be expressed syntactically through the ordering of the words. To begin with, there is no random ordering of the two-word utterances; the child doesn't say "shoe want?" for "want shoe?" or "Coming Susie" for "Susie coming." You can see a predicate construction in "want shoe," whereas in "shoe want" you'd have a subject-predicate or NP-VP construction. When one is used instead of the other, that specific one is intended. There is consistency in the order in which the words are said. This consistency has been interpreted as the child's observing and "intending" certain meaning relationships in an utterance—the meaning helped along by the word order—even though there are only two words. So syntax is developing. What the child intends is felt to determine the function of a two-word sentence. For example, there is what we call an *imperative* sentence type, which functions as a demand on someone for something. Take "me sock." It a given context with a given intonation, that could well mean "Give me my sock." Or "more pencil" (Menyuk, 1971) could mean "Give me more pencils" or "another pencil." A variety of functions have been suggested for the sentences in this stage.

Notice how children increasingly differentiate in their linguistic development. Intentions were first expressed by one word. Then two-word utterances with a set word order develop. We see the beginning of syntax and of syntactic differentiation, which finally reaches the level we think of as mature syntax. Cazden (1972) has called these two lines—semantic and syntactic—"macro" development and "micro" development. "Macro" considers the meaning intended, while "micro" has to do with the grammatical structure used to express the meaning.

Then various parts of the sentence begin to develop—again through progressive differentiation. And the system of rules for generating sentences and comprehending them approximates more and more a mature rule set. Children begin to inflect their words; nouns are made plural, possession as in "girl's hat" appears, "me shoe" becomes "my shoe." Finally, between ages three and five, transformations are developed in increasing complexity. Various types of transformations such as the question set have been studied in some detail and are described in Dale (1976) and elsewhere. Briefly, children begin to indicate syntactically that they are asking a question first by intonation. So a child may say "home" with a rising inflection to indicate a question like "Are we going home?" or "Is that home?" Different types of questions then begin to be differentiated. For *yes-no* questions (those that can be answered with a *yes* or a *no*), the next stage is still to use intonation but with far "fuller" sentences. So you may hear a child asking "You can't fix it?" or "Mom pinch finger?" (Cazden, 1972). Before we can consider this type of question to be mature, there has to be a question inversion in which "you do" becomes "do you." First, however, the auxiliary verb system has to develop, because it's an auxiliary that gets inverted, not a "full" verb. We don't say, "Want you it?" but "Do you want it?" When that system is acquired by a child, you can hear the child ask, "Can't you fix it?" or "Will you fix it?" However, you may also hear "Did I caught it?" since children still make "mistakes" with the tense and number suffixes in the auxiliary verb (Clark & Clark, 1977).

Part of the *yes-no* question system is what are called *tag questions.* The mature form is something like "You're coming, aren't you?" Notice how the sentence is not inverted, but the question is instead signaled by a tag, which is inverted. Tag questions don't appear until later in a child's language development; and when they first do, the tag takes the form of *huh?* You may hear a child say, "We can play, huh?" Then finally the full form appears: "We can play, can't we?" All these tag question forms are acquired before school age. Again, children go through the same stages of acquiring this question form but at somewhat different rates.

The evidence provided by research into a child's language system indicates just how inadequate is the explanation that children learn their language largely through imitation, which has been suggested by behaviorists as the major means of acquiring language. The imitation theory holds that the child hears the adult, imitates what the adult says, and thus learns to speak. But a child probably never hears *goed, runned, gooses,* and *mouses* or many of the other constructions he or she creates and speaks. "All gone doggie?" is not a sentence the child is very likely to have heard, but children regularly produce utterances such as that. And as Wardhaugh notes, "Babies do not attempt to imitate all the sounds in their environment but only human sounds: they seem to be 'predisposed' toward human sounds" (1976, p. 143). He also states, "Children produce in imitation only what they would say in spontaneous speech" (1976, p. 143). Clark and Clark assert, "Overall, children do not imitate new structures, even though some of them do imitate new words. Imitation per se. therefore, does not seem to involve a mechanism through which children might learn to produce more complicated sentences" (1971, p. 335).

Another explanation for syntactic development that has been offered is the concept of expansion. When a child says, "All gone doggie," the child's mother may say, "Yes, the dog is gone." Or to a child's "Throw Daddy," the mother may say "That's right. Throw it to Daddy." This method of making the child's syntactically incomplete utterances into complete adult ones is called expansion. But Cazden's research, in conjunction with that of Roger Brown and Ursula Bellugi (Cazden, 1972), found that Sara, the child who got the least parental expansion of her speech, was most syntactically developed at an earlier age. Cazden notes, "Basic grammatical structures seem to be learned despite differences in the child's linguistic environment . . ." (1972, p. 122). We will see below how, in at least one culture, parents or other adults do not expand on children's speech with seemingly little effect on syntactic development.

So what is left for the school-age child? Some students in kindergarten and the primary grades may be "mopping up" their acquisition of the *morphological system.* It's not uncommon to hear children at that age say "feeled" or "gooses," especially if the words are new to their vocabulary. Even in older students you may get the *-s* morpheme on words with Latin endings such as *hippopotamus* to give *hippopotamuses.* These over-generalzations are, of course, natural and with continued development and exposure to the complete morphological system, disappear.

A very interesting developmental trend is seen in the school-age child: the movement from connecting sentences by conjunctions (*conjoining*) to doing it through *embedding.* In the early grades you will frequently hear children say, "I have a cat and he's black and he likes hot milk" (conjoined). The embedded equivalent would be "My (I have a cat—shows possession) black (he's black) cat likes hot milk," and it would tend to be produced by an older child. Embedded sentences are characterized as ones in which the *S* (recursion) appears in the NP. The relative clause transform in Chapter 2 (see page 37) is an example of the mechanism proposed to deal with where the relative clause element in a sentence comes from. This same trend is found in students' written language (see Chapter 6).

When one conjoins, one preserves more information in the surface structure. Not that it is necessary information, because generally what's dropped are words in *identity,* that is, those referring to the same thing. Thus conjoining is the addition rather than a rearrangement of elements in the deep structure. Later, students seem better able to delete, rearrange, and substitue various elements. (See Chapter 2 for various kinds of transformations.) All of these procedures are used in embedding. However, remember that for students through grade seven, conjoining may be used more frequently than embedding as a sentence-combining device. Giving students a specific sentence-combining task, we find that second-graders connect sentence sets such as:

(1) My hat is blue.
(2) My has has flowers on it.[2]

---

[2] This sentence set, along with others, was used in a protocol a group of us in the College of Education, Ohio State University, made as part of an entire series of films illustrating concepts of language development. See "For Further Viewing" for the various titles available.

with an *and* quite frequently to produce "My hat is blue, and it has flowers on it," in which a pronoun is substituted for the second noun in identity —*hat.* The sixth-graders, on the other hand, produced very quickly, "My blue hat has flowers on it" and "My flowery hat is blue" (a rather complex set of transformations being performed to turn "has flowers on it" into "flowery"), only later producing "My hat is blue and it has flowers on it," in which the noun in identity is deleted and a pronoun substituted for it.

An important question for teachers about students' syntactic development is the kinds of syntactic forms they produce at different stages and ages—in which age is loosely linked to stage. This linkage must be loose, since it is possible to find second-graders ahead of sixth-graders in some areas of syntactic development.

There is another developmental question we can ask: what are students' emerging receptive abilities? In other words, what can they comprehend as well as produce? This is usually inferred from various comprehension tasks in which the individual manipulates something according to a set of verbal directions. The person's nonverbal behavior thus indicates how much of the verbal form is understood; can he or she follow the directions or not? Carol Chomsky (1969) has carried out research in this area that illustrates some distinct differences between children's and adult's ability to comprehend the language.

In English we have what is called the *Minimal Distance Principle* (MDP), which means that the noun closest to a complement verb (a verb in the infinitive form, i.e., with *to* + verb form) is the subject of that verb. For example, in the sentences:

Obadiah beseeched Crumbles to leave.
Obadiah permitted Crumbles to leave.
Obadiah urged Crumbles to leave.

the noun *Crumbles* is the subject of the complement verb *to leave.* In sentences of this type, the application of the MDP is required by the largest set of verbs that occur in the first verb position, for example, *beseech, permit, tell,* and *want.*

Chomsky suggests that children learn the regular set first, applying the MDP as the most general rule in order to comprehend those sentences. You will remember this is a principle of language acquisition—from general to specific. Then the children overgeneralize, as they do elsewhere in their system, to the exceptions to the MDP. *Promise* is an exception. "Obadiah promised Crumbles to leave" means that Obadiah, not Crumbles, was to do the leaving. In the earlier verb set, Crumbles was to leave. Chomsky found, in fact, that younger school-age children would often interpret the *promise* sentence as if it were a *tell* sentence, as in "Obadiah tells Crumbles to leave." They overgeneralized the MDP to those verbs that were exceptions to the principle. Later, as with morphology, they were able to "break" the most regular rule to correctly comprehend the exceptions. Dale suggests

> *Children obviously have preferences for a small number of general rules. Overgeneralizations are as common in syntax as in inflectional development. Just as American and Russian children overgeneralize past-tense, case, and other inflections, the children in Chomsky's experiment overgeneralized rules relating deep and surface structure. Exceptions to rules—sentences in which the objects occur before the subjects, sentences that violate the minimal-distance principle—are mastered only after a considerable interval (Dale, 1976, p. 136).*

This apparent behavior could also be characterized as progressive differentiation, the development of additional rules. First one rule or item is applied to all language instances, whether it be a syntactic rule or a lexical item such as *daddy*. Then the one is differentiated more and more so that ultimately *daddy* is used only for a child's father and the Minimal Distance Principle is finally broken for the small set of verbs such as *promise*. Thus the whole is broken up into smaller and smaller and smaller parts, each one differentiated in what is considered to be a more "adult" way.

Obviously, school-age children have not yet mastered (but learn to master) those syntactic forms found almost exclusively in written English. Unfortunately we know relatively little about those differences between oral and written English, but they definitely exist. Few if any of us "sound like a book" when we talk. Part of that differentiation is syntactic (discussed in more detail in Chapters 4 and 6).

One form we can pinpoint is the passive, which appears much more frequently in writing than in speech. Unless we wish to obscure the person responsible for an act by leaving off the *by* phrase as in "The window was broken," we tend to say "Billy did it," to use the active syntactic verb form. In other words, in speech the passive is a much more unusual form than the active. But in writing, especially in certain kinds of scientific writing, the passive occurs much more frequently. For example, in chemistry the actor is often not important, is completely irrelevant, or doesn't quite fit semantically. So you'll frequently find sentences like, "An explosion is produced by combining sodium and nitrogen. It is not recommended to create such a combination without taking the proper precautions." The stylistic differences between active and passive forms are not always well understood, but we know the passive form is more common in writing than in speech.

There are also some social and geographical differences in the syntactic systems acquired by students, as there are in the phonological systems. However, these differences are relatively minor in the face of the mutual intelligibility we have among varieties of American English. And they will be discussed in much more detail in the following chapter, at least in the case of the social variety called Black English. But you will find some students using a rule-governed multiple negative such as "I ain't got none," while others do not. In some parts of Pennsylvania you may hear children using a slightly German syntax, as in the song title "Throw Mama from the Train a Kiss." That is the result of the influence of German on English in that geographic area. Usually the average teacher will have students in the classroom whose speech is syntactically very similar to his or hers. Whatever the differences, they are relatively minor in the syntactic system.

The syntactic development profile described here has implications for the development of literacy as well. There is divergence of syntactic forms in speech and writing, and when students learn to read they have to learn those different forms. Unfortunately we know very little about how it affects their learning to read, but the differences do exist and should be kept in mind. At the same time, students must also learn to produce written forms as they learn to write stories, science reports, notes, and so forth. One thing is clear—speech can be written down and read, but more mature writing diverges more and more from speech. The student has to learn to deal with the syntactic differences between these modes and will look to you, the teacher, for guidance.

Development of the Semantic System

Certainly the lack of system and detail in the description of the semantics of American English is evident in a discussion of semantic development in children. Also, we must take into account that there are many approaches to the study of semantics. It certainly is not just the development of a lexicon: it is also a development of the sets of rules for combining the lexical items into recognized patterns. This area also bridges into syntax.

As far as semantic development in children up to age five is concerned, several powerful generalizations have been applied. The notion of features is one of these. Another is the concept of progressive differentiation.

There has been an increasing number of studies, Eve Clark's work among them, dealing with the application of the feature concept to semantic development. It has indeed been found to have explanatory power in the acquisition of an adult lexicon. For example, it seems as though some features of a lexical item are acquired before other features, usually in a hierarchical arrangement, with those coming first being the most general or superordinate. We have found the same thing happening in phonological development. In both cases we could also note that the features a child attends to may be different from those features an adult attends to. If a lexical item can be thought of as a bundle of features, then we can say that children successively approximate the adult sets of features for lexical items. Clark notes:

> *For example, in the acquisition of the meanings of* before *and* after, *children first learn both words have to do with time. + Time; next they learn that these words refer to sequence rather than to simultaneity of some sort,—Simultaneous. The feature—Simultaneous carries with it a specification of ordering the sequence, + Prior. This combination of features (+ Time, − Simultaneous, + Prior) characterizes the meaning of* before *but not that of* after. *The last feature that children learn is − Prior, i.e., that* after *is in fact the opposite of* before *(Clark, 1971).*

Thus a child will use *before* and *after* to mean the same thing until he or she picks up the −Prior feature for *after* to make it an opposite. First, in the developmental sequence, *before* and *after* are synonyms. Only later do they become antonyms. In fact, Clark's semantic feature hypothesis states that when children begin to use words, they will often only have partially acquired the set of features adults attach to items in the lexicon. She also proposes that the first features are perceptual in nature, based on shape or movement (Clark, 1974). French suggests animateness (capability to move) as an early feature in children's semantic development, since movement is extremely important in visual perception in the very young (French, 1976). But we also recognize that words have functional and social "meaning" as well, plus many connotations that can be attached. A cup not only has shape, but functions in a specific manner in a specific culture. So lexical acquisition is complicated by these "meanings," which are not highly perceptible in a physical sense and require exposure to a given culture. According to Anderson (1975), it's not until children reach the age of nine or older that they become less tied to perceptual features such as shape and size and can begin to operate on more functional and culturally bound ones such as those used to distinguish cups from other objects like mugs and glasses, where the perceptual boundaries between them are vague. Yet some aspects of our semantic system are *so* vague that not even adults agree on definitions or feature sets for certain lexical items. Laraine Hong conducted a study into the definitions of *woman, man, girl,* and *boy,* and found adults made no obvious boundaries between *woman* and *girl,* and *man* and *boy.* She states: " . . . adults rely on a variety of criteria, many of which are shaped by the nature of their individual perceptions and social knowledge" (1976, p. 16). The perceptual differences and functional differences between *woman* and *girl* are, thus, not sufficient to define those lexical items. Many of the salient features of lexical items are cultural in nature and may vary among subgroups in a culture.

The rules for combining lexical items must develop as well. McNeill (1970) found that five-year-old children did not do well in repeating grammatical sentences that were masked with noise. Adults and older children had relatively little difficulty in repeating the sentences. McNeill hypothesized that one of the reasons was that the young children's rule system for combining words (as well as their semantic feature system) is not well enough developed to enable them to accurately predict the word made ambiguous by the noise. Certainly the young children did not do well in repeating the grammatical sentences. Commonly, they may pick up one or two words out of the sentence but are unable to produce anything resembling a grammatical string. That their system is different and not as developed is quite obvious from the ease with which an adult can repeat the masked sentence. However, all ages have trouble repeating strings of words that are not grammatical—that aren't sentences. The development of this ability to combine words has implications for learning to read, which will be discussed in Chapter 5.

Finally, there is the idea of progressive differentiation in the acquisition of the lexicon as illustrated by the emerging definition of words such as "daddy" and "doggie." At first, *doggie* has been found to mean four legged animals of cat and dog size, stuffed animals, the house the dog lives in (our *dog house*), etc. Gradually the lexical item *doggie* comes to be applied to those animals we as adults call *dog.*

We need to know much more about semantic development, and the information available certainly is scanty, especially for school-age children and older students. We even have trouble explaining the following phenomenon: it seems as though semantic development is slower than either syntactic or phonological development. Part of the reason may be that as an individual's conceptual structure continues to develop for a long time, perhaps as long as our life span itself, semantic development is necessarily slower because it is in some way intimately connected with that development. Gibson suggests this to be the case:

> . . . The child as he observes and acts in the world around him discovers distinctive features of objects and invariant properties of events, leading him to develop first perceptions, and then a conceptual scheme of the permanent properties of his world. This conceptual structure, in turn, he learns to encode in symbols; the conceptual structure is mapped to speech. The organization of this symbolic conceptual structure is a semantic system, a system of meanings. Psychologists have made little progress in the study of meaning. But we know that every child requires a lexicon—a vocabulary of the words of his language. The words, or rather, words in proper combinations, are a kind of code of real events and things and ideas (Gibson, 1973, p. 11).

It would stand to reason, then, that some of the most crucial language development takes place in the school-age child who also makes many strides in cognitive development at that time. Students' ability to think develops dramatically during the school years.

We must also ask the question about the relationship between this cognitive development and semantic development. Can lexicon and combinations of words help students think? Or do they learn to think a certain way and then develop the lexical patterns to express it? Some researchers such as Benjamin Lee Whorf have said that language very definitely constrains thought—that it is difficult for someone to think of something if there is no word for it in the language.

But now many scholars are seeing language more as an instrument of thought. For example, Jerome Bruner (1972) suggests that language is a means of both representing and, in some ways, transforming experience. He also sees language as a system capable of helping the individual order experience. In other words, language can help us comprehend better what we did or what happened to us. As a system, language is an instrument to mediate between cognition and experience. Thinking and doing are thus connected through language. Bruner feels the mediation can take place, for example, when a child learns to handle the comparative system in the language. In other words, the child can think more "logically" when able to say, "The girl has more marbles than the boy" rather than having to say something like, "The girl has a lot of marbles. The boy has a little bit." The child is apparently able, through the vehicle of the comparative structures in language, to easily connect what is much and what is little into a scale of more to less. Bruner states:

Once the child has succeeded in internalizing (language) as a cognitive instrument, it becomes possible for him to represent and systematically transform the regularities of experience with far greater flexibility and power than before (Bruner, 1972, p. 163).

In children between four and twelve language comes to play an increasingly powerful role as an implement of knowing . . . I have tried to show how language shapes, augments, and even supercedes the child's earlier modes of processing information. Translation of experience into symbolic form, with its attendant means of achieving remote reference, transformation, and combination, opens up realms of intellectual possibility that are orders of magnitude beyond the most powerful image-forming system (Bruner, 1972, p. 165).

To support these contentions, Bruner cites several studies done by Jean Piaget and his Geneva, Switzerland, group of researchers, including Hermina Sinclair[-de Zwart], who have given us some of the most productive research in this area.

Eric Lenneberg, who is perhaps most noted for his work on the biological foundations of language, also believes that language serves a supporting role in the development of cognition. He contends that language universals, for example, are constrained by general cognitive functioning, and that in children, concept formation is primary while vocabulary learned for the concepts is definitely secondary. A word may come to signal or stand for a concept, but the concept itself definitely antedates any linguistic label. In other words, if a child doesn't know the color orange, the word *orange* won't be in the child's vocabulary.

Turning to Piaget and his group, again the question arises of the role of language. Within cognitive development, Piaget places language "at the service of thought" (1966). He describes language as a "ready-made system that is elaborated by society and that contains, for persons who learn it before they contribute to its enrichment, a wealth of cognitive instruments (relations, classifications, etc.) . . . " (1966). Later he says, " . . . it (language) is every man's indispensable instrument of thought" (1968).

Sinclair[-de Zwart], a developmental psycholinguist, has been much more explicit about what we could call the Genevan position of the role of language in cognition. She has interpreted Piaget's work in the light of these questions about language and notes two main points Piaget makes about the relationship:

1. "The sources of intellectual operations (including logical reasoning) are not to be found in language . . . " but within the beginning development of symbolic function during the sensorimotor stage, which is preverbal.
2. "The formation of representational thought is contemporaneous with the acquisition of language . . . " both belonging to the more general process of the above-mentioned development of the symbolic function in children's cognition.

To put it simply, Sinclair states that "language is not the source of logic (thought), but is on the contrary structured by logic" (1969).

In an experiment conducted by Sinclair and Barbel Inhelder (1969), they first determined which children had not acquired the principle of *conservation*.[3] The experimenters then tried to teach them the terms used by children with conservation. These were comparative sentences such as "This jar has *more* than that jar"; differentiated terms such as *big* and *fat* as opposed to undifferentiated terms such as *fat* for both *fat* and *big;* and coordinated sentences such as "This jar is longer but thinner" or "This jar is tall and thin." After teaching the children who were unable to conserve these "verbal formulas" used in talking about conservation by other children, the experimenters again presented the children with the conservation task. They found that although the children could learn all the verbal formulas, not without difficulty, they still generally were not able to conserve. Only 10 percent of the subjects made any progress in that task. The experimenters concluded that verbal training in the language used to express a set of cognitive operations will not by itself bring about the acquisition of operations; language training will not ensure that a student actually has acquired a certain level of thinking. In fact, the inability of the child to coordinate and produce sentences such as "The jar is tall *and* thin" in the preconservation phase is apparent in

---

[3]Conservation is one of Piaget's best-known cognitive findings. At a certain point in their development, children will say, when you pour equal amounts of water into different size jars right in front of them, that one jar has more water in it than another jar. The jar they choose is a short, wide one rather than a tall, thin one. They are then at what is called a preconservation stage. When they say that both jars, no matter what the shape, hold the same amount of water, they are able to conserve. In other words, they are able to comprehend that the amount stays the same.

the child's inability to coordinate freely in language in general. The child can coordinate *between* sentences but not *within* as easily, and the experimenters found that the coordination in sentences such as "This jar is longer and thinner" was the most difficult set of terms to teach the children. In this experiment, Inhelder and Sinclair, by studying the language used by children to accompany certain cognitive processes, were able to clarify at least somewhat the connection between language and cognition. We would surmise that, in some instances at least, semantic development follows congitive development. This is also one of Bloom's contentions (1975).

Paralleling emerging cognitive patterns is also a widening of experiences that influence lexical development. Certainly the student who studies space flight expands his or her vocabulary. As teachers, we can do a great deal to enhance this sort of development, perhaps simply by calling it vocabulary growth. Whatever we call it, we can think of vocabulary as part of an ever-widening system of linguistic and cognitive development. If we provide experiences, students can think and talk about them, thus expanding both their thinking and their language abilities. Clearly communicative competence is being enhanced by such study and expansion, especially if levels of experiences are provided in conjunction with new vocabulary. Thus students may take a trip to a local science and industry museum, perform experiments in class, read about a topic, talk about it, and write about it. Such levels of experience, from concrete manipulation to greater abstractness, can also help prevent the phenomena of being able to "mouth" words but not really comprehend their meaning.

Certainly lexical development has a major social component. New social situations require that vocabulary symbolize the experiences. Therefore, as students grow older, they begin to experience *dating* and the highly ambiguous lexical item *love.* They may begin to encounter *prejudice, sexism, discrimination, lessened job opportunities,* that multitude of social events we catalogue and code through the vocabulary in our language. Also, students vastly expand their lexicon through literacy—through learning to read. It is thought that a person's reading vocabulary is the largest of all—bigger than the listening, speaking, or writing vocabulary. Probably this is partly due to the fact that it's a recognition vocabulary (as is listening) as opposed to a production vocabulary—speaking and writing. In other words, we usually recognize more than we can actively produce. You may know what *heuristic* means when you see it in print but may never use it yourself; and so on with many words.

The area of social and geographical differences in semantic development has been fraught with misunderstanding and misconception, and these will be taken up in some detail in the next chapter. Suffice it to say that there are probably no or very few differences in the way children's semantic systems develop. There may be differences in the content of the system, in the set of words a child knows and uses, because experiences differ. But the stages of semantic development seem to be similar to the stages of syntactic and phonological development. Certainly it is to be assumed that all children progressively differentiate and that they operate with feature sets. We are talking about human learning patterns, which are presumed to be universal.

Development of Social Language Use System

We've just been describing and discussing the acquisition of three commonly recognized language systems: phonological, syntactic, and semantic. But there is another system that is also important and can loom extremely large in the lives of students: the social use system. It is generally assumed that most children acquire or develop the basic patterns of the languages they're exposed to, but it is not always realized that they also acquire a culturally constrained system of how to use language socially. Students learn that *what* is said and *how* it is said are not dictated merely by "correct grammar." This use system is highly important because it tends to vary more than the other language systems, probably because it is culturally bound. In other words, many cultures may speak essentially the same language—English, in our case. But each culture has a different set of rules for how language is used socially—how it functions socially. One illustration is that, in many cultures, children are to be seen and not heard. In "mainstream," middle-class American culture, children can be both seen and heard. Thus some cultures (incidentally, that's most of the world) expect children to be quiet around adults, and a few allow them to be vocal around adults. Or we find sex differences in language, and a set of rules specifying how to "talk male" and "talk female."

For preschool children, there are several areas or *domains* of behavior that are very influential in "teaching" the rules of language use socially. The first is the domain of the home, the place of primary socialization for the child. There he or she learns the first lessons in "appropriateness": when to talk and when not to, what to talk about, how to talk about it, and who to talk about it with. For example, children learn certain verbal routines such as greetings and farewells, the appropriate use of which, according to Gleason and Weintraub, " . . . depends more upon saying the right things at the right time than upon deeper cognitive structures" (1976, p. 130). So children are taught to say "hello," "goodbye," and "thank you," among other routines. In fact, Gleason and Weintraub contend that this social use of language appears as early as the referential use of language (1976, p. 135), such as the appearance of "kitty" to refer to the family cat.

There is also the domain of the playground or street where peers exert the most influence. For the young child, this may not be as important, but again cultural patterns put varying emphases on these two domains. As the child grows older, the social domains expand and may continue to do so depending on the individual's socioeconomic status, sex, educational level, race, occupation, etc.

Let's examine several different, extremely important, social language use acquisition patterns that are culturally constrained, and then in some detail examine their implications for teaching. There is a highly revealing study done by Ward (1971) of children's language acquisition in the rural black community of Rosepoint, Louisiana, not too many miles from New Orleans.[4] It's a different culture from middle-class culture, and some differences show up in the children's patterns of communication with adults, in how they use language socially.

Among Rosepoint adults, it's generally the feeling that children should be seen but not heard. "No one in the community takes seriously the chattering of a child. In fact, as the conversations indicate, the children hold their parent's attention longer *if they say nothing*" (Ward, 1971, p. 47). According to Ward, much of the burden of direct instruction is on the child's peers and not on the parents. So within the home the child may remain relatively silent, while in the street—the peer domain—the child does most of his or her talking.

Other studies also describe this silence on the part of the child in the home. "Silence is . . . highly valued in children (especially in the presence of Momma)....Within the home the child is expected to observe and, in learning tasks, to emulate the maternal figure....In this ambience words between adults and children are extremely restricted; few words are used ....The value placed on silence in the home (on the part of children) is one facet of an elaborate ideal of deference, which includes learning proper modes of address, how and when to act in the presence of adults, and how and where to look (mutely) when being addressed by an older person" (Abrahams, 1975, pp. 70-71).

Obviously parents still interact linguistically with their children. According to Ward, this interaction usually takes the form of the parents' expanding on their own speech to the child without requiring a *verbal*

---

[4] It is called *Them Children* and is a readable study of child language acquisition in a different culture from "mainstream" culture.

response from the child. For example, one mother said to her son: (Ward, 1971, p. 49)

What Scott ate today	for dinner?
What you ate	for dinner?
What did you eat	for dinner?
What you and	
Warren have	for dinner?

This was all said to the same child in sequence by the mother. Also the mother usually initiates the conversation, not the child. Finally, Ward found virtually no examples of adults correcting the *form* of what the child said; they responded only to the content of the child's utterance. For example (Ward, 1971, p. 52),

CHILD: Give me two meat.
MOTHER: Two meats! You don't never eat what I give you anyway. You leave it on the plate.

The use of *meats* by the mother was unconscious on her part; she was really responding to the child's eating patterns.

Rosepoint mothers spend very little time expanding their children's utterances. Instead the expansion patterns come from the mother's speech itself: (Ward, 1971, p. 50)

NATALIE: Now tell her what you do all day.
What do you do in the day?
What you do in the day?
What you do in the day?
You play?
Tell her that.
Tell her you play.
Tell her that!
Tell her you play!

This is all uninterrupted speech by the mother with no verbal response from the child. This lack of expectation for the child to produce a verbal response fits well the notion that children are to be seen and not heard.

In contrast, let's look briefly at Adam, a middle-class black child whose father was a graduate student at Harvard University (Brown and Bellugi, 1964; Cazden, 1972). First, Adam's mother expanded his utterances. Such expansions would look something like those presented here, although some of these were made by Eve's and Sara's mothers as well as Adam's (Brown and Bellugi, 1964; Brown, 1973):

CHILD:	Baby highchair	MOTHER:	Baby is in the highchair.
	Sat wall		He sat on the wall.
	Throw Daddy		Throw it to Daddy.
	Eve lunch		Eve is having lunch.

Second, Adam initiated many of the recorded conversations with his mother. She would follow his topic lead, thus allowing a great deal of reciprocity in the conversation. And third, mothers in this middle-class culture tend to be aware of the forms used in children's speech. All of this contributes to a certain verbal "forwardness" on the part of many middle-class children. They are used to initiating a conversation with an adult, and they are used to being rewarded for talking to them. The Rosepoint children, on the other hand, are not reinforced for that same verbal behavior. They learn a different set of social rules for language use around adults. They use language with peers and much less with adults. And when they talk to adults, the adult leads the conversation. This is not to say that they don't learn the syntactic, semantic, and phonological systems of their variety. They do as well as a middle-class child. They learn, instead, a different set of social "appropriateness" rules.

There is at least one important educational implication to be drawn from this difference. The Rosepoint child is not used to being verbally assertive with a teacher or with other "strange" adults, while the middle-class child is. So children who are quiet with adults may be labeled "nonverbal" or "backward" even though they are only using their culture's set of rules about how one communicates with adults.

How can this mismatch occur? A child from, let's say, the Rosepoint culture who enters school is also entering both another area of experience (*domain*)—education—and another culture—"mainstream" middle class. Within the educational domain exists a new set of experiences for any child, a set of expectations as to "proper" physical and verbal behavior, and a possibly vast social expansion from the child's previous experience. Many new people enter the child's life. The child is expected to learn appropriate behavior in keeping with the values held by people acting in the domain.

But a Rosepoint child's learning of this behavior may be complicated by the necessity of dealing with the different culture. And we tend to judge each other according to our own cultures. When the two don't match, and when we aren't aware of the mismatch, *cultural clash* can be the result. In such a clash situation, both parties can be quite upset about the other's behavior and not know why. For example, the lower-class black student who doesn't look the teacher in the eye may be labeled "sneaky." The teacher who demands being looked in the eye confuses the student who knows you only look at an adult when you're defying his or her authority. Respect is shown by downcast eyes. So the teacher unconsciously encourages insubordination in the student but reacts extremely negatively when that student is self-assertive in ways other than looking directly at the teacher.

Social language-use systems can also contribute to cultural clash when they mismatch. Labov (1968) gives a clear example of this when he contrasts black ghetto culture's modes of expressing politness and disagreement with those of middle-class culture. In the middle class a child does not say to an adult, "You're stupid" or "You're wrong," especially in certain tones of voice. The social rule is such that an adult may say these things to a child, but not vice versa. A child from the ghetto culture hasn't learned the same social rule set. Disagreement with adults is often expressed nonverbally in that culture or, sometimes, by certain kinds of verbal forms which, on the surface, may seem highly disrespectful but are encouraged so the child will develop the ability to assert him or herself verbally, an important part of the culture (See Abrahams, 1975). So when the child begins to be verbal in school—which is usually encouraged—he or she doesn't know all the rules for school disagreement forms and consequently makes mistakes. These mistakes can have severe consequences. There are students in Harlem schools who are labeled "incorrigible" and "troublemakers" on their permanent records because they can't disagree in middle-class modes of politeness. And this happens in many more places than just Harlem.

Obviously cultural clash can have and has had some very real negative effects in classrooms where there are several cultures. It is helpful if we understand that there are different systems of social language use that are culturally constrained. We can become aware of their existence and learn something about the specific language patterns used. We can use this insight to help various groups of students maximize their communicative competence and to not turn them into even more silent students who sit quietly simply to get through each school day with a minimum of embarrassment. Some obvious cultures we need to be aware of in this context are: black ghetto culture, Appalachian culture, the various American Indian cultures, Spanish-based cultures such as Chicano, Mexican-American, and Puerto Rican, and Chinese culture. The list could be much longer; we can extend it by extending our awareness of and sensitivity to different systems of the social use of language.

To conclude: by the time children come to school, they have an excellent grasp on three language systems: phonology, syntax, and semantics. They are also beginning to control aspects of the social language-use system, which expands greatly when the child enters and continues in school. As teachers, we can work with those aspects of the system that need to be expanded and refined. In this way, we can be extremely helpful in aiding students to expand their ability to communicate clearly with a variety of people in this multicultural society.

Bibliography

Abrahams, Roger D., "Negotiating Respect," *Journal of American Folklore, 88,* No. 347 (January-March, 1975), 58–80.

Anderson, Elaine S., "Cups and Glasses: Learning that Boundaries are Vague," *Journal of Child Language, 2* (1975), 79–103.

Bloom, Lois. *Language Development: Form and Function in Emerging Grammars.* Cambridge, Mass.: M.I.T. Press, 1970.

Bloom, Lois, P. Lightbown, and L. Hood, "Structure and Variation in Child Language," *Monograph of the Society for Research in Child Development,* No. 160 (1975).

Bowerman, Melissa. *Early Syntactic Development: A Cross-Linguistic Study with Special Reference to Finnish.* Cambridge, England: Cambridge University Press, 1973.

Brown, Roger. *A First Language.* Cambridge, Mass.: Harvard University Press, 1973.

Brown, Roger, and Ursula Bellugi, "Three Processes in the Child's Acquisition of Syntax," in *New Directions in the Study of Language,* edited by Eric H. Lenneberg. Cambridge, Mass.: The M.I.T. Press, 1964, pp. 131–62.

Bruner, Jerome, "The Course of Cognitive Growth" in *Language in Education, A Source Book* edited by A. Cashden and Elizabeth Grugeon. London: Routledge & Kegan Paul, 1972, pp. 161-66.

Cazden, Courtney, "Suggestions from Studies of Early Language Acquisition," in *Language and the Language Arts,* edited by Johanna S. DeStefano and Sharon E. Fox. Boston: Little, Brown and Co., 1974, pp. 42-47.

Cazden, Courtney. *Child Language and Education.* New York: Holt, Rinehart and Winston, Inc., 1972.

Chomsky, Carol. *The Acquisition of Syntax in Children from 5 to 10.* Cambridge, Mass.: The M.I.T. Press, 1969.

Clark, Eve V. *First Language Acquisition,* unpublished manuscript.

Clark, Eve V., "On the Acquisition of the Meaning of *Before* and *After,"* *Journal of Verbal Learning and Verbal Behavior, 10* (1971), 256-275.

Clark, Eve V., "What's in a Word? On the Child's Acquisition of Semantics in His First Language," T. E. Moore, (editor), *Cognitive Development and the Acquisition of Language.* New York: Academic Press, 1973, pp. 65-110.

Clark, Eve V., "Same Aspects of the Conceptual Basis for First Language Acquisition," in *Language Perspectives—Acquisition, Retardatiron and Intervention,* edited by R. L. Schiefelbusch and L. L. Lloyd. Baltimore: University Park Press, 1974, pp. 105-128.

Clark, Herbert H., and Eve V. Clark, *Psychology and Language.* New York: Harcourt, Brace Jovanovich, 1977.

Dale, Philip. *Language Development: Structure and Function.* Second Edition. New York: Holt, Rinehart and Winston, 1976.

French, Patrice L., "Perception and Early Semantic Learning," in *Child Language—1975,* edited by Walburga von Raffler-Engel. International Linguistic Association, special issue of *WORD, 27,* Nos. 1-3 (1971), 1976, pp. 125-138.

Garnica, Olga K., "How Children Learn to Talk," *Theory Into Practice,* Vol. XIV, No. 5 (December, 1975) 299–305.

Gibson, Eleanor J., "Reading for Some Purpose: Keynote Address," in *Language by Ear and by Eye,* edited by James F. Kavanagh and Ignatius G. Mattingly. Cambridge, Mass.: The M.I.T. Press, 1972, pp. 3-19.

Gleason, Jean Berko, and Sandra Weintraub, "The Acquisition of Routines in Child Language," *Language in Society, 5* (Aug., 1976), 129-136.

Halliday, M.A.K. *Learning How to Mean—Explorations in the Development of Language.* London: Edward Arnold, Ltd., 1975.

Hong, Laraine, "Distinguishing *Woman* from *Girl* and *Man* from *Boy:* A Problem of Semantic Features and Vague Word Boundaries," unpublished paper, 1976.

Jesperson, O. *Language.* New York: Holt, Rinehart and Winston, 1925.

Kaplan, Eleanor L. "The Role of Intonation in the Acquisition of Language." Doctoral Dissertation, Cornell University, 1969.

Labov, William. *A Study of Nonstandard English.* Champaign: NCTE, 1968. Also in DeStefano, Johanna S. *Language, Society and Education: A Profile of Black English.* Worthington, Ohio: Charles A. Jones Publishing Co., 1973.

Lenneberg, Eric H. *Biological Foundations of Language.* New York: Wiley, 1967.

Maccoby, Eleanor E., and Bee, H.L., "Some Speculations Concerning the Lag Between Perceiving and Performing," *Child Development, 36* (1965), 367-377. In *Language Development,* Second Edition, by Philip S. Dale. New York: Holt, Rinehart and Winston, 1976.

McNeill, David, "The Development of Language" in *Carmichael's Manual of Child Psychology,* edited by P.H. Mussen, Vol. 1, Third Edition. New York: Wiley, 1970, pp. 1061-1161.

Menyuk, Paula. *The Acquisition and Development of Language.* Englewood Cliffs, N.J.: Prentice-Hall, Inc., 1971.

Park, T.Z. A Study of German Language Development. Berne, Switzerland: Psychological Institute, unpublished manuscript, 1974.

Piaget, Jean, and Barbel Inhelder. *La Psychologie de L'enfant.* Paris: Presses Univer. France, 1966.

Piaget, Jean. *Structuralism.* London: Routledge & Kegan Paul, 1968.

Sinclair-de Zwart, Hermina, "Developmental Psycholinguistics," in *Studies in Cognitive Development,* edited by D. Elkind and J. H. Flavell. New York: Oxford University Press, 1969.

Ward, Martha Coonfield. *Them Children, A Study in Language Learning.* New York: Holt, Rinehart and Winston, 1971.

Wardhaugh, Ronald. *The Contexts of Language.* Rowley, Mass.: Newbury House Publishers, Inc., 1976.

For Further Reading

Brown, Roger. *A First Language*. Cambridge, Mass.: Harvard University Press, 1973.
A delightful book giving the lowdown on Adam, Eve, and Sarah by the researcher who started it all—Brown. From the horse's mouth for someone interested in detail in that classic set of studies.

Cazden, Courtney. *Child Language and Education*. New York: Holt, Rinehart and Winston, 1972.

A comprehensive, research-oriented book that covers a great many facets of children's language, specifically in the educational domain.

Chomsky, Carol. *The Acquisition of Syntax in Children from 5 to 10*. Cambridge, Mass.: The M.I.T. Press, 1969.

If you want to look in depth at certain aspects of syntactic development in school-age children, this is an excellent book. It also applies the transformational-generative mode of analysis to syntax to give you a clearer picture as to how that is done.

Dale, Philip. *Language Development: Structure and Function*. Second Edition. New York: Holt, Rinehart and Winston, 1976.

A very readable book that goes into quite a bit of detail, especially in syntactic development. An excellent background and reference volume.

Menyuk, Paula. *The Acquisition and Development of Language*. Englewood Cliffs, N.J.: Prentice-Hall, Inc., 1971.

A comprehensive, detailed volume covering not only the preschool child but also the primary age child. Much specific information on phonological and syntactic development in the school-age child.

Ward, Martha Coonfield. *Them Children, a Study in Language Learning*. New York: Holt, Rinehart and Winston, 1971.

This is an ethnographic study of child language acquisition in a rural American community, which has many implications for teachers of both the culturally different and children from "mainstream" culture.

For Further Viewing

DeStefano, Johanna, Sharon E. Fox, Martha L. King, Victor M. Rentel, and

Frank Zidonis, Graduate Reading Faculty, Ohio State University, development staff of USOE funded protocols project, "The Language of Children" (1970-1975).

Films Available:

Acquiring Comparative Structures (1974)

Color, 16 mm, 17 min.

Three children attempt to produce and understand comparative terms. The number and types of comparatives versus absolutes in their responses reveal their level of cognitive development. The teacher asks the children to comment on portions of marbles, which differ in size and number, and pencils, which differ in dimension. She also asks them to group the marbles and pencils as she specifies. For teacher training. Accompanying guide and worksheet.

Acquisition of Morphology: Group Variability (1975)

Color, 16 mm, 10 min.

Children in kindergarten, second, and sixth grades respond to sentences that require them to form the past tense of various nonsense verbs. They are then given a set of six cards with five adjectives and a noun and must put the cards in the right order. For teacher training. Accompanying guide and worksheets.

Acquisition of Morphology: Individual Variability (1975)

Color, 16 mm, 10 min.

Twelve children in kindergarten, second, and sixth grades see pictures of cartoonlike characters and then try to complete a sentence that involves inflecting or changing the ending of a nonsense word. The changes involve noun plurals, verb past tenses, and comparative and superlative forms of adjectives. For teacher training. Accompanying guide and worksheets.

Acquisition of Morphology: Sequence (1975)

Color, 16 mm, 10 min.

Children in kindergarten, second, and sixth grades respond to sentence patterns that require them to use the plural form of various nonsense nouns. They also try to form comparative and superlative forms of nonsense adjectives. In the last section the structure of compound nouns is explained. For teacher training. Accompanying guide and worksheets.

Children's Phonology (1975)

Color, 16 mm, 10 min.

Five children, ranging in age from three to four and one-half, play a word game with their teacher in which they are asked to choose between possible and impossible words. Their responses indicate whether they have abstracted and internalized the implicit ordering of English sounds. For teacher training. Accompanying guide and worksheet.

Combining Simple Sentences (1975)

Color, 16 mm, 15 min.

Groups of second and sixth graders combine two or three short sentences, which are read to them by their teacher, into one sentence. The task is structured to investigate the process of sentence combining and the complexity of the result. For teacher training. Accompanying guide and worksheets.

Promise/Tell Structures in Children's Language (1974)

Color, 16 mm, 13 min.

Children in kindergarten, second and sixth grades respond to a set of eight sentences. The verb *tell* or *promise* is followed by a noun and infinitive construction in each sentence. The child indicates the subject of the infinitive by moving the appropriate doll. For teacher training. Accompanying guide and worksheets.

Semantic Acquisition (1974)

Color, 16 mm, 8 min.

Adults and children attempt to repeat grammatical and anomalous sentences that have been masked to reduce clarity. Their ability to repeat grammatical sentences is correlated with the maturity of their knowledge of semantic feature lists and selectional restrictions on words. For teacher training. Accompanying guide and worksheet.

Shared Nomenclature (1975)

Color, 16 mm, 18 min.

The sequence of semantic acquisition is illustrated in this film. Four pairs of age-mates are shown. One member of each pair is given an illustration of the arrangement of six blocks with novel designs. After arranging his blocks, he must communicate the proper arrangement to his partner on the other side of a blind. For teacher training. Accompanying guide and worksheets.

Understanding Negatives and Passives (1975)

Color, 16 mm, 15 min.

Preschool, kindergarten, and first-grade children are shown a simple action picture and are asked several questions about it. Their responses demonstrate their understanding of the syntactic and semantic constraints that govern active, passive, negative, and affirmative sentences. For teacher training. Accompanying guide and worksheet.

Variation in Language

When we raise the question of how we can help our students maximize their ability to communicate, we need to ask about the impact of language variation on our role as teachers and on our students. We know, for example, that variation can be an important part of the *who* we are teaching and the *who* we are as teachers. Students' language and our language consistently display types of variation no matter where we live and what social class or group we belong to. Other types of variation in language may appear depending on geography, on social class, or on other social factors such as educational level, ethnic identity, sex, and so on. These types of variation in language will be explored in this chapter to acquaint you not only with what they are but also with what role they can play in the classroom.

In determining the place of language variation in the classroom, perhaps one of the most important principles for us to know about is that variation in language is natural. We expect it among languages and are not the least bit surprised that Spanish sounds different from English. We tend to accept the fact that some students will speak a language other than English. If we teach in San Francisco, we expect to have Chinese-speaking or Spanish-speaking children. If we teach in the Southwest, we expect Spanish again or various American Indian languages such as Navaho or Hopi. And there are groups of other language speakers all over the United States—French speakers in Maine, Tagalog speakers (from the Philippines) on the West Coast, to name only several.

A type of variation that seems to be generally less expected is variation within a language. Perhaps this is partly due to the pervasive concept, in our case, of "standard English." Curriculum materials in the language arts and English education include teaching something called "standard English," radio and TV announcers are thought to speak it, educated people are supposed to use it. Somehow it's "more logical," "better," and "more expressive" than other forms of English. But is the concept of "standard English" a viable one? Perhaps a historical look at the notion of a standard language will help answer that question. In England there is Received Pronunciation, RP, or "the Queen's English," which is considered standard or at least a standard by many Britishers. It is the variety of British English, including lexical and syntactic differences as well as phonological ones, spoken by the most prestigious and socially powerful who tend to cluster in the London area. Obviously the Queen herself speaks it. In the recent past, RP was even more powerful as a standard. To become a BBC announcer, it was mandatory to speak it no matter where you were from in England or where you broadcast—be it Scotland or Wales. It was taught in schools and held up as an almost absolute standard, a complete necessity for one to learn if one were to climb up the social scale.

Although British English is perhaps the closest to us emotionally and socially here in America, the idea of a "standard" variety is not at all unusual in other societies. Parisian French is advanced by the power of Paris, French mass media, and the Académie Française (located in Paris, of course). When I learned French at the university, it was Parisian, not another variety. Many Italians will tell you the "best" Italian is a Tuscan variety spoken in the Florence area, although they may still cling to their regional varieties, since Italy is not as socially unified with a strong central government as is France. If it were, it's possible that a form of Roman Italian would be ascendant—if Rome were the center of power. In China, the definition of the Chinese *language* is actually political in the sense that many of its "dialects" are mutually unintelligible[1] but are all considered "Chinese" for solidarity reasons. However, the government is promoting the teaching of one variety of Chinese for speaking purposes. Mandarin is the basis of this variety, called Putonghua, now taught in Chinese schools. Mandarin is spoken in Peking, China's capital, as well as being the variety spoken by the largest number of people in China (Lehman, 1975, p. 11). Putonghua is composed of " . . . the pronunciation of the general Peking dialect, the grammar of Northern Chinese dialects, and the vocabulary of modern colloquial Chinese literature" (Lehman, 1975, p. 11). One of the government's goals is to have all one billion plus Chinese able to speak Putonghua, now the "standard" Chinese. On Taiwan, where many dialects were brought together quickly, engineers often wrote notes to each other in face-to-face communication situations because they couldn't understand each other's spoken Chinese. Thus, they resorted to the writing system, which all understood.

How does the United States "standard" variety compare with these

---

[1] "Mutually unintelligible" means that speakers of one variety cannot understand speakers of another variety and vice versa. This is exactly the case in China. A Cantonese speaker (Canton area) cannot understand a speaker of Mandarin (Peking area) and vice versa.

other *recognized* ones? First of all, if it exists, it is not associated with one geographical location and social hub such as London, Paris, or Peking. A person from Seattle will not try to sound like a New Yorker or a Philadelphian or a Chicagoan, although all these places are nationally powerful. We have nothing to compare regionally with Tuscan Italian; we don't try to sound Northeastern or whatever. Our regions aren't that well defined linguistically. No one particularly tries to emulate the speech of our Presidents who, in turn, do not try to change their speech. John F. Kennedy remained *r*-less in certain contexts such as *cah* and added an *r* in others, to give *Cubar.* Lyndon Johnson continued to sound like a person from Texas. We have no American English Academy, as a counterpart to the Académie Française, to pass on "proper usage." Not everyone tries to sound like Walter Cronkite on the evening news. So what do we have for a standard?

Instead of having a true nationally recognized "Standard English," what we do have are more or less regional standards, although some regional varieties are not standards. The form of these regional standards is largely determined by social, economic, and political power, as they are in many other countries. Those people in a given area who are recognized as powerful are also often recognized as speakers of "good English." So if the power structure changes, what is considered "standard" may also change. Historically this has happened in many countries. In medieval France, Provençal vied with other varieties of French for ascendancy. This was the French spoken in the area of Provençe in southern France. It had an extensive literature, another mark of a standard language; the *Song of Roland,* a famous medieval poem, was in Provençal. In fact, Provençal poets were famous throughout the Western world. But Paris became the seat of the kings of France and developed a power ascendancy over the rest of France. Thus France became unified as a nation with a strong centralized monarchy rather early for Europe. Gradually Provençal lost its prestige and, by now, its speakers, since more and more people began to speak Parisian French because of economic and political necessity.

Thus we don't have a standard in the sense of one variety of American English—including its phonology, syntax, and lexicon—being taught widely in schools as an entire system. Our "standard" is much more complex than that, with variations in phonology being particularly allowed.

Since this is the case in the United States, we need to know about the variations of American English we may encounter among our students. What can linguists tell us about within language variation? First, variation in language is systematic. People who speak different varieties do not produce random forms. The variation is patterned and highly rule governed, as in the case of Black English described later in this chapter. This

83

systematic variation is the way linguists distinguish different varieties in a language, although the boundary lines are often very fuzzy.

Also, we know that language variation is judged by social groups who hear the variations used. Attitude sets are held toward the different varieties both by speakers of the varieties and by those who hear them but don't speak them. These attitudes reflect the cultural set toward different groups. In other words, if our culture "looks down on" or dislikes certain groups—as just about all cultures do—our judgment of speech in those groups follows the general attitude set. Consequently varieties may be judged "good" or "bad" depending on the status of *who* speaks them. An extreme example is Hindi-Urdu, essentially a single language but considered two because both Indians and Pakistanis speak it. Relations between the two countries are strained, to put it mildly. Thus we are told that Hindi is spoken by Indians and Urdu is spoken by Pakistanis, with mutual intelligibility often denied. In other words, a Pakistani and an Indian may claim that they don't understand one another.

It is important that these principles about language variation are understood by those of us who work with students, since we have a great deal of power over them in our judgments of their language varieties, whether they be geographical or social. These principles are part of an objective look at variation.

What kinds of variation do we have in the United States? This chapter is devoted to a description of some major types of language variation.

Geographical Variation

The study of geographically constrained varieties or dialects, as they're usually called, is an old one in linguistics. Dialect atlases were begun as long ago as the nineteenth century in Germany. These atlases, including the ones now done in the United States, show the geographical distribution of language forms (such as where people say *greasy* with an /s/ and where they say it with a /z/ here in the United States).

One of the major characteristics of geographical variation is that one linguistic feature may be used in a specific area of the country and another related one in an adjacent area, such as *greasy* (generally Northern) and *greazy* (generally Southern). When this contrast exists, a line can be drawn between the two; that line is called an isogloss. It's a boundary line showing where one feature ends and another begins. Isoglosses bundle together in a variety of ways. In fact, a dialect could be defined as a bundle of isoglosses that are more patterned than surrounding isoglosses; that is, they crisscross and "weave" together. But precise definitions of specific dialects are difficult because in the United States many features tend to be shared on the fringes of a geographical area and even in the center. Our variations of American English tend to be mutually intelligible; we can understand speakers of other dialects and they can understand us. And certainly one difference, such as *greasy* and *greazy*, doesn't indicate the boundaries between two dialects. In some regions, the isoglosses seem to crisscross each other randomly. When this happens, it's called a dialect transition area. Oklahoma is currently one such area in the United States. Generally, when a sufficient number of isoglosses bundle together, this is considered a dialect.

Dialects are often defined as mutually intelligible varieties of a language, but even that definition is problematic because vocabulary differences can render one dialect unintelligible to outsiders. I'm thinking of the time I first heard a Cornish dialect (spoken in parts of Cornwall, England), which contained a lexicon for common items that was totally unfamiliar to me. Thus such a definition for dialect clearly rests on *degrees* of mutual intelligibility. If you know no German, you probably will be able to pick out only one or two words in a German speaker's speech. But you can pick out more words in a Cornishman's dialect even though the speaker's line of thought may remain murky to you. And if the person were to talk about a scientific subject, you would undoubtedly understand more as that is a more shared and "public" vocabulary.

What factors have influenced the development of dialects in a region? It is a rather complex combination of factors, but some have been isolated. We do know, for example, that there is greater dialect differentiation and more stable isogloss bundles in areas where settlement is relatively geographically static. With language constantly changing, such change can become noticeable when there is at least some geographic isolation. In a given area, people have more opportunity to talk with one another than they have with someone from over the mountains. As you would expect, there is quite a bit of dialect differentiation in areas where the population is geographically stable. That happens particularly where there is a large rural population with relatively few migrations to urban centers. And this is a disappearing phenomenon in industrialized countries where people flock to big cities for work. So some dialects are actually disappearing in England where there is continued movement into big cities.

You will also find more variation in longer-settled areas than in newer ones. According to Carroll Reed, "Older settlements, such as those existing on the continent of Europe, often show sharp and extensive differences, while colonial areas, such as those found in the United States, tend to be more homogeneous" (1973 [second printing], p. 3). England, although very small in size, has sharper and more pronounced dialect boundaries than does the United States. Also, New England, relatively small in size, has more dialect differentiation and less homogeneous speech than does California, which is both younger in English settlement history and much more fluid in settlement patterns. In California, families more commonly moved from one part to another, especially if they weren't tied to the land. And more people came from all over the country to settle, bringing their dialects with them. New England did not experience this large influx of people from all over the United States. People may have lived for generations in one town. Such stability provides for greater language differences.

Origin of the speakers can also influence dialect patterns. Part of New England's dialect differences are based on its settlers being from different parts of the British Isles. California was settled by people from all over the United States, Europe, and Mexico. The Spanish influence is definitely felt more in those areas with native Spanish speakers, as parts of Pennsylvania were influenced by native German speakers. Spanish and German are languages that tend to be maintained by their speakers; that is, they continue to be spoken. On the other hand, Finnish has left relatively little impression on the dialects of the areas where Finns settled in the United States because the speakers have tended not to maintain it: not to teach it to their children and not to teach reading and writing in Finnish. The ability to speak Finnish has usually disappeared by the second generation born in America, although there are a few indications now that in some parts of Minneosta and other northern and midwestern states, the language is being taught to children, usually in church-related schools.

As you might expect, dialect boundaries can also be related to lines of people's movement in a country. In the United States, the Mississippi and Ohio River valleys show clusters of isoglosses of language features relating to movement up and down those rivers.

Geographic mobility tends to reduce dialect differences. Probably in the United States, geographical dialects will continue to disappear as more people travel the country and live in different areas. It is usually older people now who are the informants for dialect studies because they haven't been as mobile as the younger ones. In this country, then, it is probably fair to say that geography will increasingly diminish in importance as a basis for language variation. Other factors such as social class are assuming increasing importance. For example, large numbers of Applachian whites and Southern Blacks have moved North into large urban centers looking for work and a better life. They brought their local dialects with them, but the children are exposed to a much more varied input. Geographical dialects change under such an impact as lines of communication are established with people who don't speak the way people do "down home." In fact, in large urban centers there are often dialects of great regional prestige such as in Boston, New York, Philadelphia, and Richmond, Virginia. Features from these dialects may be picked up by immigrants to the cities and may also radiate outward to surrounding areas, thus influencing older and more rural dialects.

The speech communities children are raised in have changed. A *speech community* is a group of speakers who tend to evaluate language patterns in a consistent way. The concept is social in nature and not tied to any one variety of a language, so the community may even be multilingual. Hymes (1972, p. 54) defines it in the following way: "A speech community is defined as a community sharing rules for the conduct and interpretation of speech (including writing as well), and rules for the interpretation of at least one linguistic variety." In all probability, the Appalachian dialects are evaluated in a different way in Detroit, Michigan, than they are in Appalachia, and that evaluation is transmitted to the children with a possible ensuing change in the children's speech to features and forms more accepted by the various Detroit speech communities.

In the United States, dialect differences in the East are much more pronounced than they are in other regions of the country. Oregonians sound much more like people from Kansas and Nebraska than Philadelphians and New Yorkers sound like each other, even though these two cities are only about 90 miles apart. But it's also not accurate to characterize everyone in a region as speaking one dialect, as is sometimes done when radio announcers are described as speaking "Midwestern." In the south, for example, there are many regional differences even though to a Northern ear they may sound the same.

As a teacher, you will probably run across dialect variation in your students if you teach in an urban area. Or if you teach in a rural area other than your own, you will undoubtedly notice dialect differences. It's important to be alert to them and put them in perspective. You can begin by being aware of your attitudes toward them. For example, Southern dialects tend to have low social prestige in the rest of America, possibly because they are strongly associated with the poor immigrants to Northern urban centers or with a set of attitudes about the South in general. I once had a student who had been sent to a speech therapist in the Northern school she had moved to to get rid of her Georgia dialect. It was considered a deficient form of English. The result was that she stuttered severely for over eight years after that type of "therapy." Generally, however, there is no single ascendant dialect in America in the sense of prestige, as we mentioned earlier. Boston dialects and "Main Line Philadephese" are not emulated in San Fransisco or Los Angeles. However, unfavorable attitudes toward various geographical dialects can negatively influence students' chances to maximize their communicative competence, especially if they don't feel comfortable using language in the classroom. If it's not used, it's not developed. Those negative attitudes are generally expressed by the deficiency hypothesis: a linguistic difference is a deficiency. This viewpoint is widespread in some educational materials, and we need to be alert to its appearance and acceptance.[2]

What sorts of features of dialects are you likely to hear in students' speech? They are those sets of features that enter into defining or characterizing a specific dialect. Certainly one of the most striking sets is lexicon. I used to call the fizzy stuff in bottles *pop*. Going from the West coast to the East, I found people didn't understand me. They used *soda* for the same fluid. Some people in Boston say *tonic,* which has quite a different meaning for me. And somewhere in the middle is *soda pop.* The brown paper contraption I carried my lunch in was a *sack.* In Oregon we had *sack lunches* too. Again, in the East I wasn't understood when I asked for *sacks.* They were lunch *bags.* In Philadelphia, a *sack* is a large container for something like 50 pounds of potatoes or coal. In Oregon, we didn't make the size distinction. All these containers, big or little, were called *sacks.* You may be aware that *frying pan* is variously called *spider* and *skillet* as well. *Window shades* are also called *blinds* and *roller shades.* The grass strip between the sidewalk and the street is called *parking strip, lawn extension, boulevard, city strip*, and *tree lawn.* Furniture gives rise to different lexical items for the same object. The large, overstuffed piece in the living room is variously called *sofa, daveno, davenport,* and *couch,* to name only a few variants.

These lexical variations tend to be connected with familiar objects in everyday use or appearance. The scientific and technical lexicon is far less geographically bound. *Proton* is used all over the United States to refer to that particular atomic particle. In fact, much of the vocabulary used in school is not geographically bound, especially in upper elementary grades, middle schools, and high schools.

There are also syntactic differences among dialects in American English, but they tend to be fewer than lexical ones and largely found in the morphological system. It's not uncommon to hear, "She come tomorrow" instead of "She comes tomorrow." One can also hear past tense and past participle differences as in *climbed* and *clumb,* and *dived* and *dove.* Often, also, these variations appear in what is called nonstandard speech, mean-

---

[2] Frederick Williams has edited a volume on the deficiency-difference controversy, *Language and Poverty* (Chicago: Markham, 1970), which is well worth looking into for a detailed presentation of the various arguments.

ing they are not used by "standard" speakers in that particular region.

As you would expect, there are also phonological differences in both the vowel and consonant systems. These are the differences that yield, for example, the generally Northern *greasy* and the generally Southern *greazy* or the Southern /pIn/ for both *pen* and *pin*. Dialects may have different sets of phonemic contrasts; *hoarse* and *horse* may be contrasted in one but not in another. They do not contrast in my dialect. For me it's a homonym set; for others, the pair is not homonymous.

Vowels are most often used to distinguish phonologically among dialects, as they systematically vary the most. Recall the old joke about "poils" and "erl" in Brooklyn. Some of the major consonant differences occur in the initial sound in *these* and *them*. In some areas you will hear *dese* and *dem*, again often considered nonstandard. Or *caught* or *court* may become homophones through the nonrealization of the /r/ to give /kɔt/ for both. To teachers, these phonological contrasts may be quite noticeable. However, they are on the "surface" rather than in the deep structure. In other words, different lexical items such as *sofa* and *davenport* have the same meaning, as do *dem* and *them* (phonological differences). "That's the davenport" and "Dat's duh sofa" have the same deep structure, the same tree diagram. In American English, dialects have far more common than disparate characteristics. And what's not common is largely surface forms. The dialects of American English are far more similar than they are different. We cannot be blinded to the overwhelming number of shared features by the differences, which may stand out far beyond their importance. It's not uncommon for people to tell me they think treating a variety such as Black English like a foreign language is a useful approach. But that maximizes the differences and tends to ignore the substantial similarity. Varieties (including dialects) of American English are variations on a theme, not different symphonies.

Social Variation

It is likely that social variation in speech is of far more consequence than geographical variation to teachers and students in the United States. Let me begin to explain why by defining the term *sociolect*. It was coined to parallel *dialect* and essentially means *socially constrained* or *determined* variety of speech. It refers to those varieties attached to socioeconomic status, culture, and so forth—in other words—to social rather than geographic factors. But socioeconomic level is not the only social variable to affect language behavior. Robbins Burling notes:

nportant sociological distinction is likely to be reflected in language. We all know that teenagers and members of the older generation tend to speak differently. Women do not speak identically with men. Professional groups develop their own jargon, and so do groups of criminals. Even families often acquire a few unique linguistic symbols, such as words that are used by family members with a special twist of meaning. By our language we define certain people as inside the group, and we leave others out. Language comes to be an accurate map of sociological divisions of a society (Burling, 1973, p. 27).

Sometimes it's difficult to separate dialect and sociolect because a highly geographically marked dialect may also be associated with lower-class speakers. In fact, in the United States there seems to be a tendency for dialects to become or give rise to sociolects. As mentioned previously, large numbers of Blacks from various parts of the South migrated to Northern urban areas. They brought their dialects which, generally, were rural, lower-class, Southern dialects. Also, large numbers of Appalachian and Southern whites have moved to urban areas, again bringing their various dialects into contact. Unfortunately we have very little information about either the extent and nature of that migration into urban areas or about the resulting speech patterns that must be emerging. This could all be complicated by recent movement back to Appalachia because of increased prosperity and rising employment in that area.

Black English

Much more is currently known about the dialects-become-sociolect called Black English or black ghetto vernacular than about many sociolects. First, it is not particularly geographically constrained. Children have been found in Oakland, California (DeStefano, 1970) and in Philadelphia (DeStefano, 1972) using many of the same forms in much the same way. Other linguists have found the same ghetto vernacular spoken in Los Angeles, Detroit, Chicago, New York City, and Washington, D.C. The reasons for the overwhelming similarities in black speech in these cities is not well understood—but the similarities do exist.

Who are the persons who speak this social variety, also sometimes called Nonstandard Negro English (NNE; Labov, 1968), Black English Vernacular (Labov, 1972), or Black Vernacular? As you would expect, the characteristics are social. First, the speakers are usually lower-class blacks living in urban ghettos. They tend to be racially isolated, living among other blacks. They also tend to be residentially isolated; that is, they live in ghettos with fairly definite boundaries and may experience great difficulty getting out of these ghettos (see St. Clair Drake on Chicago's "Gilded Ghetto" in DeStefano, 1973). They also tend to be socially isolated in that they interact much more closely with one another than they do with people outside their ghetto. Black English speakers also have a distinct culture, different from middle-class "main-stream" culture. As mentioned in previous chapters, black children may have a different conception of proper behavior in meeting a teacher's eyes. This is culturally constrained behavior. If you are teaching urban black children, you are dealing with another culture with a set of values and specifications for behavior. Remember Ward's Rosepoint, Louisiana, example of different constraints on children's language behavior (Chapter 3).

Part of this culture are the systems of forms and use of the vernacular, both of which will be discussed only briefly, since detailed descriptions are available elsewhere. (See For Further Reading for some references.) First, it is now suggested that the most different form features of Black English are intonation patterns and lexical items. There is a different "melody" to Black English—a different stress, pitch, and juncture system. It has been suggested that Black English does not have a stress system pattern (see Chapter 2), but a time stress pattern instead. More time is thus given to some sounds and less time to others in this sort of system. Tarone reports that she found a wider pitch range in Black English, with higher pitch levels included than those found in other varieties. And she notes that more rising and level final contours were used in Black English, as opposed to falling final contours (fade-fall terminal) in other varieties (Tarone, 1972). You can hear these and other intonation differences by listening closely to speakers of Black English.

The lexicon also is obviously different in some ways from other varieties of American English. This is particularly evident in slang terms, which tend to come and go with great rapidity. Good-looking women are "foxes" now and men can be "dudes," but in a relatively short time those terms probably will be replaced, especially if whites pick them up. Originally "right on" and "uptight" were black terms, but they have been borrowed by a wider community and are no longer used by many blacks, who have subsequently coined other terms. There are also shared words, which are used in radically different ways by blacks. "Nigger" is one of these. Used by those outside the culture, it usually refers pejoratively to a black person. Used inside the culture it may mean "boyfriend" or "friend" as in "He's my best nigger," or it can be a solidarity term as in "We're all niggers." In black culture, it's become a word with positive connotations.

Aside from intonation (suprasegmentals) and lexicon, there are possibly other differences in the phonological and syntactic systems. However, it is generally felt that most of these features are shared with other varieties of American English. For example, you may hear a ghetto black child say, "Rufie my sister name." The use of /f/ instead of /θ/ in *Ruth* is not an uncommon phenomenon. It's sometimes developmental and sometimes linked to various American English varieties, both geographical and social. Note also the indication of possession by word order only, without the use of the possessive morpheme *-s* on sister. This pattern is part of the system of Black English and may also be part of other varieties as well. Sometimes you may also hear, "I got two cent," in which the plural noun is indicated solely by the plural adjective and not by an *-s* on the noun. Again, some of the redundancy is dropped in this system in which a number word, such as *two,* signals more than one, or plural, and not the *-s.*

Finally, there is a rule in the vernacular that goes something like, "In cases in which you contract from a full verb form in some American English varieties, you can drop the contraction in Black English." So *Ruthie's,* meaning *Ruthie is,* may become *Ruthie* to give "Rufie my sister name."

In the syntactic system, there may be some forms that are actually limited to Black English, although this view may also change the more we get to know about the other varieties of American English. One particular form is a *be* verb, which appears in sentences like "He be working now," which means something like "He's usually or habitually working at this time," not "He's working now." This form of *be* is called *aspect* rather than *tense.* We don't have an aspectual use of *be* in most varieties of American English, perhaps in only one.

There are also multiple negative forms that appear in Black English in sentences such as "It ain't no cat can't get in no coop," meaning "There isn't any cat that can get into any (pigeon) coop" (Labov, 1972, pp. 130-131). Labov (1972) deals with these forms and the rules governing them at length; he contends that some multiple negatives are particular to Black English and are not found in other varieties of American English. The rules for negation are quite complex but, suffice it to say, multiple negatives in Black English are highly systematic and rule-governed.

Finally, the indirect question form is also different in Black English, although it may appear in Applachian English as well (Cochrane, 1977). I say, "I asked Alvin if he could come." In my speech, I signal that this is an indirect question by the use of *if.* In Black English, a speaker is likely to say, "I axed Alvin could he come," in which the question is signaled by a question inversion of the noun and the auxiliary verb form—*could he.* That inversion is consistent with other question forms in American English and, therefore, is more "regular" in a certain sense that the *if* form. The *axed* for *asked* is not only a phonological sequence found in Black English but, again, is also found in Appalachian dialects. It is also an archaic English form.

One of the most important characteristics of the vernacular for teachers to know about is the variable use of these forms in actual speech—a variable application of rules governing them. I've had ghetto black children say to me, "I ain't got no book and he doesn't have one either." Multiple negatives do not appear in all possible places in vernacular speakers' speech. Nor do phonological forms or other syntactic forms. In fact, much of the verbal output of black ghetto students is probably "standard" in form. But *categorical perception*—which means if you hear a form in someone's speech sometimes you think it's there all the time—prevents many of us from perceiving this variable use of the nonstandard forms. Consequently ghetto black students tend to be sold far short on their language use and are thought to use mainly vernacular forms when, in fact, they may not in school. I will discuss their language abilities in more detail when I talk about *register* below.

So far we've been talking mostly about the formal characteristics of Black English, but one of its most striking aspects is how it functions in ghetto blacks' lives. Verbal ability—the ability to talk well, to rap as one might call it in Black English—carries great prestige. H. Rap Brown states, as quoted in Abrahams (1974), "By the time I was nine, I could talk Shine and the Titanic, Signifying Monkey three different ways, and Piss-Pot Peet for two hours without stopping. Sometimes I wonder why I ever bothered to go to school. Practically everything I know I learned on the corner.... That's why they called me Rap, cause I could rap" (1974, p. 244). Ghetto culture has many of the verbal forms found in other oral cultures, such as oral epic poems. Men can gain prestige and status in the community through their ability to *toast,* which is to recite these poems containing stock characters such as the signifying monkey (probably African in origin), John Henry (we only know the song), and Stagolee. Probably this prestige is partly due to the oral rather than written nature of black culture. Cultural information such as belief and value systems tends to be transmitted more by speech than by writing. In contrast, mainstream culture is a literary culture; its information is largely transmitted through books and other printed matter.

As part of the oral culture, little boys may "play the dozens" on the playground. It's a type of verbal one-upmanship, of verbal dueling in which one tries to "cap" another's statement. The boy who can remember the largest number of these "one-liners" is the winner. Some examples (from Kochman) are:

Yo mama is so bowlegged, she looks like the bite out of a donut.

Yo mama sent her picture to the lonely hearts club, and they sent it back and said, "We ain't that lonely!"

Your family is so poor the rats and roaches eat lunch out. (Kochman, 1970, p. 159)

There are many other verbal forms that are used in black ghetto culture: for men talking to women and vice versa, for talking to strangers and white people, for preaching, and so forth. Abrahams notes, for example: "Ideally she [the Black woman] has the ability to *talk sweet* with her infants and peers but *talk smart* or *cold* with anyone who might threaten her self-image" (1975, p. 62). And there are different audience interaction patterns as well. There tends to be much more participation and response by black audiences than by "mainstream" audiences. Middle-class people tend to sit quietly and give nonverbal cues that indicate they are listening. Black ghetto residents tend much more to give verbal cues that they approve or disapprove of what the speaker is saying. All of this verbal behavior and speaker-listener interaction is highly developed, codified, and culturally constrained. It's definitely part of the sociolect called Black English. Or, to put it another way " . . . They [young Black males on the corner] were the genius of the people, always on their toes, never missing a trick, asking no favors and taking no guff, not looking for trouble but solid ready for it. Spawned in a social vacuum and hung up in mid-air, they were beginning to build their own culture. Their language was a declaration of independence" (Abrahams, 1974, p. 240).

Lower-Class English

There is another variety of American English that could possibly be specified as a sociolect, although its features may be so limited in number as not to warrant designating it a separate variety. However, like Black English, it is not particularly geographically constrained. I call it lower-class speech or lower-class English. Its features contain many of those found in Black English, such as double negatives and an /f/ for a /θ/ in a medial or final position in a word, as in *Rufe* for *Ruth* and *Rufie* for *Ruthie*. Who speaks it? Obviously, members of the lower socioeconomic class in America. We joke about *dem* and *dese,* the /d/ in place of /ð/ in that initial position. But that's one of its features. In fact, that form is what is called a *stereotype.* A stereotype is a feature that signals to a listener that the speaker belongs to a certain group, which may or may not be the case in reality, and it is also a feature that is overtly talked about as being one used by certain groups. Both multiple negatives and initial /d/ for /ð/ are stereotypes. There are also markers, which are features that indicate which group a speaker belongs to but which don't have the strength of stereotypes. Examples of markers in lower-class speech are the medial and final /f/ for /θ/ and possibly final /n/ for /ŋ/, as in *singin.* Certainly we've all heard about those people who "drop their *g*'s."[3] In that case, it's a stereotype.

There is also another phenomenon that often appears in lower-class speech, especially in the speech of upwardly mobile females. (This is only one of quite a few sex-typed variations in language use.) It's as though the "proper rules" weren't quite learned and were mixed together. It is called *hypercorrection.* You may hear it frequently with *who* and *whom* and with other pronouns. How many times have you heard "She gave it to Felix and I." In fact, Harry Reasoner on the October 4, 1976, news said, "From now on, you'll be listening to Barbara and I." It seems as if the speaker vaguely remembers being taught to say, "It is I" instead of "It is me." So when the *I-me* pronoun appears in the object position of *to Felix and   , I* tends to "surface." Unfortunately the archaic rule still has some power, but not enough for the speaker to use pronouns in accordance with actual educated usage. You may also hear some noun plurals hypercorrected, such as /mæskəz/ instead of /mæsks/. What may happen here is that in actual usage we rarely say /mæsks/; instead we tend to say /mæs/ with a prolongation of the /s/ phoneme. However, children are often taught that /mæs/ is "incorrect," especially in spelling and reading lessons. So some children, in an attempt to "clearly" signal plurality, will say /mæsəz/ in which they phonologically match the plural form to the final phoneme, which is /s/ in this case. But if corrected "to put the *k* in," they sometimes do say /mæskəz/, which is clearly a hypercorrection. They try to get in all the phonemes as well as signal plurality. If you have students who hypercorrect, you can help them untangle the usage confusion they're in. Figure out how they arrived at their hypercorrection, as with /mæsks/, and expose them to the common forms. With plurals following consonant clusters such as *masks* and *ghosts,* you can point out that in informal speech, we do say *mass* for *masks* and only use the "full" form in specific, formal situations such as in school sometimes. This type of switching—called register switching—is discussed in detail below. It makes a good starting point for lessons considering how different people talk in differ-

---

[3] "Dropping the g" is a misnomer, because what occurs is actually a substitution of one phoneme—/n/—for another—/ŋ/. As you remember, /ŋ/ is a single nasal phoneme in English that is sometimes represented in writing by an *ng* grapheme.

ent ways and that the variation is systematic and patterned. I have found a great deal of interest in language variation by students at all levels. Geographic vocabulary differences amaze and amuse them; these differences are easy to collect and analyze. "Slang," which is associated with speech variation along a variety of parameters, such as social group, sex, age, and occupation, is also popular with students. And the exposure to systematic language variation is an important part of students' education as well as an important part of teacher knowledge. Finally, part of communicative competence is the ability to express yourself in a variety of ways, since variety is inherent in language and can be controlled for a wider range of expressive abilities.

Sex Differences in American English

A fascinating area of variation (for some of us at least) is now being widely researched and is evoking a great deal of comment even in the popular press. You'll recognize the controversy over "chairperson" versus "chairman" and "chairwoman." Does "man" include both male and female, or only male? It centers around sex differences in language, which have been classified in two ways: language *by* males and females and language *about* males and females. The above controversy—at times very lively in various newspaper columns—belongs to the language *about* category.

I will not discuss extensively this type of variation, since there are several volumes available now that describe sex differences in detail. Among them are Mary Ritchie Key's *Male/Female Language* (Metuchen, N.J.: The Scarecrow Press, Inc., 1975), Casey Miller and Kate Swift's *Words and Women* (Garden City, N.Y.: Anchor Press/Doubleday, 1976), Barrie Thorne and Nancy Henley's *Language and Sex* (Rowley, Mass.: Newbury House Publishers, Inc., 1975), and *Sexism and Language* by Alleen Nilsen, Haig Bosmajian, H. Lee Gershuny, and Julia P. Stanley (Urbana, Ill.: National Council of Teachers of English, 1977). However, it is important to consider possible educational implications arising from these differences and our responses to them. You'll remember that we make appropriateness decisions when we listen to people speak. We may do this with our male and female students: do they sound "appropriately" male and female? If not, what is our reaction?

First, a brief description of some differences noted by researchers in the area. One major difference is that females are reported to use more "careful" speech than males. This carefulness is both phonological and syntactic. It has long been noted that females tend to use /iŋ/ in word-final

96

positions more frequently than males, who tend to use /in/ as in *swimmin* more frequently. In syntax, the carefulness shows up in females' speech as the use of fewer multiple negatives than in males'. To put it another way, women and girls are widely reported to speak a more "standard" American English more than men and boys.

Other formal differences have been reported such as women's greater use of intensifiers like *so, quite,* and *such* as in "It's *so* cute" or "That's *quite* all right" (Key, 1975). In the lexicon, different expletives seem to be used by males and females. Lakoff (1973) "makes a convincing case that this set of expletives [e.g., "oh dear" and "fudge," etc.] may be a qualitative difference between women's and men's language; men simply don't say "oh dear," but instead have a lexical set that is viewed by society as much more forceful" (DeStefano, 1975, 70-71).

Also, lexical studies dealing with how females are talked about have yielded interesting results. For example, Nilsen (1973) found in a survey of dictionaries only 132 terms used to refer to females as opposed to 385 terms used for males.

A conclusion emerging in much of the research on the lexicon used about women is that these lexical items indicate relative powerlessness for women in the society. Certainly *he* used generically, for example, to include both males and females, would seem to be an indication for such a conclusion (DeStefano, 1977). Another minor signal is the lack of semantic equivalence between words such as *bachelor* and *spinster. Spinster,* according to Lakoff (1973), has negative connotations that *bachelor* doesn't have. A spinster is a woman who has somehow "missed the boat" when it comes to getting married. She didn't get a man, but a bachelor hasn't missed the boat because he didn't get a woman—a wife. Men can remain unmarried but women cannot, without somehow being devalued.

This powerlessness, which is described in the literature on women's American English, fits with the "carefulness" and "politeness" also reported for women's speech. Generally, if one is relatively powerless, one is careful and polite in dealing with those who have the power. This phenomenon can be seen in Black English speakers' linguistic behavior as well. Such a set of hypotheses needs to be more clearly formulated and tested, but the preliminary data seem to indicate a fruitful approach would be to develop the notions of powerlessness and politeness.

Another major area of research into sex differences in language is the area of language use, sometimes also called discourse analysis. Obviously much research needs to be done in this area to map the differences between what males and females say to whom, when and how. A tipoff as to the potential afforded by such study comes from the same type of research into the use of Black English, which is proving more fruitful than a mere look at the formal characteristics of the sociolect to determine differences between this variety and others of American English.

For example, Lakoff (1973) has asserted that conversational rules differ for females and males. There may be somewhat different sets of presuppositions about what is socially appropriate language behavior, sets that "allow" males more latitude and dominance than females in conversations. I'm reminded of a strategy a woman graduate student in a department of Educational Administration told me about recently. All Ph.D. level students in that department are in seminars together, with her as the only woman in one group. She was telling me that, first of all, the men control the direction of the conversation by interrupting one another with entry formulae such as "Yes, but . . . " or "That's fine. However . . ." or "Wait a minute." She felt uncomfortable about interrupting (as is reported in the literature) but finally started to because otherwise she literally didn't get a word in. When she did this, the men kept right on talking. Being interrupted by a woman was perceived quite differently than by a man. She wasn't one to give up, so she interrupted and kept on talking until finally the men would quit. Toward the end, she said they were beginning to treat her verbally like the other men—by stopping talking. But an interesting point is that at first her interruptions were ignored. Her verbal behavior was judged quite differently from the men's by the men, apparently indicating there are some different discourse appropriateness rules operating.

But perhaps one of the most important educational questions about sex differences in language is what do we as teachers make of them? Do we judge our male and female students differently, to the detriment of one or the other? Do we find ourselves insisting girls shouldn't laugh as loudly as boys? Do we find ourselves insisting that *man, men,* and *he* do include both males and females when a girl asks us "Now that we know all about our Founding Fathers, what about our Founding Mothers?" These are all sensitive areas, areas fraught with controversy, precedent and perogative. But they are, thus, all the more exciting and deserving of our interest and our students' interest. You can ask your class or classes how they feel about terms such as "Man and His World," "cavemen," "founding fathers," and so on. Do your female students feel included or excluded? How could they rewrite those phrases to include everyone, yet not sound pompous or contrived? Such close editing can also pay off in overall closer editing of written work and a greater insight into written registers.

Register

Another type of social variation that is extremely important in people's speech is called *register switching*. This means that speakers make changes in their language when the circumstances they are in change. This type of social variation is not limited to the American speech repertoire, as is Black English. Instead, it seems to be a linguistic universal (Verma, 1969) operating in all speech communities and on all varieties, although the specifics of switching are determined by a specific society and by the formal characteristics of a variety. In other words, when to switch is culturally determined, and the forms appropriate to each register also vary from society to society.

The term *register* has been applied to varieties that are set apart from others by the social circumstances of their use. If a social situation changes, the register a speaker uses may also change in its phonology, syntax, and lexicon, as well as being accompanied by nonverbal changes such as differences in gestures, facial expressions, etc. In the phonology category, I'm finding in some research I'm now conducting that many times register switching is signaled by changes in intonation patterns (supersegmentals) as well as in the segmentals (phonemes). A teacher talking to children in the classroom will often pitch his or her voice higher and, contrary to what we usually do, end questions marked by question words or inversions with a fade-rise terminal to give "And how are you doing?" / || /

Lexical or vocabulary changes are probably the most obvious distinctions among registers, at least in American English. For example, "bug" may be used in informal, peer speech as in "Ugh, look at that bug." In more formal situations, "insect" is required. An entomologist studies insects, while bugs bite us on warm summer evenings. Or contrast "Shut up!" with "Please be quiet." Think about these various switches:

Teacher to unruly student: "If you don't be quiet, you'll have to stay in from recess," or "Be quiet, Tommy."

Teacher to friend in teachers' lounge: "That kid's yackity-yaking is driving me nuts."

Teacher to principal: "Tommy is disruptive in class and a behavior problem at times."

Teacher to parents: "Tommy has a tendency to be noisy in class" (DeStefano and Rentel, 1975, p. 334).

99

Or take the example Bolinger (1975, p. 377) gives. He suggests looking up the synonyms of *crazy* in Roget's *Thesaurus* and noting the different registers some belong to. Compare "maddened," "insensate," and "demented" to "daft," "loco," "teched," "not right in the upper story" and "off one's nut."

Note the switch from ecclesiastical (religious) vocabulary to administrative vocabulary in the following poem, probably for purposes of humor:

What If An Educator Had Written the Lord's Prayer?

Our Father figure who resides in the upper-echelon domain,
May thy title always be structured to elicit a favorable response.
Reward us today, bread-wise,
And minimize our unfavorable self-concept, resulting from credit over-extension,
As we strive to practice reciprocal procedures.
And channel us, not into temptation-including areas,
But provide us with security from situations not conducive to moral enrichment.
For Thine is the position of maximum achievement in the power structure,
Not to mention the prestige-attainment factor that never terminates.
                              Amen.
Midlothian, Texas

                                        Tom Dodge[4]

A register is generally conceived to be situationally bound; switch the person's social situation and the person will switch registers if he or she has the competence to do so and if switching is called for. According to Verma, "They (registers) cut across dialectical varieties and may be used for specific purposes by all the speakers-writers of a language" (1969, p. 294). Halliday, McIntosh, and Strevens note that registers "are not marginal or special varieties of language. Between them they cover the total range of our language activity" (1964, p. 89). And not only do registers cut across dialect boundaries but they also may cut across languages. Many Chicanos and Puerto Ricans, to name only one linguistic minority group in the United States, switch from one language to another. Students may use a variety of Spanish at home to talk with their mothers

---

[4]Tom Dodge, "What If An Educator Had Written THE LORD'S PRAYER?", *English Journal,* January 1971. Copyright © 1971 by the National Council of Teachers of English. Reprinted by permission of the publisher and the author.

100

and then switch to English in school when talking to teachers. Verma (1969) calls this register-oriented bilingualism, in which the language used is constrained by the social situation, *registeral bilingualism.*

Except perhaps for bilingual or multilingual speech communities, registers have many features in common as do most American English dialects. According to Halliday, McIntosh, and Strevens:

> *No one suggests, of course, that the various registers characteristic of different types of situations have nothing in common. On the contrary, a great deal of grammatical [syntactic] and lexical material is common to many of the registers of a given language, and some perhaps to all (Halliday, McIntosh, and Strevens, 1964, p. 89).*

Thus registers used by members of a speech community may share many, if not most, features. But they will not share features of lexicon, syntax, phonology, and nonverbal behavior that are distinctive to specific registers. It may be helpful to think of registers as largely overlapping sets of features with a small portion of each set not shared. However, what is shared may also differ according to such variables as frequency of appearance in speech. For example, Claudia Mitchell-Kernan (1969) suggests that, in ghetto black vernacular, syntactic features reflect a speaker's register switching either by decreasing or increasing their frequency of use, not by their absence or presence. Yet certain lexical features may not be shared at all among certain types of registers. Witness the jargon used by a variety of professions and portrayed very accurately in the poem above. Here it has been necessary to define many words because they generally do not appear outside of linguistics or, if they do, are used in quite different ways. *Rule* is just one example of a word having a variety of definitions.

These registers have been conceptualized as being governed by the intersection of *field, mode,* and *style of discourse. Field of discourse* refers to the area of operation of the language activity; it may be a technical area such as biology or math or linguistics or it may be a domestic area. It is related to appropriate *topics* for those areas. As Halliday puts it, " . . . subject-matter is one element in it," (1976, 22). Doughty, Pearce and Thornton (1972, p. 185) also include " . . . the whole activity of the speaker [or writer] as a participant in the setting." Verma (1969) makes a gross distinction between technical and nontechnical fields of discourse. But research is needed in order to determine the existence of various fields.

It would seem that fields of discourse may be largely determined by

101

the social situations composing the various behavioral domains in a speech community. In sociolinguistics, a domain is often thought of as a cluster of these social situations that are related by common sets of behavioral rules. Scientists behave in certain "scientific," technical ways when in their work domain, while they may behave in quite different ways (nontechnical) when in their roles as, for example, father or mother in the family domain. Spanking and baby talk are generally not considered appropriate scientific behavior.

Mode of discourse has been used to refer to the medium of the language activity. Is it spoken or written, extempore or prepared? This is probably the grossest distinction we make in a literate society, although it may not turn out to be as revealing as other mode distinctions. Doughty, et al describe *mode* as " . . . the channel of communication adopted: not only the choice between spoken and written medium, but much more, detailed choices can be described under this head . . . . Such distinctions as those between text written to be read, text written to be read aloud, and text written to be read aloud as if newly received (e.g., in a letter which arrives in the action of a play), would be distinctions under mode—to the extent that these differences can be related to formal differences in the language used" (1972, pp. 185-186).

In an oral culture such as the one of ghetto blacks or American Indians, distinctions might be made between spontaneous or extemporaneous speech and partly memorized, more ritualized speech in which certain verbal formulas play a large role and in which there may be relatively little audience feedback. Undoubtedly other finer distinctions can be made between or within modes.

Finally, *style of discourse* has been used to refer to the language constrained by the role relationships between speaker and listener or writer and reader, generally along an informality-to-formality continuum. Along this continuum, style can vary from most intimate, informal language with a high shared context (participants know each other well, have similar backgrounds, and so forth) and much shared vocabulary to highly formal, ritualized, formulaic writing with very little shared context. Role relationships refer to the whole set of behaviors that accompany roles and are expected of those roles when they interact with one another. As teachers, we expect certain behaviors from students and they from us. If we or they don't get them, the situation is disrupted until the expected behaviors appear again. Generally, the teacher-pupil role relationship could be characterized as one of greater formality along the informal to formal continuum. This formality specifies certain kinds of language as appropriate and other kinds as not belonging at all.

When various styles, modes, and fields of discourse intersect, specific registers are the outcome. And all variables are influenced by the social situation the participants are in—in other words, the extradiscourse or nonlanguage features such as location, time of day, and so forth.

The Range of Registers

Within a speech community, there is probably a range of registers that encompasses those connected with each of the behavioral domains. The number and type of domains may differ among sociological analyses, but common ones are family, playground, and street (neighborhood or friendship), education, religion, and employment. The behavioral rules constraining each domain also include language behavior rules. In the educational domain, a student does not say certain things to a teacher, even when angry, that he or she will say to peers in the playground, which is another domain.

Registers tend to cluster within these domains, so that the complete range could be subdivided in that way. These clusters reflect to some degree the social situation clusters that make up the behavioral domain. A social situation is defined by an interaction of social time, setting, and role relationship. For example, in school classroom situations in the educational domain, the social time is clearly delineated by the actual time of the school day. Also, that time is broken down into smaller units devoted to different types of instruction on different subjects and to inculcation into middle-class or "mainstream" culture. The time is spent in a specific educational setting, usually a classroom that is physically different from other settings. The roles usually include those of the teacher and pupil, each with a set of expectations as to "proper" role behavior. Allen Grimshaw (1972) indicates the role relationship to be one of superordinate teacher to subordinate pupil. Dell Hymes (1967) has classified it as a formal role relationship, as opposed to the more informal ones of friendship and neighborhood. The interaction of these factors, probably in combination with others not yet identified, determines the social situation, which in turn determines the register or registers used in that situation. Finally, the specific language used between pupil and teacher reflects the situational constraints just described.

So the entire range of registers undoubtedly reflects the range of social situations in a speech community or culture. However, it is doubtful that any single adult can master the entire range, because it is unlikely that anyone could have experienced all the social situations in great enough depth to permit learning the entire set of registers. Probably an adult controls a limited range of registers within the community's total range; this sample I call an individual's *repertoire* of registers. The adult's repertoire seems to be constrained by a variety of factors such as socio-economic status, sex, age, occupation, educational level, and special interests. It is likely that an individual's repertoire includes clusters of registers in certain domains in which the person is deeply involved and fewer registers in those areas of less personal involvement. For example, a wife whose work includes managing a home and taking care of small children will, for at least a time, have a different cluster of registers in the family domain than will her husband, if his occupation demands that most of his time and energy are spent away from the home.

Undoubtedly there are also production and comprehension differences in register, as there are in other types of language activity. These differences show up quite clearly in vernacular-speaking ghetto children who may not be able to produce (in speech) selected registers they hear through the mass media but who evidently seem to understand large parts of them. Susan Ervin-Tripp makes this same point when she says that a type of bilingualism may exist at the comprehension or reception level, "as it does with those Spanish and Navaho speakers who can understand [more English] than they can produce" (1970, p. 40). Certainly I comprehend far more Spanish and Italian than I can speak.

Probably adults have mastered for use those registers required for participation in the domains in which they are most active, while they can comprehend, recognize, and expect other registers they can't or don't usually use. For example, churchgoers probably expect certain registral features in the minister's sermon and prayers that they may not be able to use themselves.

Undoubtedly also there are socially constrained rules that speakers and listeners have internalized for register switching but that have yet to be discovered. They need to be written, but since social constraints in rules have only begun to be built in and since we know relatively little about the specifics of what triggers switching, it will probably be some time before such rules can be written and considered adequate in any way.

Acquisition of Registers

As with other forms of language behavior, whether governed by form rules or by social rules, adult abilities are different from child abilities. Probably adult and child register repertoires differ both in kind and in degree of mastery, the adult repertoire being larger and containing some registers not included in a child's repertoire. The developmental aspect of register can be seen by comparing a six-year-old's repertoire to an adult's. One crucial element in this restricted repertoire seems to be the more constricted set of domains to which a child is exposed. Before going to school and thereby entering the educational domain, a child's social domains are largely those of the home and neighborhood. The child has peer relationships in the neighborhood, but a role in the family domain is one of a subordinate to the superordinate parent. But whatever the parameters of, say, a preschool child's register repertoire, the child must learn to produce the socially relevant and demanded registers at the appropriate times and must be able to switch from one to another when the occasion prescribes it. Certainly part of a child's acquisition of language is this acquisition of adult, socially constrained language patterns and an understanding of the constraints themselves.

In the acquisition of both syntax and semantics, it is hypothesized that children progressively develop and revise sets of "rules" through differentiation of the input until they reach the level of adult abilities. It may also be possible to hypothesize that, in acquiring registers, children learn through progressive differentiation of their speech community's *social* situations the language features that accompany those situations. Then we could postulate that in a rule-governed way, they modify their speech forms to fit those situations. Perhaps part of this development can be observed in children's role playing, during which they not only explore adult roles but also use adult language as well as they can. (See Cook-Gumperz and Corsaro, 1976, for more detail on language in role playing.)

Unfortunately we have relatively little information on children's acquisition of registers. However, some indications of acquisition of register can be gleaned from the literature. William Labov (1966) suggested in his Lower East Side (in New York City) study that an adult-type register repertoire is not in evidence until age 14 or 15. Even at this age, children typically still have more control over informal features than over formal ones, since formality in social situations seems to increase as one enters more adult-oriented domains. At age 14 or 15, most children will not yet have entered the work domain. However, Freedle, Naus and Schwartz (1977) report that children, at a fairly early age, adopted a "formal language-register" when talking to adults.

Variations of form in different social situations are evidently learned very early by a child, but the forms may be different from those in the adult repertoire. Jean Berko Gleason (1973) notes that the earliest form of register switching is simply a distinction between talking (infant's first words) and silence. This fits in with Ervin-Tripp's proposal (1971) that the first social features to be distinguished are major setting and addressee (person spoken to) contrasts. The infant is not afraid to talk or babble in front of familiar faces but will often fall silent in front of strangers (one type of addressee contrast). A major setting contrast could be home versus not-home for an infant. Probably infants are more readily silent out of the home than in their own familiar surroundings. Gleason also indicates that preschool children's register repertoire includes the whine. (Adults prefer to think that it has dropped out of their own repertoire.) They will whine to a parent or parent figure (Gleason, 1973) but not to other adults. So even this early there is some social distinction made among various adults in the child's life.

Other distinctions may be grossly based on age as the dominant social factor triggering register switching in preschool children. Gleason noted that older but still preschool children in her sample talked "baby talk" to infants, used a peer-group colloquial register with their age mates, and used a formal register with adults. Josephson and DeStefano also found age a dominant factor in the switching of six-and eight year olds (1977). Gleason also noted another element in a child's repertoire—a register of socialization evidently used with somewhat younger children in which the older child gives linguistic cues as to the younger child's expected behavior. So age differentiation among people coming into contact with a child seems to be important in register development. Certainly adults often have highly developed, age-graded registers for use in talking to children of different ages (Gleason, 1973).

School also seems to be a socially significant factor in register switching for the children who are in school. They add registers appropriate to the educational domain that they are finally encountering. For example, Houston (1969) reported in her study of Florida black children's language a school register, as she called it, that was distinct in many ways from nonschool language. She felt it represented "careful" speech. In my research on a specific educational register, I noted its being acquired in black vernacular speaking children's repertoire of registers (DeStefano, 1970). Thus school definitely seems to be a significant domain in children's lives, which, to some extent, controls the acquisition of new registers. Ervin-Tripp (1971) notes that school is an unambiguous setting for the child, quite distinct from home and church domains. (Unfortunately, since our knowledge of register acquisition in other domains such as work is very limited, adult ability levels are achieved without our knowing the details of that acquisition.)

This discussion of register and its developmental aspects, although the outlines of both are far from clear, is an important prerequisite to an understanding of ghetto black students' language acquisition.

Acquisition of School Register

There are several registers that are important in school and about which we know very little. One such register is what we can call the Language Instruction Register, or the LIR as it will be referred to. This register can be characterized as being one of the registers of English language learning that includes literacy learning, so important in American schools. Think a moment about the lexical items used by teachers in the teaching of reading: *sound, letter, word, sentence, beginning sound, blend,* and so forth. These are all terms children have learned in their literacy lessons; they are part of the LIR. Downing (1970 and 1976), who uses the term RIR, or Reading Instruction Register, found that some first-year British primary school children's concepts of *word* and *sound* did not match the teacher's. In other words, when the teacher used *word* in a reading and writing lesson, the children had a different understanding of what the word *word* meant. Their feature set did not match the adult feature set defining that lexical item. Such a mismatch in definitions of the same lexical item can lead to serious instructional problems based on the erroneous assumption that "everyone understands." Douglas Barnes (1969), who reports on a Math Instruction Register, expressed some of the same concerns about the teacher's use of lexicon not understood by his or her students.

What does the LIR sound and look like? First, one field of discourse in schools is language instruction, as in a situation in which a teacher is concerned with how to speak or write in certain ways. The mode of discourse for the LIR can be both spoken and written. The style of discourse for language instruction is fairly formal or "polite;" the teacher tends to pronounce words more carefully than in many other classroom situations. For example, I get a wave of recognition from teachers when I note that in a spelling lesson a teacher will say, "The first word today is *desks. Desks.*" and then a bit later may say, "All right, pull your *dess* into a circle."

Or take the way in which teachers and language arts instructional materials handle the topic of "parents" with young children. Who are they? In "Basalese", the language of basal readers, they are *Mother* and *Father.* Regardless of context, they are seldom referred to as Mom and Dad by anybody connected with schools. The following questions are all too familiar to anyone who has ever taught language arts in an American elementary school:

What time did Father arrive home from work?

107

What does Mother hand to Father on his way to the office in the morning?

How does Father help Charles and Julia when he is home?

What did Mother ask baby Jennifer?

Those questions can be spoken or just as easily written. In either case, the style is formal, polite, and careful.

The LIR is probably part of what Barnes (1969) calls the language of instruction. He found in British secondary schools in the equivalent of our sixth-grade what he called a Math Instruction Register, or MIR, which teachers used specifically while teaching math. Such specialization, especially in lexicon and pronunciation, is not surprising. Rainey (1969) noted a teacher in a Black Headstart class used /iŋ/ as in /siŋiŋ/ while story reading (a fairly formal situation) and while formally teaching. She would then switch to /in/ as in /siŋin/ when trying to get attention from or create closeness with the children. In instruction, the unmarked, formal form /iŋ/ was used.

The speech situation for LIR includes, among other features, a school building and classroom, time during the school day, a teacherlike adult (authority figure), and a school type of testing situation.

Thus we have seen at least the bare outlines of a classroom register that students are expected by adults to acquire during their school years. The educational domain, then, provides an environment in which further language development is stressed for students.

How do ghetto vernacular-speaking students do in these circumstances? Both the school environment and how they respond linguistically are very important in understanding their language development as a whole. All too often their language is perceived categorically, that is as being totally "nonstandard" [or dialect bound] by those not in their culture, which in practice means most of their teachers and other school people with whom they come in contact. But vernacular-speaking black children participate in register acquisition that includes many so-called standard features, just as in Cambridge, Mass., black and white middle-class children do.

Before school age, ghetto black children learn to control registers pertinent to the domain of family and neighborhood, but again these registers will be constrained by age, which excludes certain social experiences for the young child. However, features that can be called "standard" are expected by black adults to appear early in this repertoire. Claudia Mitchell-Kernan (1969) reports that in the Oakland, California, ghetto, a child reaching the age of five receives increased pressure from his or her parents to use more so-called standard features in speech. The school provides the most consistent input of "standard"features, and by age nine or so the black children, according to Kernan, are aware that some forms are more socially stigmatized than others. Such growing awareness is probably a feature of acquisition of the repertoire of forms and attitudes in a given speech community. Certainly it reflects reported adult attitudes. In Oakland, black adults view speech with more so-called standard English features in it as "careful" style.

Although the speech community these children live in is one of great complexity and one in which verbal ability is highly prized, the black ghetto child is also expected by family and teachers when entering school to learn to add other registers to his or her repertoire based on exposure to the educational domain. Repertoire enlargement is facilitated by expanded role relationships. One of the role relationships that begins to expand for the child is the superordinate-subordinate, adult-child relationship in which the teacher, not the parent, becomes the significant adult. Linguistic "appropriateness" is expected; if expectations are not met, the consequences for the child's success can be severe. Walt Wolfram (1969) rightly notes that the registers, or "styles" as he calls them, elicited in the speech of children to a variety of adults are among the most important in American society. He feels these registers help an individual make moves up and down the social scale.

To what degree do black ghetto vernacular-speaking students acquire registers associated with social situations in the educational domain? I have looked at black ghetto students' acquisition of the LIR. Vernacular-speaking blacks are often expected to use the LIR in the classroom when the situation demands it. In my estimation, there is a great deal of significance attached by teachers and parents to their acquisition of the LIR. They tend to see it as acquisition of "proper speech" and undoubtedly have great difficulty in separating its production from the acquisition of reading and writing. However, components of the students' vernacular registers may not be shared with the LIR. In LIR, *past* and *pass* are not homonyms, while they often are in the most vernacular registers, no matter who speaks them. They both become /pæs/. Also *mast, mask, masks,* and *mass* are hononyms in the vernacular and in some school situations, but are not in the LIR.

How did these black students do? The most general developmental finding is that the older the students, the more LIR features she or he produces. Richard Light (1971) noted in his study that the highest percentage of vernacular features was used by the youngest black children. By the fifth grade in the Oakland, California, schools where I studied the

LIR, 71 percent of all responses made were made in that register (De-Stefano, 1970). It would appear that the black vernacular-speaking students were going through the process of learning to respond in a linguistically appropriate manner to specific social demands made on them by the educational domain.

These findings lend support to the contention that the process of language acquisition is a continual one, especially when sociolinguistic factors are taken into account. Also, a vernacular-speaking student may have learned to produce more formal registers such as the LIR than he or she often is credited with. Abrahams (1972) also notes this underestimation of ghetto black children's language ability:

> *I have been convinced for some time that Black kids come into the classroom with a much wider range of registers (both productive and receptive) than we give them credit for. Informally I have tested this and had it tested by other classroom teachers by asking the kids to mark (imitate and dramatize) on some story both in "TV talk" and the way they would hear it at home or on the streets. Their ability to produce "TV talk" varies from individual to individual and from feature to feature, but is certainly much greater than anyone has heretofore given them credit for.*
> *Roger Abrahams[5]*

Even though there was a general increase in LIR production across grades, different features showed very different levels of acquisition. I found that the LIR negative verb with indefinite pronoun (I *don't* have *any*) even in the first grade showed a high level of acquisition, with only a 5 percent vernacular response (as in "I ain't got none"). By fifth grade the multiple negative vernacular form had virtually disappeared in the students' responses in a formal situation but certainly not in their vernacular (DeStefano, 1970).Light's data on Washington, D.C., black children (1971), for example, showed that when no adults were present, the children realized the multiple negative every time it was possible to do so. The virtual disappearance of the multiple negative was an interesting finding because multiple negation tends to be highly socially stigmatized throughout the United States (as we have mentioned earlier). It is possible that even six-year-old black ghetto children have some awareness of the social unacceptability of multiple negation in a formal school situation.

At the other extreme were several LIR features that even by fifth

---

[5] Roger Abrahams, quotation from a letter to Johanna S. DeStefano, 1972. Reprinted by permission of the author.

grade (age 11) demonstrated very low levels of acquisition. The lowest were word final consonant clusters -sks and -sts, as in *masks* and *ghosts.* These were atypically low; by grade 5, the LIR responses of *masks* was realized 4 percent of the time. Many students didn't produce the LIR form at all. The majority of the responses to the *masks* stimulus took the form of *mass* without the prolonged -s common in many other registers. Why the confusion? The forms *masks* and *ghosts* are virtually absent in the vernacular; instead one hears *mass* and *ghoss* with the prolonged -s.[6] I suspect there is a highly mixed input by the teacher as well; he or she probably says *mass* most of the time, so the student has no consistent pattern to follow. Mitchell-Kernan (1969) suggests that Oakland black students had no stable concepts of what the "standard" alternative was in their own repertoires. So if the teacher is relatively inconsistent in patterning, the irregularity Labov (1968) noted in Harlem boys' formal test speech could well result. Labov found that although the boys were given the same stimulus several times, their answers to that stimulus varied.

It seems, then, that black vernacular-speaking students do tend to acquire the LIR as they grow older and that they differentially control certain features within the LIR. Some features show significantly lower levels of acquisition than others do. Generally, however, this formal register acquisition is more a matter of being able to produce a higher frequency of so-called standard forms already in the vernacular registers (Henrie, 1969), which contain many more standard forms than we except, than it is learning completely new forms. I agree with Light (1971, p. 167) that "The children's [black vernacular-speaking children] productive as well as their receptive control of standard English should not be underestimated." We must be careful not to fall into the categorical perception trap, which does tend to underestimate the student's speech forms.[7]

Attitudes Toward Language Variation

Another important area of sociolinguistic inquiry and an important area for teachers is the attitudes people hold toward the varieties of a language and different languages. Attitudes can be so powerful they can actually dictate what is considered a language. For example, remember the earlier

[6] See the earlier discussion of hypercorrection.
[7] Johanna S. DeStefano, "Some Parameters of Register in Adult and Child Speech," *ITL,* 1972. Copyright © 1972 by the Instituut voor Toegepaste Linguistiek. Reprinted by permission of the publisher.

discussion of Hindi-Urdu. For religious and political reasons, Hindi-Urdu is considered two languages by its Hindu speakers (Hindi) and by its Moslem speakers (Urdu). Many of its varieties are mutually intelligible, and it is readable by anyone who is literate. But India (Hindi) and Pakistan (Urdu) have deep rifts between them, so deep they wish not even to have a language in common.

Attitudes can also almost deny that a language that is commonly spoken even exists. This has been the case among some Haitians who maintain they speak French, considered upper class, while in fact they most often speak Haitian Creole, which is a mixture of French and African languages. I've also spoken to black adults who say that Black English is merely a "bad language" or "bad speech," in other words, not a linguistic system in its own right. Many of them want to eradicate it in favor of other American-English varieties.

Dale makes the assertion that many of these attitudes are remarkably stable as well. He says:

> In American society, even the most radical and revolutionary figures do not use nonstandard syntax in public speaking or in print ....There is a new trend [in the American black nationalist movement] toward using some aspects of the nonstandard dialect [sic], but it almost always involves vocabulary items, not sentence construction (Dale, 1975, p. 272).

All of these attitudes, which are invariably held all over the world, are sets of judgments that place relative values on the "worth" of some languages or varieties. An attitude toward language is a judgment about linguistic variation along a continuum of "least worthy or valued" to "most worthy or valued." These judgments are culturally constrained; each culture has its set of values concerning the varieties of a language and the languages it comes in contact with. Prerevolutionary Russian aristocracy spoke French to one another rather than Russian, since French was considered far superior to the "language of the peasants and serfs." Remember the attitudes held toward English we mentioned in Chapter 1. Ammon (1977) notes that speakers of a regional dialect of Swabian German (a region in Southern Germany) are rated as generally less intelligent than those who can speak standard varieties of German. The list of attitude sets could proliferate endlessly, all culturally constrained and probably strongly based in *ethnocentric* views of other cultures or subcultures. *Ethnocentrism* is the attitude that one's own culture is best; other cultures are judged using one's own as a standard, and the others usually fall far short.

In the United States, we have an example of an ethnocentric judgment about language variation—part of the attitude set of many members of the dominant, "mainstream" culture. Put simply, it is "a difference in language is a deficiency." (This attitude has been mentioned earlier in this book; see Chapter 3). In our society, it has been particularly applied as part of the attitude set toward black ghetto vernacular. We have been told that black ghetto children are largely nonverbal and that when they do speak, they are illogical. We've been given the example "Tree green." This is an illogical utterance because the *copula* (*to be* verb) has been "dropped," and therefore the relationship between *tree* and *green* is not clear in the way it would be if *is* were between the two words. What *is* means is not all clear to me; in fact, it's considered an empty form—one that doesn't carry lexical meaning. It's there as part of the syntax of a language but doesn't impart further information. In many languages the copula is not used in constructions with *noun + adjective*. Russian is one of these, and to call Russian "illogical" because it specifies "Tree green" is simply ethnocentric. But in American black children's speech, it is often considered to be illogical and therefore constitutes another reason why black ghetto vernacular is "deficient." A major reason why this variety is considered to be "deficient" is because it's spoken by poor blacks. The variety is guilty by association with the people who speak it. If prestigious Americans spoke it it would probably be judged quite differently.

Obviously teachers have attitudes toward language variation, too, and they tend to mirror those held by the dominant culture in the United States. In some cases, it's been found that teachers are even more normative than the general public: that is, they hold to the norms for language behavior more strenuously than do nonteachers. Such an attitude set has important consequences for students from different subcultures and cultures who speak different varieties of English, as well as for "mainstream" students who may have developmental features still in their speech or who have not yet acquired certain formal registers used in the educational domain.

What are the parameters of teachers' attitudes in more detail? Frederick Williams and his colleagues at the University of Texas have conducted investigations on teachers' attitudes toward Black English-speaking children and found that:

> . . . *some teachers tended to judge children's speech along two main dimensions: confidence-eagerness and ethnicity-nonstandardness. In subsequent research, Williams and Whitehead found that teachers typically rated middle-class children, both black and white, higher on both dimensions. But most important was the*

113

> *finding that many teachers were making responses on the basis of the child's speech patterns. Black children's speech patterns were consistently rated less confident and eager and more non-standard and ethnic than white children's speech, irrespective of social class status. Consistently, the teachers studied by the authors tended to assign the nonstandard and ethnic labels to a child's speech if, evidently, certain cues were present. This stereotyped response pattern by teachers, irrespective of the actual speech evidence, has important implications for classroom teachers who work with black children (Williams and Whitehead, 1973, p. 169).*

Another excellent discussion of Williams and others' work on attitudes appears in *The Sounds of Children* by Williams, Hopper, and Natalicio, 1977.

Certainly the stereotyped response pattern may in some way be connected with hearing what we have called stereotyped features of lower-class speech, such as multiple negatives, or with markers that are also used to "socially diagnose" someone's speech.

Another survey of teachers' attitudes, as well as those of parents and students, was conducted in city schools across the United States (Hayes and Taylor, 1971). The researchers found that teachers of three to five years' teaching experience were found to regard such variation much more positively than others, although teachers in training, especially black ones, were found to be more positive about language variation than teachers in predominantly white schools, although most feel negatively toward the syntax of various so-called nonstandard varieties. A majority of the teachers interviewed felt that students' speech should be corrected, not left alone, although they didn't particularly reject the child's culture—at least that's what they said. But 10 percent of the teachers did reject outright minority group cultures and language. One final conclusion seems to be very important:

> *The majority of teachers rate the speech of their students as poor to fair, and inappropriate for the classroom. This critical attitude remains fairly constant throughout the grades and was true regardless of race or socioeconomic class (Hayes and Taylor, 1971, p. 2).*

As a group, teachers tend to hold a highly normative, *corrective* view toward students' language—*all* students' language. What consequences on the maximization of communicative competence in students might this attitude set have? One consequence I have seen and that has also been reported by many other teachers and educators is that students may stop producing speech and writing. It is difficult to help someone maximize productive language competence when there is no language being produced. But it happens all the time. When I first taught a class in a Philadelphia ghetto school, I had a student who hid under his desk whenever I asked the children to do some writing. He stayed there until everyone had finished. How much would he learn about writing if he never did any? I later discovered that he had had a teacher the previous year who had insisted that the children's papers be virtually "perfect" in their mechanics, spelling, and syntax. This boy thought he failed so badly in those areas that he gave up.

The same thing can happen orally. If forms in a student's speech are constantly corrected, the student may well fall silent to avoid the pain of being wrong again. Failure tends to breed failure and a sense of hopelessness.

You can already sense the emphasis on *form* that seems to be so highly related to the negative consequences of an all-too-common attitude set. How many of us remember painful moments in English classes caused by a professor grading strenuously on form and not paying any attention to how well the paper functioned as exposition or persuasion or narration?

This, then, is a first suggestion to help overcome the influences of negative attitudes: as a teacher, concentrate on how the student's language is functioning as communication rather than on form. Dell Hymes suggests that for perspective on language:

> *What is crucial is not so much a better understanding of how language is structured, but a better understanding of how language is used; not so much what language is, as what language is for (Cazden, John, and Hymes, 1973, p. xii).*

What some language functions are will be discussed below. Obviously it is more difficult to evaluate the effectiveness of function than it is to pinpoint form in students' language, either spoken or written. But since we are concerned about communicative competence, we make that attempt. I also have serious doubts that children in elementary school are cognitively developed enough to respond to instructions on form; instead they respond to content. The separation of form from content is a high-level cognitive function; if a student is not at that level of functioning, he or she probably will not even "hear" many formal distinctions in language.

Another suggestion to help disarm negative attitudes toward language variation is for teachers to put such variation into a developmental framework of register acquisition. A student exposed to new social situations with attendent registers will generally learn the forms used in them given enough exposure and time. Part of communicative competence certainly is an expanded register repertoire, an ability to make one's language fit the social situation. As teachers, we can help students expand their repertoires and also learn the forms associated with those registers.

Functions of Language

Dell Hymes' admonition above—to understand the uses of language better—reflects both a renewed interest in language functions and an attempt on the part of some sociolinguists and educators to describe this type of language variation. I can only applaud these studies as, after all, we all know that we use language in certain ways to accomplish certain ends. Using older terminology, we may exhort, beg, wheedle, needle, order, command, demand, question, assert, and sometimes just plain fool around. We vary the function to fit our goal, some of us doing a better job than others at it.

But how can we be more effective in our language use—more precise, more clear, etc.? And how can we help our students grow and mature in their language use? These studies, in being descriptive, can help us gain insight into the nature of functions and into possible classroom strategies for maximizing communicative competence.

What do we know about this type of variation? M.A.K. Halliday (1975) has described at least seven universal functions of language that have importance for us and our students. They are:

Instrumental language: "I want" or "I need." Language used to satisfy needs or desires. Often takes the form of a request.

Regulatory language: "Do this," or "Get out of here!" or "Stop it!" For controlling others.

Interactional language: "Will you play with me?" or "Let's go for a walk together." For establishing relationships, defining them and maintaining them. Also for participating in social behavior.

Personal language: "I'm going to be a doctor." or "I think...." For expressing individuality, to give personal opinions and feelings.

Imaginative language: "Let's pretend" or "Once upon a time," etc. Used to create a world of one's own.

Heuristic language: "Why," "What's that for?" or "Why is the sky blue?" or "Why do people talk different?" For exploring the world, for finding things out.

Informative language: "I've got something to tell you." For conveying information.

Halliday stresses the need for students to learn to control all these functions, " . . . that the *full* range is necessary for the development of a fully communicating human being" (Pinnell, 1975, p. 319). Pinnell (1975) reports, however, that she found in her study of classrooms that some functions didn't appear as frequently as we might expect or hope, such as the heuristic one, which is crucial to intellectual and emotional development. She has thus pointed up a potential problem area in maximizing communicative competence.

A major factor complicating the study of language functions—and one making it also a fascinating study—is that several functions can be served at once in one utterance, with one or more rather hidden. For example, don't we sometimes hear "If we all get quickly lined up for lunch, we won't lose any recess." On the surface, this is informative language. But I submit its function is at least twofold—instrumental and regulatory. It could be paraphrased, "If you don't get lined up right now, I'll punish you by taking away some recess time." The teacher wants the students quiet and orderly. And a threat is implied—loss of recess time. As we grow up, we learn to hear these "hidden agendas" and we learn to use them ourselves.

However, to extend their communicative competence, we know our students need to learn to inform clearly, ask questions, soften their regulatory language from "Stop it!"—raw commands—to a more transactional mode, and so on. In other words, we know we need to help them broaden and deepen their ability to use different functions, to become more "sophisticated" in their expression. A classroom suggestion: analyze the type and number of functions of language used in your classroom. Are some missing or at least not very frequently used? If so, plan situations to elicit them so that the students will be able to explore the function and refine their uses of it.

Bibliography

Abrahams, Roger D., personal communication, 1972.

————, "Black Talking on the Streets," 240–262 in *Explorations in the*

Ethnography of Speaking, edited by Richard Bauman and Joel Sherzer. London: Cambridge University Press, 1974.

———, "Negotiating Respect, Patterns of Presentation Among Black Women," *Journal of American Folklore, 88,* No. 347 (January-March, 1975), 58–80.

Ammon, Ulrich, "School Problems of Regional Dialect Speakers: Ideology and Reality. Results and Methods of Empirical Investigations in Southern Germany," *Journal of Pragmatics, 1,* No. 1 (April 1977), 47–68.

Barnes, Douglas, "Language in the Secondary Classroom," in *Language, the Learner, and the School.* Harmondsworth, England: Penguin Books, 1969.

Bolinger, Dwight. *Aspects of Language.* Second Edition. New York: Harcourt, Brace, Jovanovich, Inc., 1975.

Burling, Robbins. *English in Black and White.* New York: Holt, Rinehart and Winston, 1973.

Cazden, Courtney, Vera John, and Dell Hymes, editors. *Functions of Language in the Classroom.* New York: Teachers College Press, 1972.

Cochrane, Ruth B., "Production of Selected Features of Appalachian English in a Sentence-Repetition Task by Children in Columbus Public Schools," unpublished Masters Thesis, Ohio State University, May, 1977.

Cook-Gumperz, Jenny and William A. Corsaro, "Social-Ecological constraints on Children's Communicative strategies," paper presented at the American Sociological Association Meeting, August 31, 1976.

Dale, Philip. *Language Development.* Second Edition. New York: Holt, Rinehart and Winston, 1975.

DeStefano, Johanna, "A Sociolinguistic Investigation of the Productive Acquisition of a School Language Instruction Register by Black Children," Ph.D. Dissertation, Stanford University, 1970.

———, "Black Attitudes Toward Black English: A Pilot Study," *The Florida Foreign Language Reporter, 9,* Nos. 1 & 2 (Spring/Fall 1971).

———, "Productive Language Differences in Fifth Grade Black Students' Syntactic Forms," *Elementary English, 49,* No. 4 (April 1972a), 552–558.

————,"Sex Differences in Language: A Cross-National Perspective with Emphasis on English," paper presented at the International Studies Association Meeting, St. Louis, Missouri, March 20, 1977.

————, "Some Parameters of Register in Adult and Child Speech," *Review of the Institute of Applied Linguistics, 18* (Spring, 1972b).

————. *Language, Society and Education: A Profile of Black English.* Worthington, Ohio: Charles A. Jones Publishing Co., 1973.

————, "Women's Language—By and About," in *Views on Language,* edited by Reza Ordoubadian and Walburga von Raffler-Engel. Murfreesboro, Tenn: Inter-University Publishing, 1975, 66–76.

DeStefano, Johanna, and Victor Rentel, "Language Variation: Perspectives for Teachers," issue entitled "Language Use and Acquisition," edited by Martha L. King, *Theory Into Practice,* Vol. XIV, No. 5, (December, 1975), 328–337.

Doughty, Peter, John Pearce, and Geoffrey Thornton. *Exploring Language.* London: Edward Arnold, 1972.

Downing, John, "The Development of Linguistic Concepts in Children's Thinking," *Research in the Teaching of English, 4,* No. 1 (Spring 1970), 5–19.

————, "The Reading Instruction Register," *Language Arts, 53,* No. 7, (Oct. 1976), 762–766.

Drake, St. Claire, "The Social and Economic Status of the Negro in the United States," in DeStefano, Johanna. *Language, Society and Education: A Profile of Black English.*

Ervin-Tripp, Susan, "Social Dialects in Developmental Sociolinguistics," in *Sociolinguistics.* Washington, D.C.: Center for Applied Linguistics, 1971.

Freedle, Roy, M. Naus, and L. Schwartz, "Prose Processing from a Psychological Perspective" (1977) in *Discourse Production & Comprehension,* edited by Roy Freedle. Norwood, N.J.: Ablex Corp., in press.

Gleason, Jean Berko, "Code Switching in Children's Language," in Timothy E. Moore, editor, *Cognitive Development and Acquisition of Language.* New York: Academic Press, 1973.

Grimshaw, Allen D., "Sociology, Sociolinguistics, and Language Teaching," paper presented at TESOL convention, 1972, Washington, D.C.

119

Halliday, M.A.K. *Learning How to Mean—Explorations in the Development of Language.* London: Edward Arnold Ltd., 1975.

Halliday, M.A.K., and Ruqaiya Hasan, *Cohesion in English.* London: Longman, 1976.

Halliday, M.A.K., Angus McIntosh, and Peter Strevens. *The Linguistic Sciences and Language Teaching.* London: Longmans, Green and Co., Ltd., 1964.

Hayes, Alfred, and Orlando Taylor, "A Summary of the Center's 'BALA' Project," *The Linguistic Reporter, 13,* No. 4 (Fall 1971), 1–4.

Henrie, Samuel N., Jr., "A Study of Verb Phrases Used by Five-Year-Old Nonstandard Negro English Speaking Children." Berkeley, Calif.: University of California, June, 1969 (Mimeographed).

Houston, Susan H., "A Sociolinguistic Consideration of the Black English of Children in Northern Florida," *Language, 45,* No. 3 (September 1969), 599–607.

Hymes, Dell H., "The Functions of Speech," in *The Psychology of Language, Thought and Instruction,* edited by John P. DeCecco. New York: Holt, Rinehart and Winston, 1967.

———, "Models of the Interaction of Language and Social Life" in *Directions in Sociolinguistics,* edited by John J. Gumperz and Dell Hymes. New York: Holt, Rinehart and Winston, 1972, 35–71.

Josephson, Judith P., and Johanna S. DeStefano, "Children's Productive Ability to Modify Their Speech as a Function of the Listener," unpublished manuscript, 1977.

Key, Mary Ritchie. *Male/Female Language.* Metuchen, N.J.: The Scarecrow Press, Inc., 1975.

Kochman, Thomas, "Toward an Ethnography of Black American Speech Behavior," in *Afro-American Anthology,* edited by Norman E. Whitten and John F. Szwed. New York: The Free Press, 1970, 145–162.

Labov, William. *Language in the Inner City: Studies in Black English Vernacular.* Philadelphia: University of Pennsylvania Press, 1972.

———. *The Social Stratification of English in New York City.* Washington, D.C.: Center for Applied Linguistics, 1966.

Labov, William, Paul Cohen, Clarence Robins, and John Lewis. *A Study of the Non-Standard English of Negro and Puerto Rican Speakers in*

120

New York City, Vol. I and II, 1968. Final Report, Cooperative Research Project No. 3288, USOE.

Lakoff, Robin, "Language and Woman's Place," *Language and Society, 2,* No. 1 (1973), 45–80.

Lehman, Winfred P., (editor). *Language and Linguistics in the People's Republic of China.* Austin, Texas: University of Texas Press, 1975.

Light, Richard L., "Some Observations Concerning Black Children's Conversations," *The English Record, 21,* No. 4 (April 1971), 155–167.

Miller, Casey, and Kate Swift. *Words and Women.* Garden City, N.Y.: Anchor Press/Doubleday, 1976.

Mitchell-Kernan, Claudia, "Language Behavior in a Black Urban Community," University of California, Berkeley: Language-Behavior Laboratory Work Paper 23, 1969.

Nilsen, Alleen Pace, "The Correlation Between Gender and Other Semantic Features in American English," mimeo, paper presented at Linguistic Society of America Meeting, December, 1973.

Pinnell, Gay S., "Language in Primary Classrooms," *Theory Into Practice* issue entitled "Language Use and Acquisition," edited by Martha L. King, Vol. XIV, No. 5 (December, 1975), 318–327.

Rainey, Mary, "Style Switching in a Head Start Class," University of California, Berkeley: Language-Behavior Laboratory Work Paper 16, 1969.

Reed, Carroll E. *Dialects of American English.* The University of Massachusetts Press, 1973 (second printing).

Tarone, Elaine E. "Aspects of Intonation in Vernacular White and Black English Speech," unpublished Ph.D. dissertation, University of Washington, 1972.

Thorne, Barrie, and Nancy Henley, (editors). *Language and Sex.* Rowley, Mass.: Newbury House Publishers, Inc., 1975.

Verma, S.K., "Towards a Linguistic Analysis of Registral Features," *Acta Linguistica Academiae Scientiarum Hungaricae, 19* (1969), 293–303.

Williams, Frederick. *Language and Poverty.* Chicago: Markham, 1970.

Williams, Frederick, Robert Hopper, and Diana S. Natalicio. *The Sounds of Children.* Englewood Cliffs, N.J.: Prentice-Hall, Inc., 1977.

121

Williams, Frederick, and Jack L. Whitehead, "Language in the Classroom: Studies of the Pygmalion Effect," in *Language, Society and Education: A Profile of Black English.*

For Further Reading

Abrahams, Roger D. *Deep Down in the Jungle,* revised edition. Chicago: Aldine Publishing Company, 1970.

This is an ethnographic study of the toasts, or epic poems of Black culture, as Abrahams recorded them in Philadelphia. It will give you an in-depth look at the folk characteristics of Black culture as well as the form of the poetry itself.

I also recommend his article "Black Talking in the Streets" in *Explorations in the Ethnography of Speaking,* edited by Richard Bauman and Joel Sherzer, Cambridge University Press, 1974. He very clearly details various modes of Black street talk—which you may hear your students use.

Abrahams, Roger D., and Rudolph C. Troike, (editors). *Language and Cultural Diversity in American Education.* Englewood Cliffs, N.J.: Prentice-Hall, Inc., 1972.

This readable volume covers several important bilingual situations in the United States as well as some crucial concepts on language variation.

Cazden, Courtney, Vera John, and Dell Hymes. *Functions of Language in the Classroom.* New York: Teachers College Press, 1972.

This book of readings has an important cross-cultural aspect plus its emphasis on the use of language in the educational domain. The articles are generally quite readable. Of special interest is the group of articles on American Indians, a neglected group for educational studies.

DeStefano, Johanna S. *Language, Society and Education: A Profile of Black English.* Worthington, Ohio: Charles A. Jones Publishing Co., 1973.

This volume of readings covers not only the forms of Black English but also gives a cultural description of speakers, of verbal behavior, and discusses in detail educational implications for literacy learning in particular.

Doughty, Peter, John Pearce, and Geoffrey Thornton. *Exploring Language.* London: Edward Arnold Publishers, Ltd., 1972.

This small volume gives a British perspective on language in education, including a more detailed look at functions of language.

Thorne, Barrie, and Nancy Henley, editors. *Language and Sex.* Rowley, Mass.: Newbury House Publishers, Inc., 1975.

This book of readings also contains a comprehensive annotated bibliography on sex differences in language.

Williams, Frederick, Robert Hopper, and Diana S. Natalicio. *The Sounds of Children.* Englewood Cliffs, N.J.: Prentice-Hall, Inc., 1977.

This very readable book on language variation includes the Spanish-speaking student and a set of records illustrating varieties of American English and Spanish spoken in the United States.

Language and Reading

There are cultures, not all of which are literate; but there is also a world-wide culture of which writing [and reading] is a part. Literacy, for better or for worse, will have to be taught, for all of the foreseeable future.

Dwight Bolinger, 1975, 497

One of the major extensions of communicative competence in our society is literacy. Learning to read is a major achievement in a student's language development, and the ability to read plays a major role in many people's lives, since the written word has a central function in our society as a primary transmitter of the culture. In fact, the place of reading instruction is probably questioned less than almost any other aspect of the school curriculum. Parents, teachers, national leaders—almost everyone—express concern about students learning to read. Gibson and Levin (1975) note that "reading has received more attention than any other aspect of education. The ability to read *well* (my emphasis) is the basis for success in school and later, so there is small wonder that instruction in the early grades is organized around learning to read" (1975, p. 3).

Moira McKenzie, speaking of reading in Great Britain—but applicable here in the United States as well, asserts rightly, I think, that "there is no controversy about the fundamental importance of becoming literate. The argument wages around the most effective and long lasting way in which this can happen" (*Contact,* 1976). This question of how to teach reading most effectively has engendered a variety of reading methods and materials, research studies and countless articles and books on the topic. It is also a crucial question for us as teachers that remains a sometimes puzzling one to answer, despite all of the time spent on it, in the face of certain students' difficulties in learning to read—at all curricular levels. And in the face of certain other students who know how to read when they come to school—the "early reader" group.

owever, we do know the answer—or answers—is one that encompasses a variety of factors including fitting a learner with appropriate materials and learning strategies. We include learner-specific factors such as previous exposure to reading (and degree thereof), motivation to learn to read and interest in reading, and possible cultural differences and attitudes toward reading. We also include the reading process—what does one do when one reads? What is highly skilled reading? And what does one do when one learns to read well? How do we mesh this process with instructional strategies and materials for successful reading? What strategies, techniques, and materials are useful for which individual students?

And we will ask, of course, what contributions can linguistically based studies make to our answers to the question of how to teach reading—of expanding communicative competence in one of the most crucial ways in a person's life? First, answers to how to teach reading must include information on the nature of the learner. Much current research is being done on the reading process—what one does when one reads. Also, we now know much more about possible cultural influences on learning to read and on the motivation to learn to read—another aspect of the learner.

To elaborate, linguistic and psycholinguistic studies in particular have begun to give us insight into the reading process, both in the sense of decoding (being able to recognize the words on the printed page) as reading and in the sense of comprehension as reading. Much emphasis has been placed on comprehension or getting meaning from the written language, because we recognize that decoding simply doesn't go far enough. We don't want our students to "bark at print," as it's sometimes rather graphically put. (I get an image of trained seals lined up in rows balancing flash cards on their noses.) How many of us have heard students read orally, sometimes fluently, and then not be able to answer comprehension questions? What has broken down in the reading process, in the development of literacy, so that a student can't understand what he or she has read? (And this does not refer to a fifth-grader decoding a college physics text; it refers to conceptually "appropriate" material.) We are now beginning to be able to answer some of these questions.

Also the teacher's behavior in this process of learning to read and of reading itself is a major factor. Some studies have shown, in fact, that teacher behavior may be one of the most crucial factors in reading success. If this is the case, linguistic findings—to be useful—will have to influence that behavior in some way. We will explore some possibilities for teacher behavior here.

Discussed below in some detail is the sociocultural environment of both the learner and the teacher with attendant influences on the learning and teaching of reading. In recent years, an awareness of the importance of these factors in success in reading has been growing among teachers and educators. This awareness is partly because of a broader understanding of the concept of cultural clash as it enters into the area of reading. We know we need to understand where, geographically and socially, the students come from if we're to maximize communicative competence, including competence in literacy.

Answers must also provide information on methods and materials, even if they are negative instances of what materials aren't too useful or what strategies aren't particularly productive. And sometimes it is not that the information provided by linguists is not perhaps helpful, but that the specific applications made by the linguists are not useful. For example, because of linguistics, we know quite a bit about how the phonemes of American English correspond to patterns in the written language that must be "deciphered" in reading. But materials based on very high regularity between phonemes and letters of the alphabet—"A fat cat sat on a mat"—have been found to be less effective in teaching reading than was hoped. This whole area of linguistic contributions to methods and materials will be dealt with in detail later in this chapter.

The Reading Process

What does one do when reading? A good question, as it is not something we can see or hear unless the reading is being done aloud. We can ask questions about the material. But we can only infer what the reader *does* when reading silently. This is where we need a theory to propose the outlines of the process and to explain the observable behavior. The theory must also take into account the printed page, which becomes the input instead of speech. In reading we've moved to another language mode— that of writing rather than speaking. The theory, then, must take into account the learner, the task—reading, and the medium—the written language. From these specifications—who the learner is, what goes on during reading, and what the characteristics of the printed page are—a teacher can form hypotheses about reasonable instructional procedures and materials. These hypotheses, in turn, may be linguistically based in a broad sense. The teacher can then test the hypotheses with students, see the results, and either modify or have the theory confirmed in some aspects.

This is the prime importance of any theory—to serve as a system of "explanations" for observable behavior, which serves as a basis for making hypotheses and as a coder of events. It serves as an organizer of experience and provides a set of "suggestions" for further organization of experience. In Chapter 3, children and students learning language were characterized as hypothesizers and organizers. In a rule-governed way they modify their sets of language rules more and more toward the adult set, but in their own way. It is postulated that they make hypotheses about what these rules are (unconsciously, of course) and modify them according to input from the environment sifted through their developmental patterns.

Teachers can also be characterized as hypothesizers. They, too, must look at the environment—the students in the room—and check their hypotheses against the students' behavior. A more efficient hypothesizer has an articulated theory or set of theories about, for example, students' reading behavior. This is the importance of theory: to provide as sound a base as possible for hypothesizing about what will help students learn to read—that is, to acquire the mature process of reading—and then to provide an interpretive framework for the data collected or observed about the students' reading. Theory should not justify practice, as it has all too often been used to do in the classroom, but it should perform the two above functions at least in the light of observation. The problem of theory being used to justify practice is mentioned because linguistic theory has sometimes been used in just this way in education. And when any theory that has not been translated thoughtfully into practical applications is applied directly, the results are often less than educative. What generally happens is that the content of the theory is directly taught to students who may see few implications in it for them. What should have remained teacher knowledge was made student knowledge as well. And the actual lessons were justified by the assertion that they reflected the latest theory.

Theories About the Reading Process

With that preamble about the role of theory in teaching reading, what sorts of theories are there about the process of reading? As you can well imagine, there are many—too many to be covered in a book of this type and size. But there are parts of several that seem to have quite a bit of hypothesizing power as well as explanatory power for teachers of reading.

To begin with, reading can be characterized as a "conceptual process, a tool for thinking and learning that can take the place of first-hand experience" (Gibson, 1972, p. 3). Gibson and Levin also define reading as ". . . extracting information from text" and further, ". . . as an actual process, self-directed by the reader in many ways and for many purposes"

(1975, p. 5). The perceptual part of the process or processes is thus put in perspective vis-à-vis the meaning aspect. This is important because some definitions of reading largely rest on "code-cracking," in which certain perceptual aspects are primarily stressed. In other words, some scholars would maintain that when a student has learned to decipher words and letters from the printed page, the ability to read has largely been acquired. But In the above definitions, meaning is heavily stressed as a part of the reading process.

In reading, as with speech, meaning is carried by means of language. However, the eye is the major receptor rather than the ear, especially with accomplished readers. And the graphemic system (letters and their combinations) is primary in the written language instead of the phonemic system (sounds and their combinations) as in speech. These differences have implications for learning to read, that is, for the acquisition of the reading process. However, the basic process is part of our language system as a whole, and many of these strategies employed by children learning to speak are probably employed by those same children learning to read.

Reading Strategies

What are some of these strategies used by the learner? Certainly we can again place the student in the role of hypothesizer as we did for language acquisition. Information comes to the student about those marks on the printed page. This information comes on a variety of levels—semantic, syntactic, graphophonic (meaning the phoneme-grapheme, sound-symbol correspondence), perceptual, and simply mechanical in the sense of learning to move your eyes from left to right when reading English. Ultimately the student learns to coordinate all these levels, connecting the various processes to " . . . extract a sequence of cues from printed texts and relate these, one to another, so that he understands the precise message of the text" (Clay, 1972, p. 8). Probably this is done by the student's formulating hypotheses and then testing them through experience with reading. And again, we assume that the student moves through a series of hypotheses, constantly moving toward an adult set for reading.

Remember, of course, that the beginning reader may make use of radically different hypotheses from those of a mature reader. You have probably noticed students who move their lips when they are reading silently. This is evidently a residue from making overt phoneme-grapheme correspondences in the early reading stages. This is when the child would say "cat" when c-a-t was presented. Children spend a great deal of time *saying* what they see rather than *nonverbally* recognizing it. This is not "acceptable" adult reading behavior. These stages will be examined in more detail later in this chapter.

Hypothesizing is a process of seeking patterns, a very general human activity. Any theory of the reading process should "plug into" some of the most general processes of human cognition and behavior.

But a theory also must give explanatory power to actual reading behavior, which is observed by you as the teacher. In order to do this, we need more specific concepts within the theory. One concept you are already familiar with is that of distinctive features (Chapters 2 and 3). There are many different types of distinctive features, based upon the various linguistic, psychological, and physiological systems in the reading process. One set is perceptual features in letters and printed words. For example, there are feature contrasts in letters such as straight versus curve (*l* vs. *c*), horizontal or vertical versus diagonality within straight as a category (— vs. /, as in *Z*), and open versus closed within curve as a category (*c* vs. *o*). Gibson also includes redundancy as in *W*, where one half the letter is like the other half versus discontinuity as in *L* (Gibson and Levin, 1975).

Often with beginning readers, you can see the general language process of progressive differentiation among features taking place. First a student may confuse *b* and *d,* not taking into account the *direction* of the round part of the letter in relation to the straight part. Later that is sorted out with little difficulty by most students. (A few may have perceptual problems, which make those discriminations difficult.) So at first the similarity between *b* and *d* is noticed, then the difference that makes the difference. Progressive differentiation may also operate on letter positions in a word. It is not at all unusual for beginning readers to confuse *saw* with *was.* It's as though as long as all the letters are there, the specific arrangement doesn't matter. Later it does, as the student comes to know that *saw* and *was* are letter sequences that signal two different words with very different meanings. There are distinctive differences in the positions of the *s* and the *w*. Another example is the pair *mane* and *mean,* although Fries would also add *man* to that set (1962, p. 201). The difference between *man* and *mane* is one letter; the difference between *mane* and *mean* is one of letter placement differences being distinctive.

The skilled reader actively searches for distinctive differences, with knowledge of the rules supplying information on where to look for them. But remember that a skilled reader's rule set is different from a beginning reader's. The former probably doesn't perceive single letters but, instead, clumps of them, which are distinctive in English orthography, such as *th* and *ch*. This perceptual information is then skillfully organized into higher-order units, which ultimately yield meaning. Gibson (1973) notes that beginning readers often have trouble grasping the meaning of what they're reading. It's as though the perceptual tasks are almost too much for them, and they haven't learned to process the features that will yield the meaning. Certainly this is not surprising; it's a type of "not seeing the forest for the trees." Again, *saw* and *was* are similar perceptually but not semantically. And phonologically no one would confuse the two. Yet those two systems may be ignored in face of the perceptual similarity—the student reading *was* as *saw* or vice versa. But rule systems are built to handle the entire reading process, and it's not surprising that many beginning readers start with a piece of the system. A very real burden is on the beginning reader, who has these hierarchies of distinctive features to learn and sort out.

Feature Analytic Theory of Reading

Probably one of the most direct applications of the concept of features to the reading process is Frank Smith's feature-analytic theory of reading (1971 and 1975), which postulates feature lists for virtually all the aspects of reading from decoding through meaning. The semantic feature lists are the same as those described in Chapter 2: they consist of a bundle of features, some distinctive and some not, that specify the meaning of the lexical item or *word,* this latter term being more common in discussions of reading. There are also the feature lists identifying a phoneme and the lists identifying a letter in the alphabet and, presumably, sets of letters. Such a model takes the place of the more traditional explanations of reading and gives a more unified explanation to the phoneme-grapheme correspondences than does the traditional phonics approach.

It is proposed that the skilled reader bypasses the acoustic cues or features and uses the visual set to determine the meaning of a word or phrase or sentence. As I have noted elsewhere, "Sound is evidently bypassed for a direct use of the visual system." (Destefano, 1977) In other words, there is little or no "inner speech" while the person is reading and *no* lip movement. The individual instead has another set of cues that are *not sound* cues. Certainly that would help to explain the speed a skilled reader can achieve without sacrificing meaning. But there are other sets of features that enter into "reading for meaning." Syntactic features also enter into extracting meaning from the printed page. In other words, we use knowledge of how words pattern in English to predict the next group of words. If you were to read, "She ate ——— and butter," you'd probably

131

fill *bread* in that slot. Part of your choice would rest on syntactic restrictions specifying a noun in that position, and part would be semantic. If you were to read, "She ate bread ———— butter," you'd undoubtedly put in *and.* If you read, "She ———— bread and butter," you'd be likely to add *ate* rather than *made,* but this position has perhaps fewer restrictions on it than the others above. A less mature reader may not make the same predictions with the same ease, presumably because the feature sets are not fully acquired. Data from the above procedure and sentence repetition tasks do in fact seem to indicate that young children's feature sets are not complete; therefore, they cannot predict as well as older children or adults lexical items that fit the already begun pattern. Remember the inability of children to repeat grammatical sentences when they were masked by noise (Chapter 3).

Obviously we need to know much more about features of various types—semantic, syntactic, visual, acoustic, and more—before we can delve into detail about the ways in which a beginning reader's lists are incomplete. However, the concept of features as presented by various psycholinguists is a unifying one, with far more explanatory power about the reading process than many of the more traditional views. Sound-letter (phoneme-grapheme) correspondences don't explain enough, especially in a mature reader. Perhaps this oral-visual schema explains virtually nothing about what a fluent reader normally does. Gibson and Levin contend that " . . . the reader processes the largest structural unit that he is capable of perceiving and that is adaptive (has utility) for the task he is engaged in" (1975, p. 23). Smith asserts that "Fluent reading requires the constant making of hypotheses about meaning in advance that are tested with a minimum of visual information . . . " (1974, p. 238). Notice he doesn't even allude to sound-symbol correspondence, but only allows visual information from the printed or written symbols.

Another psycholinguistic (and psychological) concept with explanatory power for the reading process is the notion of *redundancy,* which allows in another powerful notion—prediction. A mature and fluent reader makes predictions (or hypotheses) about the printed page—meaning predictions. And redundancy helps reduce uncertainty and narrow the field of possible predictions, thus speeding up reading. Redundancy occurs when we get the same information from more than one source. "General consensus" is redundant because "consensus" already carries in its meaning "general." Repetition of words and phrases is obvious redundancy and can be very effective as in poems, children's stories, and the like. We have old saws like "Practice (repetition) makes perfect." In natural language, we also have a great deal of redundancy of various types. In speech we have acoustic, syntactic, and semantic redundancy. In the written language we have visual, orthographic (spelling system), syntactic, and semantic redundancy (Smith, 1971). Let's look closer at redundancy within the written language:

The student didn't know the an————.

Visually, if that came at the end of the page you could simply turn it and find the last letters. Orthographically, you "know" the *an* won't be followed by certain letters such as *f, h, p, a, r,* or *z* because those combinations don't occur often or at all in English spelling patterns. Syntactically, we would expect the word to be a noun or adjective, since it follows an article *the* and is in a common English noun or adjective position. We wouldn't expect another verb or adverb there. Semantically, we know something about what happens to students in classrooms. They are asked questions and expected to give *answers.* It could be *anagram* possibly, but not *antibody,* which you don't *know* but may *know about.* All this information is redundant; the skilled reader doesn't need four different sets of cues as to what the rest of the word is. Smith, who explains this process very clearly (1971, pp. 20-1), suggests that the skilled reader needs much less visual information than the beginning reader. The former's three systems—orthographic, syntactic, and semantic—are more complete than the latter's. Thus the beginning reader may need much more redundancy—from a variety of systems—in order to extract meaning from the reading material—or may rely heavily on one type of redundancy, which is not optimal for reading, but over which he or she has some control.

There are two other types of redundancy commonly discussed. One is distributional redundancy, which has to do with the probability of a certain event or item appearing. For example, in the English orthographic system, not every letter has the same chance of occurrence in words. Some letters are far more common than others. That is part of the reason for the keys of a typewriter being arranged as they are with the *z* and *q* in extreme corners. Commonly occurring letters are the vowel letters *a, e, i,* and *o* and the consonant letters *n, s,* and *t.* According to Smith (1971, p. 22), *e* occurs 40 times more often than *z,* the least frequently used letter of the alphabet. As mature readers, we probably have a good sense of what we expect to see on the printed page based at least somewhat on distributional redundancy not only of letters but also of words. That is, given a certain topic, certain words will appear far more frequently than others. And in general writing, function or "empty" words such as *is, the, a, and,* and *so* will appear far more frequently than "content" words.

Sequential redundancy is the type of redundancy having to do with the predictability of events or items in sequence, as the term would imply. The examples:

She ate bread and ———.
She ——— bread and butter.
She ate ——— and butter.
She ate bread ——— butter.

would all be sequential redundancy. It also occurs within words, as in g_rl. No skilled reader of American English would have trouble reading that word. In fact, sequential redundancy is recognized in Hebrew and other Semitic language writing systems to the extent that the vowel sounds are not indicated in writing, only the consonants. In English as well, consonant letters and groups probably carry a far higher information load than the vowel letters. Compare g_rl to_i_ or c_ll to_e_or_a_. In c _ ll, you can reduce the uncertainty at least to *cell* or *call* or *cull* (if you know that word), and context would certainly reduce even those uncertainties to one choice. Given the sentences:

She will ——— me on the telephone.
and
She studied a ——— under the microscope.
and
She ———ed walnuts by hand.

you can assign *call, cell,* and *cull* accurately. But a beginning reader whose language systems are not as developed could have more trouble making the assignments as the sequential redundancies could not be exploited—they haven't yet been recognized as redundancies.

A skilled reader can be far more economical in reading than a beginning reader because he or she can employ the various types of redundancy to increase reading speed. Smith states:

> . . . the more redundancy there is, the less visual information the skilled reader requires. In passages of continuous text, provided the content is not too difficult, every other letter can be eliminated from most words, or about one word in five omitted altogether, without making the passage too difficult for a reader to comprehend—provided that he has learned the rules related to letter and word occurrence and co-occurrence[1] (Smith, 1971, p. 23).

It would seem then, that as teachers of beginning readers, we can help them discover the redundancies in the printed language and help them learn to exploit them. What can they use? According to Smith (1971), first graders can use sequential redundancy in the sense of being able to more easily identify single letters appearing in three-letter words than in isolation. By fourth grade, students could equal adults in the use of sequential redundancy of identifying letters in words. But there are other redundancies in the language that may not develop as quickly but could be exploited by students. Hopefully research will begin to reveal more specifics about these redundancies.

Diagnosis of Reading

We have described only briefly some characteristics of the reading processes of the skilled reader that have been revealed in psycholinguistically oriented research and theory. As teachers you must know what a mature reader does before you can effectively help a beginning reader become fluent. And you also need to know about strategies students use to learn to read and to help them make the match with more mature strategies. What are some things they do? How can we diagnose their level of development of the ability to read? Kenneth and Yetta Goodman and Carolyn Burke have done a great deal of work on what they call the *miscue,* which they feel reveals the "psycholinguistic guessing game"—that is, the process of learning to read. In other words, students when they read *orally* attend to certain features on the printed page in correspondence with their own language systems—the phonological, syntactic, and semantic. They "guess" in trying to make all these sets match so they can derive meaning from the written material. Sometimes, since the "guesses" are not quite accurate or adequate, the student reads something that isn't actually on the page. That is called a *miscue* in the sense of *miss-cue-ing* from the material and from the student's own language and experiential systems. For example, Yetta Goodman and Burke (1974) cite the following:

> Text: *To get her poor dog a wig.*
> Child reading: *To get her poor dog play hair.*

This is obviously a high-level response, but indicative of some feature sets

[1]*Occurrence* and *co-occurrence* are used in the sense that when a certain letter or word appears, we expect another particular one, or one from a particular set of others. So, in English, nouns or adjectives follow an article such as *the,* but not verbs or prepositions.

that don't quite match those of more fluent readers. It wasn't that the child didn't know *wig*, but her *play hair* indicates a different concept of what a *wig* is.

Generally, the miscues made by students reading orally are patterned, and the patterns of miscues change with the skill of the reader. Less skilled readers tend to make miscues that are syntactically at variance with the text they are reading, while more skillful readers will tend to stay within a given syntactic pattern, even if it requires correction on their part of their initial reading. For example, a second grader read "Then Tiny played firmly pushing Shiny . . . " while the text read "Then Tiny playfully pushed Shiny . . . " The syntax in the oral reading definitely does not fit the syntax of the text. A fourth grader read "Tame birds may be given gravel . . . " while the text was "Tame birds *must* be given gravel . . . " Even though the meaning was changed, the syntax of the original was adhered to.

We know from Chapter 3 that a child's grammatical system continues to develop during school age. Knowledge of what follows what syntactically or which elements pattern with which other elements becomes refined, and patterns are probably much more apparent to a more syntactically mature student. This knowledge is revealed in the reading process through certain types of miscues.

Another developmental aspect shown in the type of miscues made is that of the semantic system. The more proficient a reader, the fewer changes he or she will make in the meaning of the text in oral reading. For example, the same second grader read "things Fox" for "Shiny Fox" with no attempt at correction. At another point he read "tribe" for "tardy" in "We are going to be tardy." (It is unlikely that he meant *tribe*—he was probably miscueing somewhat on the grapheme-phoneme relationship.) He corrected *tribe* to *tried,* again not a happy semantic choice. On the other hand, the fourth grader read "Birds have to eat gravel" while the text was "Birds have to eat *the* gravel." Looking at the whole text, the omission of *the* did nothing significant to change the meaning.

The correction of a miscue can also help to reveal stages in the acquisition of reading. A student miscueing without correcting, especially the semantic ones, may not be reading for meaning. If a student miscues but corrects to either the text or something close to the text, then some comprehension probably can be assumed. In other words, the student has gone beyond simply decoding. The corrections of the more proficient readers are in that direction—correction for meaning. Also, the more skilled readers tend to produce more complex miscues that " . . . involve more integration of the meaning, the grammatical and sound systems of the language with the graphic input and the experience and background of the child" (Goodman and Burke, 1974). Many of these miscues tend to point out strengths in a student's acquisition of reading because the tendency of mature readers to miscue to preserve the meaning of the text indicates their ability to derive meaning from the printed page. Also, staying within the same syntactic category on a miscue indicates the reader's ability to exploit at least some of the redundancies and feature sets of the syntactic system of the language.

However, I must point out that oral reading—reading aloud—is different from silent reading. There is another skill set overlay in oral reading that doesn't exist for silent reading. Thus miscues may illuminate certain aspects of the reading process, but cannot be taken to be totally revealing. They are, in my estimation though, useful as a diagnostic tool at the early stages of learning to read.

As you can see, the areas and branches of linguistics offer preliminary work on the reading process and a student's acquisition of that process. These bits and pieces have strength because of their origins in a more general linguistic theory. Obviously a great deal of research is needed—which in turn may change the existing theories substantially. But such modifications are not problematic in and of themselves. They are merely part of the entire process. However, both data collected from students who read and theory are needed, since the field of reading needs them both to pull itself out of the methods-materials quagmire onto more solid diagnostic ground where instructional behavior is motivated by a well-founded theory instead of a series of alinguistic or nonlinguistic assumptions about what it is to read.

Cultural Influences on Learning and Teaching Reading

As teachers wishing to maximize communicative competence through reading, we need to be aware of what cultures both we and the learner come from. The phenomenon of cultural clash (described in Chapter 4) all too often influences behavior in the classroom to the point of blocking learning. This clash situation can and does exist for literacy learning far more than is commonly anticipated. Why, we ask. Doesn't everybody want to learn to read? Isn't this a national goal? Yes, this is a national goal; but the motivation to learn to read is a complex one, often modified by a variety of cultural and developmental factors. As a national goal, reading has been introduced to certain groups whose cultures are either not literate or, if literate, see reading in English as destructive to their culture.

Let's look at oral cultures first. There are several in the United States, which have long oral traditions: black culture, various American Indian

137

cultures, and some aspects of Chicano culture. As mentioned previously in Chapter 4, cultural information is passed largely by word of mouth and by doing—children working alongside their parents or other adults. Oral culture also contains many traditional oral forms. The toasts, or epic poems, of black culture are one example. In Finland, the national epic, the *Kalevala,* was until the late 1800s a collection of oral poems in a distinct metric pattern. These oral tales were told by people called *kanteles* (meaning, literally, singers) who would travel from village to village chanting the tales, accompanying themselves on a zitherlike instrument. The story lines of the tales were all memorized; the actual wording and use of stock phrases to finish the metric pattern of a line was up to the individual kantele. The better turn of a phrase, the more witty the kantele, the more famous he or she was. Elias Lonnröt, the man who first collected most of the oral tales and wrote them down, found one woman who knew *several hundred* with all the twists and turns of plot. With the coming of literacy to Finland, which is now about 99% literate, the kanteles are no longer to be found, since the tales are written down for all to read—and all can read them. The Finns accepted literacy in Finnish, which was, until relatively recently for Europe, an oral language, not a written one. With the coming of literacy most of the oral traditions are disappearing.[2]

In the United States many oral traditions have also disappeared with widespread literacy. But several cultures still hold to theirs, such as the toasts and other verbal forms in black culture. These remaining oral forms have an ancient history, so ancient as to antedate by far the *Iliad* and the *Odyssey,* originally oral poems themselves, which were written only later. Such venerable beginnings indicate that oral traditions are not inferior to literary ones; they are simply older and different.

In an orally based culture, reading has little place or may be seen as peripheral to the cultural reward system. In other words, you get no special status by being able to read or to read well. Status accrues instead to the proficient "rappers" and toasters, those verbally facile who can turn a good phrase. (Remember how H. Rap Brown got his name—Chapter 4.) Or other cultures may value the faultless recitation from memory of long sagas and rituals. There may even be taboos against writing any rituals down, much like the ban on being photographed laid down by some members of the Amish religious sect here in the United States. However,

---

[2] The documentation for this comes from a variety of conversations I had with various Finns when visiting Finland. The *Kalevala* holds a central place in the national identity, and all school children learn large amounts of the epic by heart. We have nothing really comparable to it in our culture.

some materials are being produced that are written versions of toasts, oral poetry, and so on. Conceivably, if this trend continues, the oral cultures in this country will become literary as well—as happened in Finland. But this is only a supposition on my part, and no one knows how long it would take. However, oral cultures in the United States are surrounded by a literary culture—as Finland was too.

The dominant culture in the United States has a literary tradition; black culture and Indian cultures are oral. What does this mean for the motivation to learn to read for a child from one of these cultures? It may mean that there is relatively little, since reading is a largely unrewarded activity in his or her culture or in the subculture. Many black parents want their children to learn to read. They have adopted many of the "mainstream" values, including reading. But in the subculture of the child, there are other signals that essentially communicate a lack of value for reading. Labov and Robins (1973) found among black male adolescents in Harlem an almost total lack of interest in reading, particularly among those who were well integrated into the peer group, street subculture. Upon questioning it was found that members of a certain street group didn't have any idea how well each other read. Generally their reading ability was at least several years below grade level, and not one in that group was able to read above the fifth-grade level. Thus eighth graders were reading at no more than a fifth-grade level. Within the group, status and position were assigned totally independently of reading ability. As a matter of fact, any *school* success was irrelevant to the street subculture and its set of values.

What does this mean for teachers of students whose peer subculture or even adult culture is either hostile or oblivious to reading? It means that motivation certainly cannot be stirred merely by saying it's wonderful to learn to read. What satisfaction will these students get out of it *now*? How can you motivate a six-year-old by talking about the importance of reading in creating job opportunities when he or she is 18? And another problem: reading is seen within the matrix of the school subculture, toward which there may be great hostility on the part of the students and possibly the parents. It is often seen as alien to and alienating from the parents' culture. William Labov and Clarence Robins' Harlem street groups saw school as hostile and irrelevant to their lives. They tended to associate reading with feminity, as the teachers are mostly female, and girls often are able to read better than the boys. Thus if they read well, they would appear unmasculine. The boys in these groups value intelligence, but do not see any connection between intelligence and reading ability. They also value language ability, but that is oral rather than written. Motivation for reading? "Teachers in the city schools have little ability to reward or punish members of the street culture, or to motivate learning by any means" (Labov and Robins, 1973, p. 319).

It is highly unfortunate that when these boys grow older, they begin to subscribe to the adult values, which do hold more with the "mainstream" value set. But they lack necessary reading skills at least partly because of the cultural clash during the developmental reading years. So cultural clash can be extremely damaging and can contribute materially to failure as an adult when value sets shift.

How do we cope with such a clash? Labov and Robins suggest a cultural intermediary in the school, someone the boys can identify with and who also values reading—for example, a literate black man from their area who was once in a gang. What else could be done by the teacher individually? Certainly a realization of the clash is extremely important: the students are not "lazy" or "bad." Instead they are subscribing to a set of values that is much more important to them at that time. Also, school can be made to be a less hostile environment for these children. Cultural differences can be taken into account, and behavior appropriately evaluated. Perhaps with less hostility there can be more acceptance of the value of reading or at least a tolerance for it. Also, materials could be generated from the students' culture. The oral tales ("toasts") could be written down—along with song lyrics and other oral forms—and used as basic reading materials. In that way, one form the students know and understand could help make a bridge to literacy instruction; their culture would appear in the school. Obviously, cultural clash is a very real and difficult problem, but it is one we can deal with in order to maximize communicative competence for all students.

But what of cultures in which the adults are also hostile to literacy in English? In these cultures the problem is compounded. In black culture many of the parents are sympathetic if not extremely positive about literacy, and they speak English as their first language. On the other hand, in the Cherokee culture in Oklahoma, the adults are sympathetic to literacy in Cherokee but not in English. Among the Cherokees (Walker, undated), there has long been a literary tradition begun by Sequoya, an individual who created a syllabary for the Cherokee language evidently between 1809 and 1821 (Bolinger, 1975). A syllabary is a system of symbols in which a symbol stands for a syllable in a language rather than a single sound (phoneme). The Cherokee syllabary consists of 85 symbols, one representing the phoneme /s/, and the rest representing either vowel syllables or syllables consisting of consonant plus vowel sounds such as *sa, do,* and *lu* (Bolinger, 1975, p. 487).

It has been found to be common for an adult Cherokee to teach himself or herself to read. And the children quickly become literate. According to Williard Walker, who has researched Cherokee literacy, the Cherokees were estimated to be 90% literate in their own language *by the 1830s.* By the 1880s, it is also estimated that the Western Cherokee had a higher English literacy level than the white population of either Texas or Arkansas.

Walker states: "Since the federal government took over the Cherokee school system in 1898, Cherokees have viewed the school as a white man's institution which Cherokee children are bound by law to attend, but over which their parents have no control....Most Cherokee speakers drop out of school as soon as this is legally possible. While in school, they learn relatively little due to the language barrier and also due to this unfortunate, but accurate, definition of the school as a white man's institution. As a further complication Cherokee parents are well aware that educated children tend to leave the community, either geographically or socially. To them the school threatens the break-up of the family and division of the community, precisely those consequences which no genuinely tribal society can tolerate...." (undated, p. 6).

"It seems clear that the startling decline during the past sixty years of both English and Cherokee literacy in the Cherokee tribe is chiefly a result of the recent scarcity of reading materials in Cherokee, and of the fact that learning to read has become associated with coercive instruction, particularly in the context of an alien and threatening school presided over by English-speaking teachers and controlled by English-speaking superintendents and PTA's which conceive of Cherokee as a 'dying' language and Cherokee school children as 'culturally improvised' candidates for rapid and 'inevitable' social assimilation. Indians and whites alike are constantly equating competence in the school with assimilations into the white middle class....For the Cherokee community to become literate once again, Cherokees must be convinced that literacy does not imply the death of their society, that education is not a clever device to wean children away from the tribe. This is not a uniquely Cherokee situation. Identical attitudes toward education and the school no doubt can be found in Appalachia, in urban slums, in Afro-Asia, and, indeed, in all societies where the recruitment of individuals into the dominant society threatens the extinction of a functioning social group[3]" (undated, p. 10).

We have already discussed the hostility toward school in the urban slums. School, then, is often seen as an enculturating tool of the dominant society. Since reading and literacy are a major part of "mainstream"

[3] Willard Walker, "An Experiment in Programmed Cross-Cultural Education: The Import of the Cherokee Primer for the Cherokee Community and for the Behavioral Sciences," undated mimeo. Reprinted by permission of the author.

culture, they are seen as part of that enculturation. But all too often reading failure and difficulties are blamed on physiological or psychological problems, and the cultural input is largely, if not entirely ignored. (Ethnocentrism again?) How can we talk about decoding problems if the child comes to school perhaps overtly hostile to the idea of learning to read or learning to read English? Where is the initial motivation to learn to read? And if the school is hostile to a student's culture, as all too many are, where is that motivation going to come from in school? If the teacher is also hostile, the classroom situation itself will not provide the motivation either.

What can we as teachers do? First, we can realize that the cultural hostility is only partly manifested in the school situation: cultural clash occurs 24 hours a day and not just in the school building. Generally the schools reflect the values of the dominant culture, which does negatively assess many other cultures. As teachers, you can be alert to the possibility to such clash in your classroom and in the school as a whole and examine in depth your own feelings and attitudes toward the students who come from cultures other than your own. Reading is learned in a cultural setting of which you and your students are a part. This cannot be overlooked if we are to be successful in helping more students maximize their communicative competence.

Language Variation and Reading: Dialect and Sociolect Considerations

Since students speak a variety of American English as their native language, what input might their sociolect or dialect forms have into the learning of reading? This is an extremely complex question, fraught with much controversy and having available relatively little research to help settle it. Kenneth Johnson and Herbert Simons (1973) have recently done research into black vernacular-speaking students' ability to read materials written in so-called standard English and in black vernacular to try to discover the consequences of that sociolect's forms in the reading process. Their preliminary findings indicate the children read no better in the vernacular materials than they did in the so-called standard material. They suggest one factor contributing to this lack of difference might be the fact that the students had already learned to read the so-called standard, being in the second and third grades in Oakland, California, schools. Therefore, they were already acquainted with "standard" forms in certain material and had little or no trouble comprehending them. Johnson and Simons propose that a group of students should be taught from the beginning with vernacular readers and then compared with those reading "standard" texts from the beginning. These are only some of the complexities and controversies emerging from the question about the influence of sociolect on reading.

There are reading researchers as well as teachers who feel that materials written in a vernacular variety—whether it be dialect or sociolect—are not necessary. To begin with, these varieties are oral; generally, they have no written form. So when they have to be written down, there are difficulties in deciding how to spell certain forms as well as in deciding how often to put in forms such as multiple negatives. First, the spelling problem: it seems simple, but how should /Iŋ/, a frequent ending set of phonemes, be written—as *swimmin'* or *swimmin?* (The apostrophe is sometimes used to indicate something is "left out." But some linguists feel nothing is in fact left out. The /n/ is simply an alternate form of final /ŋ/. Hence the controversy.) Or how does one write *will,* which is often pronounced something like /wIw/? Do you write *wiw* or *wi* or *will?* And does the student recognize *wiw* any better than *will* as being what he or she says? A study by May (1976) indicated that children who spoke Black English experienced no interference from their variety in identifying words spelled in traditional orthography. So *wiw* may be no clearer than *will.* And do we do this for so-called standard speaking students who also say /wIw/ in certain sound environments? No, we don't. So what forms of a variety are important in reading? We don't know. And how do we spell them? How close a phoneme-grapheme correspondence is useful? A study by Gillooly (1975) may shed some light on these questions. Initially, close correspondences such as those found in i.t.a. (discussed below) had some advantages over traditional spelling; word recognition skills were better as was spelling, but *not* paragraph-meaning scores. But by fourth grade, students read traditional orthography better than any system of closer phoneme-grapheme correspondences.

A second point is the frequency of certain forms. Remember that there is inherent variation in speakers' speech. No one uses multiple negatives all the time; the incidence of use of the form depends to a great extent on the social situation the speaker is in. Therefore, how often should multiple negatives appear in the written materials? And this question applies to other forms in a given oral variety. What is the frequency of appearance that will seem realistic to a vernacular-speaking student? We have no answer to that question at this time.

These problems, added to a variety of other factors, have lead to serious questioning of vernacular reading materials. Other factors have to do with the reading process itself. Students learn to make sound-symbol correspondences. Is there any reason to think that a so-called closer correspondence would make learning to read easier? Many researchers feel there is not, that the connection between letters and sounds is arbitary enough to begin with for all students, so that a variety of strategies is necessary and *useful.* Richard Rystrom (1973, p. 4) has found indications that beginning first-graders have very little idea of the adult connections between sounds and letters. Furthermore, these first-graders he studied were both vernacular and nonvernacular-speaking children. They seem to start at the same point, and many end up at the same point—being able to read "regular" reading materials.

There is another very practical problem arising from teacher reaction to the sociolect. It has been noted that students when reading aloud will often put in certain forms from their sociolect. For example, I've heard black vernacular-speaking students read, "I axed Susie could she go wif me" for "I asked Susie if she could go with me." That sentence is a sociolect rendition of the second; they mean the same thing. So is it a mistake? Should it be corrected by the teacher and pointed out to the student that he or she did not read what was on the page? I suggest not. First of all, it is not a mistake. The student is obviously reading with meaning, since the sentence is being reproduced, although in the student's own variety. That means some sort of processing has taken place. In fact, these variety renditions can be looked at very positively as a sign that the student is in fact comprehending at least something he or she is reading. Strict adherence to the forms on the printed page means relatively little in the reading process, therefore, it need not be stressed that much. This means that you as a teacher need to be very aware of the various forms in sociolect and dialect renditions in oral reading in order to assess an individual student's progress in the acquisition of the reading process. Information on these forms is available in a variety of sources, one of which is DeStefano, 1973 (see "For Further Reading").

Register Switching and Reading

Register switching is another type of social variation in language (see Chapter 4). What is its place in the learning and teaching of reading? First, in English we have registers in both the written and spoken modes with attendant differences (see Chapter 4 for some of these differences). These differences are learned by students who must deal with these forms not found or found only infrequently in the spoken language. And we as teachers should be as aware as possible of the differences in the forms found in the written language.

In a very real sense, all students, no matter what sociolect or dialect they speak, are a certain "distance" from the forms they must learn to read, particularly in more advanced reading in the upper grades. For example, passives are not used frequently in any spoken variety of American English. Nor are poetic inversions, such as "came the dawn," found to any great extent in speech. Long appositive phrases such as "my uncle, the one who now lives in Paris when he isn't touring the world in his yacht . . . " are also more common in writing. These are only some of the syntactic differences between speech and writing that must be dealt with by students reading the written language. Constrastive comparisons between forms in the spoken and written modes would be helpful to all students learning to read. In fact, Carol Chomsky (1972) has proposed that children's exposure to the written forms of the language by their own reading as well as by adults reading to them positively influences their language development between the ages of 5 to 10. Evidently students do take advantage of the variety and complexity of the written language as they read it or as it is read to them. No matter what level I taught at, I read aloud to my students almost daily, bringing to their ears usually more difficult material than they could comfortably read at first (in high school, it was Shakespeare).

Second, learning to read can be put in a register acquisition framework. A student learning to read more and more difficult material will learn to read descriptive prose, poetry, scientific writing, newspapers, and so forth. Little, if any, of this may be *produced* by the student, but the receptive competence can be there. The acquisition framework can also be useful for students with different varieties of American English. You can see them expanding their repertoire of registers, which calls for a higher use of certain socially unmarked forms, and they can see themselves doing this, too. There is really no need to put a maximum emphasis on language differences, but all students need competence in various facets of their native language.

Sociolinguistic research and perspective have a great deal to offer that is important in the area of reading. Language use is a social act that takes place in a social context. Reading is part of that social act in a social context. If the factors contributed by a social situation with all of its cultural constraints are forgotten, a great deal of reading is also forgotten. We have already mentioned that unfavorable social conditions may make it almost impossible for reading to be learned. As teachers we cannot forget the social setting and its influence on teaching and learning to read. We cannot forget the Cherokee students' response to reading in English (Walker) and the Harlem black adolescents' response to reading (Labov and Robins, 1973). What influences may we have operating in our own classroom?

-Grapheme Correspondences and the Teaching of Reading

It is perhaps in the area of phoneme-grapheme or sound-symbol corre-spondences that we are most familiar with the contribution of linguistics to reading. The knowledge of phonology and its relationship to the written language is the linguistic basis for this contribution to the teaching of reading and is most represented in materials development. Hence you find reading books with patterns such as "Nan can fan Dan" and "The fat cat sat on the mat" in which the vocabulary is highly controlled in order to keep clear phoneme-grapheme correspondences.

This area applies to teaching decoding primarily rather than compre-hension. And it is generally viewed as playing only a temporary role in the learning of the reading process. In other words, the skilled reader is not thought to make sound-letter correspondences but instead is thought to deal more directly with the concepts expressed by the written language in the comprehension process.

The importance of helping students make phoneme-grapheme corre-spondences in beginning reading instruction is now under close scrutiny. When it was first suggested by linguists such as Leonard Bloomfield (Bloomfield and Barnhart, 1961) and Charles Fries (1963), it seemed an intuitively obvious aid to teaching reading. Thus you can find in many first-grade classrooms flashcards with the -*at* family on them, as in *fat, cat, mat, hat, sat, rat,* and *bat,* or the -*it* family, as in *bit, hit, fit,* and *sit.* After all, English has an alphabetic writing system. Letters more or less stand for sounds, although there isn't a one-to-one correspondence. But, the reasoning goes, there is enough correspondence to warrant work based on the phoneme-grapheme correspondences that do exist.

Some individuals, such as Sir James Pitman in England, felt a new alphabetic system that offered an even greater phoneme-grapheme corre-spondence would be of more help to students learning to read. This alphabetic idea was behind the creation of the *i.t.a.,* or the Initial Teaching Alphabet, which has 45 symbols instead of the 26 of traditional orthogra-phy. It was intended to regularize the correspondences even further by having each phoneme represented by a single symbol thus, the reasoning went, making decoding easier. However, as Dale (1976) points out, the phoneme /u/ is represented by a single i.t.a. symbol ω but spelled "in no less than seventeen distinct ways (in ruby, rule, do, more, fruit, bruise, group, through, moon, wooed, loose, rheumatism, flue, maneuver, grew, canoe, and two)" (p. 226).

The notion of sound-letter correspondence also helps the student to see the connection between speech and writing, to see that the printed page is really what someone says written down. Probably this is an important connection for the learner to make. But the question is whether this can be done best through teaching phoneme-grapheme correspondences. We still have many students in the United States who have trouble learning to read even though they learn word families and go through a variety of other reading exercises.

Savin (1972) suggests that many of these students are not able to segment sound into phonemes—that is, discrete bundles. He found this to be the case with some inner city students he taught in Philadelphia. They were not able to use the alphabetic principle of connecting discrete sounds with letters. Briefly, the spelling system of English is based on an alphabetic principle. One letter or a small group of letters stands for a sound in the language. Most modern writing systems are alphabetic in nature. However, there are other systems of writing. The Cherokee system and parts of the Japanese system are based on a syllabic principle, with each symbol more less being associated with a syllable in the spoken system. Interestingly enough, Savin found these children could function fairly well in making distinctions among syllables that were more than minimally different (where there is only one phoneme that is different). For example, they could tell *cat* from *dog* but not from *rat*. They showed no comprehension of the statement as, again, they evidently do not hear single sounds, "*Cat* and *cow* begin with the same sound." According to Savin, these students also couldn't learn pig Latin, which involves phoneme shifting and adding. (Remember that this "language" involves dropping the first sound of a word, putting it at the back, and adding /e/ to give something like "Ankey ouey aktey igpey atinley?" This is difficult to write, since it is only a spoken form.) In other words, for them, the syllable was the smallest auditory perceptual unit. Such evidence raises serious questions about the usefulness of units smaller than syllables for some students. If they can't make use of the information, it's not going to help them to learn to read. And we should expect such differences, knowing what we do about the variation present in human abilities and behavior.

Thus, it must be remembered that in the decoding process of some students, phoneme-grapheme correspondences may have only limited value. This is why diagnostic, learner-centered approaches are so crucial in teaching reading. We cannot afford to assume that the alphabetic principle, which is so obvious to us as fluent readers of English, is obvious to all students. Their rule systems and the features they attend to may be strikingly different from more developed systems and cueing features. Also, the other types of writing systems that exist should raise questions about the alleged "naturalness" of the alphabetical writing system. The Chinese system is logographic (which means that a symbol usually stands for a whole word), and segments of Chinese society have been literate far longer than most European societies. The Japanese writing system consists of some logographs in a basically syllabic system. Some preliminary research has even indicated that in brain-damaged Japanese, the logographs were better retained than the syllable symbols (Sakamoto and Makita, 1973). They are considered to be far more distinctive to the eye than are the syllable symbols.

Thus the linguistic contribution of phoneme-grapheme correspondences must be put in perspective in relationship to the teaching of beginning reading and decoding. With this important constraint in mind, let's look at the patterns of sound-symbol correspondences discussed by linguists such as Bloomfield and Fries, since the alphabetic principle undoubtedly does function effectively in many children's decoding processes. Charles Fries (1963) found a variety of common patterns in American English that display great regularity in the graphemes standing for certain phonemes. One of the most common is the single syllable *c v c* (consonant-vowel-consonant) sequence in which the vowel retains the "short" quality. You can find a large number of words following that pattern, and there are variations on this basic pattern that still retain a great deal of regularity. For example, consonants can be added to the initial *c* or to the final *c* or both, producing such words as *shift (cc v cc)*, and *chit (c c v c)*, and *salt (c v c c)*. Another pattern suggested by Fries as an important one for reading, especially reading aloud, is the *c v c e* pattern, which indicates that you change the "short" vowel to a "long" one when reading. It is demonstrated in sets such as:

rat	rate
fat	fate
can	cane
dun	dune
run	rune
bit	bite
sit	site

You will notice that none of these pairs except for *bit-bite* have any meaning correspondences. This is purely a spelling pattern in English.

You have probably already realized that these patterns are of one-syllable words that are common in English. However, as experienced readers, we come up against many multisyllabic words, many of them being of Latin and Romance language origin. Remember the example of *nation, national,* and *nationalize,* etc., in Chapter 2. Readers must deal with prefixes, suffixes, many syllables—often far from the patterns suggested by Fries. We recognize a connection between *nation* and *nationalize.* Yet there is no one-to-one, phoneme-grapheme correspondence preserved to show the connection exactly. There are two different initial vowel phonemes in the two words, which probably doesn't bother any fluent reader. Have you even noticed the difference? Chances are you note the similarity without noting the differences. In other words, the surface differences don't make a difference; they are not distinctive.

Below the Surface—Beyond the Phoneme and Grapheme

All of this would suggest that we may have at least another correspondence system. Some words have a direct relationship, which is obvious in actual utterance. The relationship of other words or lexical entries is below the surface. Carol Chomsky (1970) has explored this relationship, basing it on the transformational-generative framework discussed in Chapter 2. The conventional spelling of words (traditional orthography) corresponds more closely to an underlying abstract level of representation within the sound system of the language, than it does to the surface phonetic form that the words assume in the spoken language (1970, p. 287). Thus the spelling system has already abstracted away irrelevant phonemic information that could even hinder word recognition. For example, there is quite a bit of phonemic difference between *photograph* and *photography,* again which we probably don't notice. Stress plays a part in the pronunciation, as well as phonemic differences. But we recognize *photography* as a variant of *photograph* immediately and do not have to discard stress and vowel differences, which are irrelevant to the process of gaining meaning from the printed page. So the meaning relationship is clarified at the expense of greater sound-letter correspondence. However, reading theorists such as Smith postulate the fluent reader goes well below the "surface" anyway, largely bypassing sound-letter correspondences. The implication is that skilled readers do not utilize the "surface phonetic form" but instead the underlying levels in the decoding process. There is no need to make the complete sound-symbol correspondence, which could even hinder our recognition of variant forms of the same lexical item. It is suggested that we help students make these same correspondences; certainly it would extend their repertoire of reading vocabulary from a level of "obvious" phoneme-grapheme correspondence patterns. Remember the Gillooly research (1975) reported above in which, by fourth grade, surface correspondences are among the least important. This seems most reasonable to me, as it seems obvious that a fluent reader "chunks" units far larger than words when reading. Meaning lies at a larger unit level than words; for example, words usually take on meanings in context. So fluent readers must process phrases, clauses, etc. in order to comprehend what is on the page. Word discrimination based on sound-letter correspondence *may* be useful in the beginning, but rather quickly falls away as even a useful reading strategy.

Chomsky also points out that most of the phonemic variations in word families are highly patterned and therefore can be ignored when reading. Again, we are dealing with nondistinctive differences:

/k/ to /s/ as in medicate—medicine
critical—criticize
dramatic—drama*ticism*

The distinctive differences to which a reader must attend while reading are below the surface. The automatic variation can be ignored in favor of those differences that make a difference.

Students should be helped to recognize these underlying similarities for themselves. You could utilize word lists that pair related words such as those above to make clear the visual similarities. Certainly they rely more on the eye, the visual process, than on the ear—*photograph* and *photography* look alike more than they sound alike. This bypassing of the ear undoubtedly adds to reading speed and represents more mature reading, which is to be sought by both the learner and the teacher. This underlying construct also has implications for spelling, which will be discussed in the final chapter.

It is crucial to place the phonological component of the language system in perspective in the reading process. Because so much attention has been given to it in recent reading materials and suggestions for instruction, it is doubly important that we don't overemphasize it in the decoding process to the exclusion of other strategies that may actually contribute more to the development of the fluent reading process.

A Short Note—The Language of Reading Instruction

In Chapter 4, I presented some information about the Language Instruc-

150

tion Register (LIR), indicating its existence and some facets of its acquisition. The LIR is used in instruction about language—including literacy instruction. And, as mentioned, students need to acquire at least receptive control over it so that they will understand the terminology used by the teacher. However, productive control is also often expected, which becomes part of a person's metalinguistic system. Metalinguistic essentially means the ability to see language as a system, to consider the *what* of language, not just know *how* to—as in how to talk, to write, to read. Thus we are able, as mentioned, to talk *about* talk, writing, reading, and spelling. Or as Papandropeulou and Sinclair (1974) stated, "Language is a means of expressing knowledge and at the same time an object of knowledge."

In the LIR, a teacher will use terms appropriate to the register. Students are expected to understand these terms (receptive competence) and later to use them (productive competence). Terms common to the LIR include *sound, sentence, word, letter, writing, reading,* and the like. But do students understand them? If not, what do they mean? John Downing (1976) has done some research on specific LIR terms such as *word* and *sound* and reports that four-year-olds couldn't pick out a word from a list of such things as a bell ringing, someone saying /ε /, someone saying "milk," someone saying "fish and chips," and someone saying "She's a funny girl." (Of course, "fish and chips" could be considered a word, since it functions much like a single word.) However, some thought *word* was any meaningful unit of speech; therefore, at least they separated language from nonlanguage, for example, sounds such as bells ringing. Yet others simply made random guesses. He goes on to indicate that among young children, so much confusion exists that we cannot take for granted that they have begun to acquire some of the vocabulary of the LIR. Clay (1972) found the same thing to be true in New Zealand, that only about half of the six-year-olds she studied could, at the *end* of the first year of school, correctly *show* her a word, a single letter, or the first letter of a word. Since the terminology of the LIR is so central to so much instruction designed to extend students' communicative competence, we, as teachers, should check our students' understanding (receptive competence) of these terms and help them learn what we mean by them, how we use them. Clay's test "Concepts About Print" (see For Further Reading) can be of great help in the early grades. Later, students' metalinguistic development can be enhanced by their ability to use them precisely as well. This is a relatively new area of research, but watch for continuing information to be revealed about this kind of language development and its implications for teaching and learning literacy.

This chapter has attempted to indicate what at least some findings in linguistics that have relevance to reading might be and what applica-

151

tions they might have. Obviously we need to watch for continuing developments in this crucial area of the language arts curriculum, since reading is a major component of communicative competence in a literate society.

Bibliography

Bloomfield, Leonard, and Clarence L. Barnhart. *Let's Read.* Detroit: Wayne State University Press, 1961.

Bolinger, Dwight. *Aspects of Language.* Second Edition. New York: Harcourt, Brace, Jovanovich, 1975.

Burke, Carolyn. Audio tape of children reading selected passages for miscue analysis, including a selection entitled "Smart Birds." No date.

Butler, L.G. "A Psycholinguistic Analysis of the Oral Reading Behavior of Selected Impulsive and Reflective Second Grade Boys," Unpublished doctoral dissertation, The Ohio State University, 1972.

Chomsky, Carol, "Reading, Writing and Phonology," *Harvard Educational Review, 40* (1970), 278–309.

————, "Stages in Language Development and Reading Exposure," *Harvard Educational Review, 42* (1972), 1–33.

Clay, Marie M. *Reading, The Patterning of Complex Behavior.* Aukland, N.Z.: Heineman Educational Books, 1972.

Dale, Philip S. *Language Development.* Second Edition. New York: Holt, Rinehart, and Winston, 1976.

DeStefano, Johanna S., "Oral Language Development and Learning to Read and Spell," lecture given at the University of Victoria, British Columbia, March 1, 1977.

Downing, John, "The Reading Instruction Register," *Language Arts, 53,* No. 7 (October 1976), 762–766.

Fries, Charles C. *Linguistics and Reading.* New York: Holt, Rinehart and Winston, 1963.

Gibson, Eleanor J., "Reading for Some Purpose: Keynote Address," in *Language by Ear and by Eye,* edited by James F. Kavanagh and Ignatius G. Mattingly. Cambridge, Mass.: The M.I.T. Press, 1972, pp. 3–19.

Gibson, Eleanor J., and Harry Levin. *The Psychology of Reading.* Cambridge, Mass.: The M.I.T. Press, 1975.

Gillooly, W.B., "The Influence of Writing-System Characteristics on Learning to Read," *Reading Research Quarterly, 8* (1975), 167–199.

Goodman, Yetta, and Carolyn L. Burke, "Do They Read What They Speak" in *Language and the Language Arts,* edited by Johanna S. DeStefano and Sharon E. Fox. Boston: Little, Brown and Co., 1974.

Johnson, Kenneth R., and Herbert D. Simons, "Black Children's Reading of Standard and Dialects Texts," *Reading News, 2,* No. 3 (August 1973), 2.

Labov, William, and Clarence Robins, "A Note on the Relation of Reading Failure to Peer-Group Status in Urban Ghettos," in *Language, Society and Education: A Profile of Black English,* by Johanna S. DeStefano. Worthington, Ohio: Charles A. Jones Publishing Company, 1973, pp. 312–323.

May, L., "Black Second Grader's Perception of Their Dialect Speech and Their Ability to Recognize Traditional Orthography," paper presented at the annual meeting of the International Reading Association, May, 1976.

McKenzie, Moira, "Learning and Literacy," *Contact, 29,* 1976.

Papandropoulou, Ioanna, and Hermine Sinclair, "What's in a word?", *Human Development, 17* (1974), 241–258.

Rystrom, Richard, "Perception of Vowel Letter-Sound Relationships by First Grade Children," *Reading Research Quarterly.* Vol. IX, No. 2 (1973–1974), 170–185.

Sakamoto, Takahiko, and Kiyoshi Makita, "Japan," in *Comparative Reading, Cross-National Studies of Behavior and Processes in Reading and Writing,* by John Downing. New York: The Macmillan Co., 1973, pp. 440–465.

Savin, Harris B., "What a Child Knows About Speech When He Starts to Learn to Read," in *Language by Ear and by Eye,* edited by James F. Kavanagh and Ignatius G. Mattingly. Cambridge, Mass.: The M.I.T. Press, 1972, pp. 319–326.

Smith, Frank. *Understanding Reading.* New York: Holt, Rinehart and Winston, 1971.

————. "Reading," in *Language and the Language Arts,* edited by

Johanna S. DeStefano and Sharon E. Fox. Boston: Little, Brown and Co., 1974.

———. *Comprehension and Learning.* New York: Holt, Rinehart and Winston, 1975.

Walker, Willard, "An Experiment in Programmed Cross-Cultural Education: The Import of the Cherokee Primer for the Behavioral Sciences." Mimeo, No Date.

For Further Reading

Burke, Carolyn L., and Yetta M. Goodman. *Reading Miscue Inventory, Teacher's Manual.* New York: Macmillan Educational Services, 1972.

This is an extremely thorough and comprehensive introduction to the miscue and miscue analysis in relationship to children's reading. Recommended for the teacher who wants to begin to do the inventories for diagnostic purposes.

Chomsky, Carol. "Reading, Writing and Phonology," *Harvard Educational Review. 40* (1970), 287–309.

This is a comprehensive and revealing article on the implications of transformational-generative theory applied to the phonological system for both reading and spelling.

Clay, Marie. *Reading, The Patterning of Complex Behavior.* Aukland, N.Z.: Heineman Educational Books, 1972, and *A Diagnostic Survey* (Heineman, 1972).

An interesting presentation of beginning reading by a New Zealand psychologist who has devised a diagnostic instrument called the "Concepts About Print Test."

DeStefano, Johanna S. *Language, Society and Education: A Profile of Black English.* Worthington, Ohio: The Charles A. Jones Publishing Company, 1973.

Chapter Six in this volume deals with the controversies surrounding the teaching and learning of reading vis-à-vis black vernacular-speaking children. There is quite a bit of detail and many suggestions made for teaching reading to this group. Also Chapter Two contains descriptions of many of the forms that are part of the vernacular.

154

Gibson, Eleanor J., and Harry Levin. *The Psychology of Reading.* Cambridge, Mass.: The M.I.T. Press, 1975.

This is an advanced research volume, but an invaluable resource for the student who wishes to know more detail about a vast number of experiments on reading.

Smith, Frank. *Understanding Reading.* New York: Holt, Rinehart and Winston, 1971.

This volume is undoubtedly one of the most influential in reading at this time. Again, it's advanced, but offers a fine development of a theory of reading.

155

6

Language and Writing

In our society, being able to write is also considered a major part of communicative competence, as is reading. We expect students to learn to write letters and reports, write up science experiments, record observations, and perhaps write poetry and stories. Thus they become able to contribute to the transmission of culture by the printed word—an important part of a literary culture such as "mainstream" United States culture. Writing is so important, in fact, that we are now seeing front pages and covers of national magazines devoted to "Why Johnny Can't Write." The October 18, 1976, issue of *The Chronicle of Higher Education* featured on its front page the following: " 'Writing Crisis' Spurs Big Corrective Effort." The article was about remediation efforts at the university level. We are currently witnessing national concern over students' ability to write—or lack thereof.

Although writing is part of a literate individual's verbal repertoire, to write well is considered an accomplishment with no little prestige. Think of the awe many of us feel when we meet an author. In much more practical terms, the writing of letters is an effective and inexpensive method of communication; and collections of letters have even been published, provided that the writer or recepient are famous enough. But I dare say most of us write to others to maintain relationships, to convey feelings, as well as to transact business—without much thought to our potential for "going public."

The written word has a great deal of power in a literate society. When we've been promised something, we're frequently cautioned to "get it in writing." The proverb "Don't believe any of what you read and only half of what you see" was probably coined to counteract this power of the written word. You know the old feeling "If it's in print, it must be true," or "If it's down in black and white...." Writing gives us pleasure and information, and serves a host of other functions. In mainstream culture at least, it has a well recognized place and is considered a mark of the truly educated.

Thus, as teachers, how do we help students acquire the ability to write, to extend their communicative competence to include power over the written language? One traditional way has been through the teaching of grammar. An often emphasized goal for the teaching of grammar is the improvement of usage in writing and in speech. How well does that goal stand up to linguistic scrutiny? As discussed in Chapter 4 and elsewhere in the book, "correct" usage is a social distinction based on cultural standards and not on the grammar of English, which encompasses all the various social and regional forms. Samuel Thurber stated clearly the distinction between grammar and usage linguists make today—and in 1891!

> With respect to English grammar, the state of the teacher who is not also a student is especially pitiable. To know grammar only from the school textbooks ("school" grammar type) is not to know it. Grammar is not universally conceived as a science. Its business is to infer laws from observed facts. The rules of good breeding with regard to speech are not laws of the language. Educated persons are less likely in their speech to reveal laws of the language than are ignorant, simple people, who unconsciously represent traditional usage. What are called the common errors of uneducated persons the historical investigator often finds to be ancient forms that once had good standing. Language being an organism, subject to its own laws of growth, it cannot be said that there has been a standard of correctness, from which the forms which the schoolmaster calls errors are departures. Good society speaks so and so, and inflicts the penalties for non-conformity, masking its rules and regulations under the guise of grammatical laws. But a grammatical law is not a rule of conduct. A scientific law is simply a generalization. The attempt to generalize may have been unsuccessful and may leave facts unaccounted for, in which case the grammarian must try again; but the speech-rules of good society in this or that district, exist as a code and are infringed at personal risk.

But, unfortunately, usage is often what is stressed in school grammar lessons. It's not that certain forms in speech don't normally appear in writing, especially expository prose—because we know they don't. Multiple negatives usually aren't part of the written language, for example. In fact, the more complex the writing, the more it may diverge from certain spoken structures. In a sense, students learn different usage patterns for the written language, since it's a different set of registers requiring forms specific to them.

However, such lessons must go far beyond a consideration of various matters of usage if communicative competence is to be maximized in students. If usage is removed from where it doesn't belong, what is the justification of teaching grammar, or "generalizations about the language"? Over the years, one particular justification has emerged in language arts and English education curricula as the most powerful: grammar study improves writing. So there it is. Grammar is linked to composition, a handmaiden to the written word.

If grammar is studied for the purpose of improving writing, the major question is, does it? For the justification to be valid, it must in fact do that. But before we can decide, we have to determine what is improved writing. Unfortunately, most linguistic studies have been largely confined to the sentence and its structure. As of yet, there has been relatively little work by linguists on larger units of written discourse (although much more is done on spoken discourse) or on the functions of various types of writing. What we know most about so far is sentence structure. However, as teachers, we know structure in and of itself is not the measure of effectiveness in writing, although we feel a sentence is "improved" if it is structurally clear as opposed to unclear. Fortunately, individuals such as William Rutherford (1976) have been working on specifying "shapes" of sentences based on the larger context of one piece of writing and on helping students understand how the context exercises that restraint.

Broad-based definitions of improved writing and writing with heightened effectiveness are needed to guide curriculum planning and classroom practices but are presently beyond the scope of this book. Beyond the sentence, linguistic literature does not yet yield enough insight into effectiveness and function in writing to be able to offer clear suggestions for teachers of composition. Therefore, when we discuss improved writing here, we will essentially mean improved sentences. A definition of "improved" is developed in detail below.

Thus it is clear that although linguistics has made a contribution to answering certain pedagogical questions about composition, there are currently distinct limits to that contribution. It is ironic that the area of grammar and composition was perhaps one of the first to receive linguistic applications and is, apparently, one of the areas to benefit least, due mainly, I feel, to hasty applications of theories not suited to the kinds of problems they were asked to solve. For example, transformational-generative theory has never presumed to determine "What is a good composition?" or "What is improved writing?" Yet it has been assumed in many pedagogical materials that teaching some transformational-generative "facts" will directly affect students' ability to write well. Do they? Let's look at this question in some detail.

159

The Role of Grammar

What role has grammar study by students played in the hopefully increasing ability to create sentences that are not fragments or run-ons or incomprehensible? Again, we must ask another question: what type of grammar? There are at least three well-recognized types that surface in English series. (They will be discussed in detail later.) The first and oldest is popularly called "school" grammar and is based on the traditional grammar provided by early linguists who suffered from the lack of a cohesive theory. It is also strongly Latinate in its description of English and can be quite normative in its approach. Typical lessons on sentence analysis are characterized by diagramming, a technique with which we are familiar.

Structural grammar is based on the description of language offered by the structural linguists briefly described in Chapter 2, and transformational-generative grammar is based on transformational-generative theory and its description of English also discussed in Chapter 2.

Has the study of one of these three types of grammar helped to improve writing at the sentence level? Knowledge of "school" grammar rules has been shown by a large body of research to be uncorrelated with the ability to write well, however one defines this ability:

> *In view of the widespread agreement of research studies based upon many types of students and teachers, the conclusion can be stated in strong and unqualified terms: the teaching of formal grammar has a negligible or, because it usually displaces some instruction and practice in actual composition, even a harmful effect on the improvement of writing (Braddock, Lloyd-Jones, and Shoer, 1963).*

There has been much less research on the other two types of grammar, but some recent work has indicated that even knowledge of these grammars have little effect on writing (Elley et al, 1976). Thus, we must ask the same questions that have been asked of school grammar. They are: will knowledge of the structure of the language, if it is better revealed by approaches other than school grammar, improve "sentence sense"? Will this knowledge of "what," of form, transfer to knowledge of "how to," how to write sentences? We will deal with these questions throughout this chapter.

Another rationale for teaching grammar, this time based on transformational-generative theory, has rather recently appeared: that it is part of humanistic study. The rationale for teaching this theory is that it promotes a rational approach toward making conscious our unconscious rules about language. That inquiry is seen in turn as helping students learn to perform other kinds of rational inquiry. If we bear in mind the description of language in Chapter 2, we may be led to question the use of such a theory especially in the elementary grades. Again it concentrates on form, not function or content of language; it concentrates on *what,* not *how to,* and again it can be used for no units larger than a sentence. Perhaps in the later years of education, the rules and elegance of the theory could have some meaning for students. At present, however, I think it wise to heed James Moffett's statement:

> *Now that we are barely beginning to exorcise the grammar ghost, I would hate very much to see it conjured from another quarter ("grammar as humanistic study"), certified by the prestige of some of our finest thinkers and licensing a notorious weakness of many schools, which can now feel free to play the old grammar game but with new texts and a clear conscience (DeStefano and Fox, p. 348).*

What then, if any, is the place of teaching and learning grammar? To help answer this question, we first need to know something about the three types we frequently run across in school materials.

Three Grammars

What types of grammar are available to teachers? The three mentioned above—school, structural, and transformational-generative—are the three major types a teacher has to choose from for a description of language. However, many of the instructional materials created for students' use are a combination of these types, even though the teacher's manual for a series may make a claim for one "pure" approach or another. You need to be able to sort out the threads of various types, which often tend to be interwoven with little discernible pattern. Certainly the all-too-usual effect of combination is not to reveal the structure of the language by combining the strengths of the various types but instead to accentuate their respective weaknesses by using conflicting definitions for parts of speech, for example. Perhaps this unfortunate state is partially due to the ambivalence toward the place of grammar in relation to composition and in the language arts/English education curriculum as a whole.

161

School Grammar

Much of this type of grammar is based on attempts to describe English in terms of Latin grammar. For example, you may remember that English is described as having the subjunctive verb form, which survives only in some constructions such as "If I *were* you, I'd . . . ." In actual usage, the *were* form plus the noun or pronoun rarely survives. We tend to say, "If she's going to do that, then I'd suggest she...." But the Latin verb system has the subjunctive form, and therefore—the reasoning goes—so does English. Or at least it should.

Perhaps the most well-known surviving attempt at describing English in terms of Latin forms is the "It is I" ruling. In Latin when a "to be" verb is used, the second noun or pronoun after the *to be* form is in the nominative case, as is the first noun or pronoun. Both nouns or pronouns are in the same case. This rule was applied to "It is I," declaring that both must be nominative. Such an edict could work to some extent, since the pronoun system in English is one of the few that still has nominative and accusative cases (in object position). But obviously we most often say, "It's me," so usage flies in the face of the rule again. Also, that specific *it* is what is called an *empty* form, one that simply holds a structural place but has no meaning. Certainly we're not referring to ourselves as "it" to mean something like "I is I," which is precisely what the rule implies. To say *it* is in the nominative case is incorrect, because it does not function as a pronoun. The construction parallels that of "It's hot today" or "It's going to rain." The *it* in this case does not actually refer to weather, as we might suspect, and so is not a pronoun. Thus it's clear that the English structure of "It is I," is not parallel to the Latin structure. In fact, the position of a form in a sentence is often crucial in English, but is not in Latin. So even with pronouns, we usually find the accusative or objective case forms at the ends of sentences, for example, "Give it to *me*," "We found *her*, "We" (nominative) have taken care of *them*," etc.

Unfortunately this rule has also tended to lead to *hypercorrection* in speech. As Frank Palmer (1971) puts it, people evidently have begun to think, "when in doubt use *I*, not *me*" (p. 17). This produces such forms as "She decided between he (him) and I." Perhaps the use of *I* will become widespread in that position and thus the norm. It is thought that hypercorrection does have some input into language change. At any rate, Latin grammar has certainly influenced the description of English grammar, especially in the area of pronoun usage.

Another important part of school grammar is the definition and identification of *parts of speech*. Students through the years have spent much time identifying nouns, verbs, adjectives, adverbs, prepositions, and conjunctions and learning definitions concerning them. The definitions as they are traditionally phrased have overwhelming problems for the purposes of identification. To begin with, the definitions are both vague and switch the bases of definition, at one point using meaning and at another using syntactic function. This will be discussed in more detail below. According to Palmer, "It would in fact often be quite impossible to judge from these definitions whether a particular word is a noun, a verb or an adjective without knowing the answer already!" (1971, p. 59). In other words, you must already know that the word is a noun, for example, because the definition is no help in making the categorization.

Take a common school grammar definition of *noun:* the name of a person, place, thing, or idea. A *verb* is a word that refers to a state of being or is an action word. Looking at those two definitions, we find they are mutually exclusive. If a word is a verb, it can't be a noun, and vice versa, according to these definitions. A state of being is not the name of a person or idea. An action word is not a name, and so on.

Given these meaning definitions, how do we classify *skin*? At first glance, we might say, it's a noun—but on what basis? That it's the name of a thing? But it's certainly not a thing in the sense that a pencil is, since a pencil is a discrete item with properties of length and horizontalness. Skin does not have those properties: it's a continuous covering on bodies of animate beings or can be used perhaps metaphorically to denote a covering on such items as cream or an airplane. So what is a *thing*? Is it merely a catchall for those words that are not names of persons, places, or ideas? Probably.

But the problem with this definition of a noun does not end there. Considering again the mutual exclusiveness of the definitions of noun and verb: if a word is a noun, it shouldn't be a verb, and vice versa. But can *skin* be a verb? Definitely. We talk about there being more than one way to *skin* a cat. Some people *skin* rabbits and other fur animals. The ability *to skin* a deer properly is important if the meat is not to be tainted. And so on. What about *hit*? Many of us might say it's a verb—an action word. But it functions as a noun in "The *hit* went into centerfield" and as an adjective in "It was a *hit* play." Mutual exclusiveness in definitions is not an accurate description of English; many words do function as both nouns and verbs.

Another problem mentioned above with parts of speech definitions in school grammar is that their basic characteristics vary. Some are meaning definitions and some are function definitions, at least in a loose sense. For example, adjectives are words that modify nouns, and adverbs are words that modify verbs. These definitions do have a meaning component if *modify* is taken to mean "change the meaning" or "clarify the meaning" or the like. But *modify* usually means something like "being close to the noun or verb." The inconsistency in the way the parts of speech are usually defined in school grammar illustrates the confusion over what the parts of speech are. Within a given system, definitions should be consistent and consonant with the assumptions behind the system itself. The lack of a systematic approach to language shows up very clearly in school grammar through these definitions.

There is one further definition that must be dealt with, that of *sentence.* In school grammar, a sentence is usually defined as a complete thought. Have you ever found an adequate definition of "complete thought"? Usually what happens is that the definition becomes circular: a complete thought is obviously a sentence. But when does a thought become complete? Are there one or two thoughts in "If it's sunny, I'll be there"? Or what about a paragraph? Couldn't it also be a complete thought?

If we can't define a complete thought, then why are we so sure we know what a sentence is? I tend to agree with Palmer (1971), who suggests that because we write and visually indicate where sentences begin and end by punctuation, we feel we know what sentences are. Visually that's probably true, but what about linguistically? We're hard pressed to define a sentence in terms of meaning. And even when we specify a grammatical or formal definition, we run into some problems. If you ask, "What color is the tree?" and the student answers "Green," you can recognize that as a perfectly satisfactory answer to the question—and a grammatically well-formed one for English. But school grammar can define that reply only as an adjective. It takes a different sort of grammar to explain the "completeness" of the single word.

Generally, school grammar as it's commonly taught in elementary schools, junior high, and high schools does not reveal the systematic nature of English and often serves to confuse students with vague definitions that don't fit what they intuitively "know" about the language as native speakers. I once had a student—a junior in high school—identify *institution* as a verb. She wasn't able to take into account the clear morphological evidence of the suffix *-tion,* which as a final suffix is a dead giveaway for a noun. We don't institution anything, but we may institutiona-*lize* something. For this student, parts of speech as she had been taught certainly revealed nothing about the language, although she could write a clear and cogent business letter.

Also, the contribution of school grammar rules to improved composition has been seriously questioned. Research has not shown any correlation between conscious knowledge of these rules and the ability to write. In other words, knowledge of these rules will not *cause* a student to write more effectively. This information should cause us to question the influence on writing of all types of rules that make "conscious" certain aspects of language. Of course, it's possible that it is the school grammar rules specifically that have no relationship to writing. After all, since they are not descriptive of or revealing about the language, we would not necessarily expect them to have an influence on students' compositions. But will other types of "rules" or descriptions of the system of American English influence writing growth?

Structural Grammar

Another fairly common description of American English found in school materials is based on structural linguistics. However, this type of description is much less common than the school grammar approach and is perhaps even less prevalent than a transformational-generative description. This approach was briefly described in Chapter 2, in which we noted that it concentrates on a surface description of sentences. How revealing is this description? Structural linguists have classified parts of speech in ways that are much more revealing than the quasi-Latin definitions we find in school grammar.

A great many words can be classified according to the ways in which they function in sentences. And sentences tend to be defined by a description of common patterns rather than by the vague, meaning-based "a complete thought." For example, sentences are:

Noun Verb	The mongoose coughed.
Noun Verb Noun	The mongoose killed the cobra.
Noun Verb Noun Noun	The mongoose names her baby Riki-Tiki-Tavi.
Noun Verb Noun Noun	The mongoose gives her baby the cobra's head.
Noun Verb Adjective	The mongoose became hungry.
Noun Verb Adverb	The mongoose coughed quietly.
Noun Linking Verb (LV) Noun	The mongoose is a carnivore.

165

Noun LV Adjective   The mongoose is gentle.

Noun LV Adverb   The mongoose was in the bathtub.

These are only some of the possible sentence patterns in English, but they are considered "basic" in some way. Notice, however, that this description is already not very revealing, since the two NVNN patterns do not specify in any way the difference we know to exist between "The mongoose names her baby Riki-Tiki-Tavi" and "The mongoose gives her baby the cobra's head." Only on the surface are the patterns similar. We can show the difference simply by paraphrasing:

The mongoose gives the cobra's head *to* her baby.
*The mongoose names Riki-Tiki-Tavi *to* her baby.

The second sentence is not structurally similar to the first.

But the structural linguists did attempt to define *sentence*—by example through specifying patterns. And we do recognize the patterns far more easily than we can a complete thought. Furthermore, the N, V, Adj, and Adv are used to designate *function* rather than form. For example, the N LV Adjective pattern is the pattern of "Painting is fun." *Painting* is a word we recognize as having a common verb form, but it functions as a noun. We can get even more complicated phrases or clauses functioning as nouns: *"Killing cobras with my sharp little teeth and quick feet is my reason for existence."* The whole segment "Killing cobras with my sharp little teeth and quick feet" functions as a noun in that sentence. Certainly a structural grammar explanation avoids the trap laid by the school grammar definition of a noun (the name of a person, place, thing, or idea), which seems to imply one or, at most, a few words. Naming must be stretched to absurdity to cover "Killing cobras with my sharp little teeth and quick feet," since we recognize that whole phrases and clauses can function as nouns or as adverbs like "in the bathtub."

In English how a word functions is important in determining what part of speech it is. In some pedagogical materials, pattern sentences have been set up to determine which words are nouns, verbs, adjectives, adverbs, and so forth. For example, if a word could go into a slot like *The ——— sat down,* it was a noun. So you could put in words like *girl, man, child, dog,* and *cat.* Obviously since you can't put in other nouns such as *rock,* other sentences have been devised as test patterns. Note that syntactically *rock* could go in the pattern *The ——— sat down,* but it would be semantically anomalous. Such anomaly is not dealt with directly

166

in the pedagogical applications of structural grammar, in which syntax is the major emphasis.

Other tests have been devised to classify words; some are morphological in nature and others are not. For example, there is a marker category that includes words that "mark" or commonly pattern with nouns and verbs. Thus a student wanting to know if *energize* is a noun or verb can try:

the energize
an energize   noun marker tests

was energiz*ing*
has energiz*ed*   verb marker tests

Note that a morphological inflection for tense is also used in the verb test.

Articles are the common markers of nouns, and auxiliary forms such as will, shall, have, etc. are common markers of verbs. But word tests such as these do not work well with the other common parts of speech or even with some words within a class. So morphology is pressed into service, as we have mentioned. If the word is a noun, you should be able to inflect it for the plural. You can say: *institution, institutions.* But that doesn't work for mass nouns, only count nouns. We don't say *wheats* or *milks* or *rices.* For mass nouns, another test is needed, as in *wheat—much wheat.* Contrast that with count nouns—*girl, many girls*—where you can have both the plural inflection plus the determiner *many* indicating plurality.

If the word is a verb, you should be able to inflect it for tense: go, went, gone: walk, walk*ed:* institionalize, institutionaliz*ed.* Or you can inflect it for number: I walk, she walk*s.* In this case, the third person singular is the only present tense inflection left in English for regular verbs. Notice however, that position information or tense inflection is needed as a further test, since the *-s* inflection is also the plural noun inflection. Thus a word in isolation may still be difficult, if not impossible, to categorize, unless it has a marked affix such as *institution.*

In English, position in a sentence is an important indication of the function of a given word. We can say *The mongoose killed the cobra,* but not *The cobra killed the mongoose* and continue to mean the same thing, or *Killed the mongoose the cobra.* A noun appears first followed by a verb, which is followed by another noun, giving one of the common patterns of English sentences. We expect a noun or a phrase functioning as a noun to appear at the beginning of a sentence; this is structural information.

167

The definition of an adjective is also largely structural. It usually appears before a noun and after the determiner: D+Adj+N. So we have "A beady-eyed mongoose" or "The shifty-eyed senator" or "I have some new bumpers." However, there is also a morphological test that can be applied to many adjectives. Adjectives usually can be made comparative, either by inflection or by the addition of words to indicate the comparison. Both have the same function. So we have: new, newer, newest: beady-eyed, more beady-eyed, most beady-eyed. The -er and -est inflections, then, can help you decide if a word is an adjective, as can the use of *more* and *most* for adjectives that don't take the morphological inflection.

Adverbs are a group of words fraught with many problems of definition. The inflectional definition of -*ly* making a word an adverb is not always useful. We recognize *lovely* as in "She's a lovely person," as an adjective, not an adverb. So the inflection test alone fails. Position is often used to identify adverbs. Does it follow the verb in certain sentence patterns? If so, it may be an adverb. Yet *usually,* which is often categorized as an adverb, doesn't follow a verb successfully: *He ran away usually. Further problems: the word looks like *quickly,* but doesn't pattern like it (Palmer, 1971, p. 60):

He ran away quickly.
*He ran away usually.
*He was quickly good.
He was usually good.

Palmer (1971) goes so far as to say that the classification of a word group such as adverbs is merely a rag bag or dust bin classification into which words have been swept because nothing else could be done with them. I tend to agree with this: the class *adverb* remains one of the most problematic to identify. I would suggest that few, *if any,* exercises be given on the identification of adverbs, if for no other reason than that they are so difficult to specify for so little return. It's like teaching a phonics rule that applies only 50% or even only 25% of the time. What is the utility of the endeavor? Will identification of adverbs help students to write better, become more humane, or discipline their minds? I doubt if such a vague definition will help. In response to the claim of mental discipline, Moffett said, " . . . ordinary language is far too ambiguous for training in formal logic. Instead, let's offer a course in symbolic logic itself and not fool around with an inferior system" (1974, p. 349). The difficulties with *adverb* as a concept and class illustrate that ambiguity very well. Language is definitely rule-governed, but some traditional constructs obscure rules with more explanatory power.

As a descriptive approach to language, structural grammar is definitely more revealing than school grammar. The stress on how words, phrases, and clauses function is much better placed for a language such as English, and certainly the stress on the structure of English makes a great deal more sense than stress on a traditional, Latinate grammar. However, if students are still exhorted to do exercises identifying nouns, verbs, adjectives, adverbs, and the like, there is serious question as to the utility of structural grammar, at least at the elementary school level. The pedagogical applications of this type of grammar are inadequate to deal with describing not only the sentences students read but also the ones they write. The descriptions of English sentences are often too simple to help illuminate the sentences students may produce in their own writing and are also too simple to deal with sentences appearing in their reading material. If such description is largely inadequate for analysis, its utility is thus questionable for younger students especially. Again, knowing *what* (information about sentence parts, etc.) is not the same as knowing *how* —to write, to read. And which type of knowledge is most important for students?

Transformational-Generative Grammar

Is transformational-generative grammar any better in its descriptive or explanatory power? Many linguists believe that it is. But we must remember that the explanations are continually being modified in light of new inquiry into the structure of American English. For example, adjectives were once thought of as being derived from sentences such as N + LV + Adj or N + be + Pred. Therefore, a derivation was written in this way:

She wore a dress.
The dress was green.
She wore a dress which was green.
She wore a green dress.

Such a derivation worked well for certain types of adjectives. But can we do such a derivation for "She is a good teacher"?

169

She is a teacher.
The teacher is good.
She is a teacher who is good.
She is a good teacher.

That derivation does not preserve the meaning of the original sentence. "The teacher is good" does not mean the same thing as a "good teacher." In the first case, "good" seems to refer to good as a human quality, such as a good person. It has nothing to do with quality as a teacher—that is, ability to teach—as does a "good teacher." Thus the original derivation is not explanatory of the source of some adjectives.

For more details you can refer to the description of American English syntax in Chapter 2, which is based on transformational-generative theory. Such an explanation of syntax is more revealing than the other two descriptions offered: school and structural grammar. However, it is in no way complete and is changing as linguists continue to work and develop the theory. Explanation of structure—especially relationships among structures—is complex. So even though transformational-generative grammar is a more explanatory approach to language, the question must remain as to its place in the language arts curriculum, or even in the English education curriculum.

If the rationale for grammar teaching is improving composition, we must look at research on the use of t-g[1] and structural grammar for that purpose. Such research will be discussed in detail later in this chapter to determine if help is forthcoming from these approaches. If the rationale for teaching grammar is anything else, it is likely that at least some parts of t-g grammar are more useful than the other approaches in describing American English. But again we must question stressing form over content with students at ages at which attention to content evidently has a much greater hold than attention to form. This again is the question of knowing *what* and knowing *how*. Form is more associated with *what* and content with *how*.

Perhaps some of this controversy over the teaching of grammar can be resolved by examining first the structural development of students' writing and secondly the research in the application of grammar description to the structural improvement of writing. Then at least the reason of teaching grammar to improve writing can be accepted or rejected more rationally.

---

[1] For the sake of simplicity, transformational-generative will be abbreviated t-g in this chapter.

Development of Students' Writing

Register Repertoire Expansion

Fortunately for teachers, the development of students' writing, especially syntactic development, is being studied more and more. Such development can be placed within the context of expansion of an individual's repertoire of registers. In a literate society, the written mode is part of education and is used widely. Within the educational domain the business of learning to write is conducted. Formal instruction is used, then, to expand the repertoire of registers a person commands in a literate society. For some students, those who do not speak English as their first language, since learning to write means learning to write in English, they become what Verma (1971) calls "registral bilinguals." Many students may never become literate in their first language, especially if the language is traditionally not written (as many American Indian languages are not).

Why do we make a distinction between oral and written registers? For one, the mode of discourse changes from the oral to marks on a piece of paper—the written. Important changes take place when language is written instead of spoken. The false starts and "tangles" found in much speech disappear. The writer has a chance to consider what is put down and how to do it more than with speech. There is usually a greater planning element in writing than in speech. To quote Bolinger on more differences between speech and writing,

> . . . if the purpose is silent reading he [the writer] can make his sentences more complex, knowing that the reader who misses them the first time will go back. Writing is language in edited form, differing not just in the mechanics imposed by spelling and punctuation but in its polish and deliberation. "Developed prose" depends on our ability to write.
>
> Elaborate language becomes less the province of a few; more intricate ideas can be grasped and more elegant expression attempted by every user of the language (Bolinger, 1975, p. 479).

When modes change, certain syntactic elements may change as well (see Chapter 4). For example, the passive construction, as in "The milk was drunk by the black cat" or "The milk was drunk," is more prevalent in the written mode than in the oral. More elements at the beginning of sentences may be used in writing. You are more likely to write something like "By the feeble light of the early breaking dawn she began to do her chores" than you are to say it. Sentence adverbials such as the above "By the feeble light . . . " are generally at the *end* of spoken sentences—you'd say, "She began to do her chores by the feeble light of the early breaking dawn." Elements used as nouns tend to be longer in writing, and there tends to be a greater variety in the types used in written language. Sentence adverbials also occur more frequently in writing than in speech. To quote Bolinger again,

> *Above all, writing is characterized by amplification. One rarely finds parenthetical clauses in speech, but they are frequent in writing: The President, who as we know has been under great pressure to reduce three of his budgetary requests (the last having to do with public housing, but excepting the military), finally submitted a revised report, prepared by a specially appointed staff, to the joint meeting of the two committees last night (Bolinger, 1975, p. 479).*

There are even more differences, but this is presently a poorly researched area.

Field of discourse may also be different for written and spoken language, although many of our activities are carried on both in speech and in writing, and the two modes reinforce each other in a great deal of learning. How many times have you found that when you write something, it is clarified? That greater insight can then be used in speaking about the same topic. However, day-to-day activities that are spoken about may not be written about—such as housework, commuting to work, and shopping. A grocery list is an interesting piece of shorthand as a memory aid, but it's not writing in the usual sense. Some fields of discourse traditionally are oral, some are both written and oral, and some may be largely written.

Style of discourse may also vary, with a more formal set of styles associated with writing than with speech. Most of us tend not to use very formal styles orally: we aren't practiced in them and are not expected to be. We don't usually know oral rituals and other types of formal oral discourse. However, some of us are capable of writing quite formal discourse, as in business letters and technical reports.

Certainly vocabulary differences between oral and written discourse are obvious. We recognize that we see certain words in print far more than we hear them spoken. Certainly most of us don't use in speech the legalistic vocabulary we read in contracts, mortgages, and credit forms, for example.

These differences between oral and written language begin to be learned by students when they become increasingly literate. But it is not just the differences that are important; a student learns to command a new medium of expression, one that has its own strengths and weaknesses but is also part of communicative competence as a whole. Writing becomes an extension of the self, a way to project the self through time and space that is not normally attainable with oral language. It can also be a very private form of self-expression, one with relative permanence. If someone were to ask me what I *do* think disciplines the mind, I would reject "grammar study" and answer "writing." You can rewrite to your heart's content and study what you've written even years later. This repertoire of registers can be examined, rearranged, and rewritten. This permanence and opportunity for manipulation are important factors for students to learn about in acquiring the ability to write.

Syntactic Development

What do we know about students learning to write, acquiring this written range of registers as part of the development of their communicative competence? Most of our information deals with syntactic development rather than the development of different writing modes such as the expository, narrative, or argumentative. The most revealing information we have so far on syntactic growth deals with the development of sentence structures within a transformational-generative framework. Such information is crucial to an intelligent and informed diagnostic approach to students' writing since, if a teacher can't assess the developmental level of sentences, how can he or she create instructional strategies designed to help students write more maturely? Of course, some people would maintain that since writing is a developmental process, it is useless to try to accelerate it. Indeed, we still know relatively little about how much students of various ages benefit from syntactic instruction aimed at teaching them to write more complex sentences. Before we can discover that, however, we need some idea of the developmental trends found in the syntax of students' written sentences.

First you'll undoubtedly recognize as common in students' writing something like the following: "I have a cat and he's black and he likes hot milk," or "I have a cat. He's black. He likes hot milk." In the first sentence, the combining process was one of *conjoining* or *coordination.* The conjunction *and* was used to link sentences together. In the second set, no combining was used; the connection is achieved simply by one sentence following another with no attempt at syntactic combining. The use of *and* is extremely common in students' writing, especially younger students' writing, while *embedding* as a combining technique begins to appear only later in written sentences. Combination through embedding is achieved through elements or sentence parts being transformed and placed within other elements. The prenominal adjective derivation on p. 00 is an example of an embedded element, as is "The black cat" example used in Chapter 2.

According to Kellogg Hunt's findings (1974, p. 368), even sixth-graders do not use embedding as a sentence combining technique as frequently as tenth-graders. In his study, which involved a specific rewrite task to promote embedding, fourth-graders (9- and 10-years-old) embedded on the average only about one tenth of the time they could have. Out of 30 sentences, they embedded about three. (But Hunt also suggests that conjoining as a combining device begins to wane at this age.) Compare this to "skilled" adults who had written articles for *Harper's* and *Atlantic,* who embedded on the average 25 of the sentences under 5 main clauses. Hunt gives the specific example of the following embeddings:

Aluminum comes from bauxite.
It is a metal.
Bauxite is an ore.
Bauxite looks like clay.
It is abundant.   (*It* means aluminum)
It has many uses.

The adult sentence was: "Aluminum, which is an abundant metal with many uses, comes from bauxite, an ore which looks like clay" (1974, p. 367). Note the redundant elements that have been dropped and the placement of other sentence elements into the original "Aluminum comes from bauxite." We have two *which* clauses plus an adjective *abundant* from a predicate nominal position placed in the postnominal position. This higher "density" of combinations is considered more "mature" writing by many researchers. Hunt defines syntactic maturity in writing as more embedding, since he found that the adult writers we mentioned embedded more than children. Taking the adult written syntax as a base line or developmental "end point," he suggests a developmental profile for syntactic maturity that is largely corroborated by other research.

Increased embedding is thus a sign of growing syntactic maturity. Coordination through *and* drops out. The more sentences embedded into one, the more mature the syntax. However, there is also another consideration: the degree to which clauses (containing subjects and predicates)

174

and phrases are reduced for inclusion in a "main" or other clause. For example, you could combine:

The cat likes hot milk.
The cat is black.

into:

The cat which is black likes hot milk.

This would be an embedded sentence, not a coordinated one, but it would not be reduced as far as possible. The obvious combination is:

The black cat likes hot milk.

The original full clause (or sentence) "The cat is black" has been reduced to one word in a prenominal position in another sentence. According to Hunt, as children get older, they do more and more of this reduction. In other words, they retain fewer of the items in *identity,* those that give no new information. Or to put it another way, they retain fewer unreduced sentences.

What is a popular device for reducing sentences and embedding them into others? Hunt found that by age 12 or 13, students tended to use subordinate clauses. For example, you could expect to see quite a few "The cat *which is black* likes hot milk" type sentences in which a relative clause is used. The use of this device then begins to decline or remains constant as other embedding and reduction forms are learned and increasingly used.

According to the above research, the least mature sentences would be:

The cat is black.
The cat likes hot milk. (uncombined)

and:

The cat is black and it likes hot milk. (coordinated)

A more mature combination would be:

The cat which is black likes hot milk.

The most mature would be:

The black cat likes hot milk.

We could expect younger students to produce more of the coordinated sentences and fewer embedded ones than older students who in turn would not produce all the complete reductions of sentences adult writers could. In turn this means that there is increasing complexity of noun and verb phrases of sentences, if complexity is defined in some relationship with types and amount of embedding or even by meaning. Certainly "Aluminum, an abundant metal with many uses, . . . " is a more complex noun phrase than "Aluminum" alone. In an earlier study of Hunt's, he reports that a major finding was an increase in the use of "nonclause" modifiers of nouns such as adjectives, appositives, and the like. He also reported an increasing *nominalizing* tendency in students' writing. Thus you would begin to find more sentences such as "Painting portraits of my pets is one of my hobbies" in which a verb phrase "Painting portraits . . . " becomes the noun phrase of the sentence.

Diagnosing Developmental Levels

Generally, older students tend to write longer sentences than younger students, and the increased length is largely derived from increased embedding of elements into a main clause. There may be subordinate clauses, adjectives, or adverbials, as well as other elements, used to increase the length. But how do we count sentences in order to diagnose various levels of syntactic maturity in students' writing? If we take sentences as they're often punctuated by beginning writers (and also sometimes by those who should know better), we can find extremely long coordinated sentences with the clauses strung together by *ands.* But we know those are not particularly mature sentences. So how can we determine what are sentences in order to count the words in them? Hunt suggests the use of the T-unit or *minimal terminable unit,* which is a main clause with subordinate clauses and nonclauses attached, if there are any. It's the smallest unit we as adults would recognize as a grammatical sentence. Using the T-unit concept for analysis, "The cat is black and it likes hot milk" is two T-units: The cat is black.
It likes hot milk.
These are obviously two sentences, both four words in length. "The black cat likes hot milk" is also one T-unit of six words in length. The more

176

mature sentence is longer, the length being achieved by an adjective embedded prenominally. The earlier sentence "Aluminum, which is an abundant metal with many uses, comes from bauxite, an ore which looks like clay" is also one T-unit, 18 words in length. "Which is an abundant metal with many uses" is obviously not a sentence but is a relative clause, a subordinate clause. "An ore which looks like clay" is also not a T-unit but is a nominal construction instead. So the entire sentence is a minimal terminable unit just as is "The cat is black." Again, embedding has been used to achieve the greater length.

But length is not related to maturity in any one-to-one relationship. "If it's longer, it's more mature" is not literally the case. I think we could agree that the "which is" after "Aluminum" is not necessary to preserve the meaning of the sentence and thus could be dropped. If dropped, it would result in a shorter sentence but one that could be judged more mature because of a redundant element being deleted. The *trend* is that longer sentences or T-units are more mature, but it should not be taken too literally.

Once you have determined the average length of T-units a student writes, you can then look at the units internally to determine the amount of embedding and the type a student uses. Of particular importance is what is going on within the noun part of the sentence since, in English, verbs themselves are not particularly expanded. But I would use all this largely as an evaluation of expository prose, as this is the type of writing that has been studied in connection with syntactic development. We cannot be at all sure that the same standards apply to what we traditionally call creative writing: stories, poetry, and the like. There is a different function in that type of writing, which probably dictates different syntactic forms.

Thus, as far as studies of the development of students' writing are concerned, the researchers have begun to look at the development of syntax within an expository mode framework. Also, much of the analysis is within the framework of the t-g model, which has been found to have more explanatory power vis-à-vis nominalization, longer noun parts, etc., than a structural approach, which does not do much more than classify parts of sentences or sentence types. Since it's been found that children tend to use virtually all the common sentence patterns at a relatively early age, different patterns are of little use in determining developmental trends (DeStefano and Fox, 1974). It's what happens within a given sentence pattern that shows development in writing. For example, the use of adverbs, particularly sentence adverbs, increases with age. So you'll find more constructions such as "In the Democratic Republic of China, the Taiwanese have few rights" or "The Taiwanese have few rights in the

177

Democratic Republic of China." (The phrase "in the Democratic Republic of China" is a sentence adverbial.)

Instruction in the Development of Writing Ability

Partly in conjunction with research such as that done by Hunt and O'Donnell, Griffin, and Norris (1967), and partly in conjunction with the development of the t-g grammar theory, research has been done on instructional strategies for helping students learn to write more "mature" sentences. Again, *mature* is largely defined on the basis of syntax, since that area is the most theoretically and practically developed. A more mature sentence or T-unit is one that is longer and has more subordinate clauses and other kinds of embedding in it. One tendency is to say a more mature sentence has more transformations in it, but that is a problematic index of maturity as transformational rules are constantly being rewritten. So there is a good possibility that as soon as one analysis is taught, another will have been devised, which renders the whole exercise a bit futile. But certainly we can and do recognize that some sentences seem more mature to us; that recognition is not based on an awareness of the number of transformations the theory ascribes to certain constructions but on our own knowledge of English.

The instructional question has been, "What can be done to hasten the development of more syntactically mature sentences in students' writing?" This question of hastening is what Jean Piaget has called the American question; we always seem to ask, "How can we do it faster?" Nonetheless, as teachers we are concerned with helping students develop and maximize their communicative competence. In our society, writing is part of that competence and usually has to be taught in the sense that most people do not learn to write in the same way they learn to speak. It's an overlay from a literary culture. So we want to know what we can do to help students learn to write more mature sentences.

Again, we come back to questions about the relationship between grammar and composition. For a long period of time, it was accepted that teaching school grammar rules would transfer positively to writing. The research shows us there is no correlation between knowledge of these rules and the ability to write. So we ask what about other sets of rules, other approaches to grammar. We know school grammar suffers from a lack of theory and has relatively little descriptive power for English. This was precisely the question asked about t-g grammar by a series of researchers. Donald Bateman and Frank Zidonis (1966) were among the first to study if a knowledge of this type of grammar had an effect on syntactic maturity in students' writing. They used the early Chomsky model of t-g grammar and designed a series of lessons that were taught to ninth graders. They tied syntactic maturity to a reduction of errors in the sentences students wrote. They did find that the students wrote more well-formed and error-free sentences after the instruction than those students who did not receive t-g grammar lessons. These findings were promising about the value of teaching certain formal constructs about American English syntax and their impact or writing.

Later John Mellon (1969) not only taught t-g grammar to students but also had them practice sentence combining. In these exercises, students combined various sentences in a variety of ways to produce one longer and more complex sentence. Conjoining was not used as a device, but various types of embedding were. A complex example (O'Hare, 1973) is given below. The students were asked to combine the 11 sentences into one.

The heron tensed its wings for the plunge.
The heron was princely.
The heron was perched high on a ledge.
The ledge was rocky.
The ledge's height enabled the bird to survey the waters.
The waters were swirling.
The waters were blue-white.
The waters were below on three sides.
The plunge would be spectacular.
The plunge was soon to be triggered by a school of fish.
The school of fish was fast approaching.

A possible combination is:

The princely heron, perched high on a rocky ledge whose height enabled the bird to survey the swirling blue-white waters that were below on three sides, tensed its wings for the spectacular plunge soon to be triggered by a fast approaching school of fish (p. 91).

The T-unit length of the combined sentence is 45 words, far longer than any T-unit length of the constituent sentences, the longest being 12 words. Yet economy is achieved as the constituent sentences total 74 words compared to the 45 of the combined T-unit. So almost 30 redundant words were deleted as the combinations were made.

Mellon found that the students who had received instruction in t-g

179

grammar and practice in sentence combining wrote more syntactically mature sentences than those students who didn't. But notice that the practice element has been introduced. So what is the contribution of the grammar lessons to increased syntactic maturity and what is the contribution of the sentence combining practice?

Miller and Ney's research (1968) may begin to throw some light on this question. They had fourth graders (Mellon used 7th graders and Bateman and Zidonis 9th graders) *orally* combine sentences. Some writing was also involved, but the basic emphasis was oral. The results indicated that children who had the oral practice used those structures much more in their writing than did the children who didn't receive the experimental treatment. This time there was no teaching of t-g grammar rules at all.

Now we have three studies: one that taught t-g grammar but no sentence combining (Bateman and Zidonis), one that taught both t-g grammar rules and sentence combining (Mellon), and one that only had sentence combining practice (Miller and Ney). All of these combinations were correlated with increased syntactic maturity. Does knowledge of t-g grammar "rules" help students write more syntactically mature sentences?

To help answer this question, Frank O'Hare (1973) conducted a study with seventh graders in which he gave *only* sentence combining practice to the experimental group. He states he abandoned *completely* formal grammar study for both the experimental group and the control group that did not receive the sentence combining practice. The group who got sentence combining exercises had short lessons during which they embedded sentences into others. The complexity of these embeddings increased over time until the students were working with combining the above 11 sentences about the heron into one. They wrote all their combinations but also worked with them orally. And no terminology was used to explain why certain elements were deleted or to label those elements. The findings were that the students who had the practice of combining sentences wrote significantly more syntactically mature sentences than those students who did not; the T-units were longer, the clauses within them were longer, and there were more clauses within a T-unit. In fact, O'Hare found the experimental group of seventh graders attained a level of syntactic maturity " . . . well beyond that typical of eight graders and in many respects quite similar to that of twelfth graders" (O'Hare, 1976). He also found the experimental group's compositions were judged significantly better in overall quality than those of the control group. He concludes, " . . . it has been judged that sentence-combining practice that is in no way dependent on formal knowledge of grammar has a favorable effect on the writing of seventh graders" (O'Hare, p. 68). Combs (1976) found that a delayed posttest given four months after sentence-combining exercises were terminated showed some writing loss by students, but that those who had those exercises were still judged to write significantly more syntactically mature sentences.

O'Hare has developed some specific patterns of presentation for the sentence combining activities. He says to have the students do the combining both orally and in writing in short practice sessions. He also stresses giving *no* explanation of any grammar rules but encouraging the students to read widely so they will come in contact with many forms of the written language (1976).

One instruction set he gives in writing is:

The Old Man and the Hen

DIRECTIONS: Read the passage all the way through. You will notice that the sentences are short and choppy. Study the passage, and then re-write it in a better way. You may combine sentences, change the order of words, and omit words that are repeated too many times. But try not to leave out any of the information.

Once there was a man. He was old. He lived alone. He became lonely. Someone gave a hen to him. She became his companion. Each morning the hen laid an egg. The man fried the egg. He ate it for breakfast. He liked eggs. He wanted more eggs. He decided something. He would try an experiment. Perhaps he could get more eggs. He would feed the hen more grain. Perhaps she would lay more eggs. He could eat two eggs each day. He doubled the feed. The hen became fat. She became lazy. She laid no eggs at all. The man was disappointed. He became angry. He killed the hen. He was lonely again. He was also hungry. He had no companion. He had no eggs.

Professor Roy O'Donnell,
University of Georgia
(O'Hare, 1976[2])

Several other examples are:

DIRECTIONS: Make the following sentences into one sentence. Take them in the order they are given and add no extra information.

181

The pitcher looked up intently.
The pitcher glanced at first base.
Then he threw a hanging curve which the batter knocked out of
the stadium.

(O'Hare, 1976²)

[Possible combination: The pitcher looked up intently, glanced at first base, then threw a hanging curve. . . .]

Helen raised her pistol.
She took careful aim. (,)
She squeezed off five rapid shots to the center of the target.
(, AND)

(O'Hare, 1976²)

O'Hare notes the students don't have to be told what the directions in ( ) mean: it's obvious what to do. He uses this technique to teach the colon and dash (—) as well as complex syntactic forms.

What are some implications of this research vis-à-vis the teaching of t-g grammar in particular? The most obvious is that conscious knowledge of a syntactic description of the language doesn't seem to help students at least up to grade seven learn to write more syntactically mature sentences. O'Hare's study seems to make this relatively clear. Such a finding means we must seriously question grammar study having a positive transfer to composition at certain grade levels and should question that rationale when it appears in texts. It gets back to the old question of the differences between *knowing how* and *knowing what*. Do you have to know physics, aerodynamics, and the like before you can learn to fly an airplane? Obviously not. Do you have to know—at least consciously—that a usual sentence has a noun phrase and verb phrase before you can speak and write? Obviously not. There are different kinds of knowing, and students "know" intuitively how to generate sentences we recognize as American English. It is this intuitive knowledge and expansion of it that the *practice* in sentence combining seems to enhance. This practice is an active *doing* that a student can be successful at because of his or her intuitive knowledge of the language. Conscious knowledge of the structure of language is something even adults have difficulty acquiring; abstract form is not always that easy to deal with. And as I mentioned previously,

---

²Frank O'Hare, untitled sentence-combining activities in mimeograph form, 1971. Reprinted by permission of the author.

we have good reason to suspect that students in elementary school at least are developmentally not very able to abstract form from content and deal with it alone.

There are also other implications from O'Hare's research. The sentence combining activities do seem to be able to hasten or at least promote syntactic development in students' writing. Developmental studies have shown that as students grow older, they write longer, more embedded T-units. This is what the students did in O'Hare's study, only sooner than what the developmental profiles showed. Evidently this sort of development is more open to successful intervention than some other types of linguistic development such as the oral acquisition of a first language. Remember in Chapter 3 the child who said "holded" no matter how many times *held* was patterned for her? Since writing is definitely a divergent language system, it is perhaps not so determined in its development by maturational factors within the student as oral language seems to be. But by how much can we hasten development? In other words, when is it profitable to begin sentence combining activities? We haven't much research in this area, but the Miller and Ney study used fourth graders who seemed to benefit by the oral exercises. O'Hare suggests grade four as a reasonable starting point for *written* sentence combining. To begin with, the sentence sets would be simpler than the 11 sentences about the heron embedded into each other. But they could concentrate on embedding to counteract the conjoining tendencies found in so much writing. O'Hare also suggests second grade as a possibility for beginning oral combining exercises. I've found that some second-graders experience great difficulty in embedding sentences. They tend to conjoin much more frequently or even say things like, "Say the two (sentences) together real fast. Don't stop but say them together" as a response to the instructions "Make these sentences into one sentence." But these are children who had received no practice in sentence combining; it's not that they can't learn to do it and benefit from it. Other second-graders were able to combine quickly and gave me such mature combinations as "The black cat likes hot milk" for "The cat is black" and "The cat likes hot milk." As a teacher you could diagnose students' ability to combine in that way and then create exercises to give them practice in embedding.

There are many sources of sentence sets to combine, the two most important begin with you and the student. For example, from experience stories dictated by the student or from compositions written by a student, you could extract sentences that could be combined by various embedding techniques. You yourself can create sentence pairs or triplets or whatever that the students would then combine. And since it seems clear that no terminology is necessary to accomplish this, you can rely on your own intuitive knowledge of the language to help the students make more mature combinations. But one caution: although there's no need for them to learn terminology, the more you know about how English sentences embed, the more sophisticated the exercises you can create and the more sophisticated the combinations you can help your students create. It's the old difference between teacher knowledge and student knowledge. One is not necessarily the other. It is as part of teacher knowledge that the study of grammar obviously has a role in the curriculum. For you to be able to help students gain insight into language, you must know about the structure of that language. Modern grammatical studies of a descriptive, not prescriptive, nature can help you gain that insight for yourself.

Two further suggestions: O'Hare counsels integration of the exercises into other language activities such as free writing, choral reading, and the like. This way it takes its "natural" place because it's for something instead of being an empty exercise to fill up time. Put in perspective, such activities will also have more transfer to actual writing. This is something we cannot take for granted—transfer to the activity intended. Placing such practice in a writing context will insure more transfer and make the exercises meaningful.

Finally, don't overdo the practice. O'Hare's students did not spend much more than an hour a week throughout the year at such exercises. If it's given much more emphasis, especially as an isolated activity, it could begin to be seen as "the same old thing" by students. If "the same old thing" is taught in "the same old way," it could be as ineffective as many other exercises used for writing.

Punctuation

Although not much work has been done on learning punctuation as a part of acquiring the ability to write, it nevertheless is a part of the process. One of the major questions to ask is what sort of bridge exists between the spoken language and the punctuation marks in writing? Since we've tried to make as much connection as we could between speech and the written page in both the reading and writing process, it seems logical for punctuation.

The connection between speech and written punctuation is not a simple or straightforward one in all its dimensions. For example, there's really no obligatory vocal signal that corresponds to capital letters as in names and the first word of written sentences. German, for example, has a marked tendency to capitalize nouns, but that they are capitals is not signaled vocally. Neither a German or English speaker gives greater stress to capitalized words than to uncapitalized ones. You don't hear people say, "*The* girl already came" unless they intend "the" to have a special significance. Thus obligatory capitalization, such as the first letter of the first word in a sentence or someone's name, is part of the written language but not of the oral.

A major part of the connection that will be obvious to the student is the correspondence between intonation patterns and written punctuation. For example, the fade fall terminal /↘/ we use to orally signal many sentence ends corresponds to a period or to a question mark. It is a mistake in English to counsel, "When you see a question mark, raise your voice at the end of a sentence." Do you say, "Where are you going?" / ‖ / No, because a question word (*where*) and a question inversion (*are you going*) signal it's a question. So a student can turn to structural information in the case of punctuating questions. Only when there is no question word or inversion does the voice rise terminally to signal a question, as in making "it's three o'clock" into a question, "It's three o'clock?" / ‖ /

But a /↘/ terminal indicating a falling contour often signals a period. However, most punctuation problems creep in within sentences—between the capital letter at the beginning and the period or question mark at the end, especially with older students who begin to need to handle commas and other such marks. Is there any intonation relationship between punctuating with commas and vocal signals? One of the most obvious is that of the rising contour signaling a series:

I see mongooses / ‖ /, cobras / ‖ /, weaver birds / ‖ /, and flowers /↘/. The commas correspond quite directly to a rise and stop of the voice.

Also, students can work with disambiguating sentences vocally and learning the corresponding punctuation.

In which sentence is the questioner a polite murderer?

Shall I kill Master?   Shall I kill, Master?

Note in this case the comma stands for a falling and stopping contour while the ? stands for another.

In which sentence did Chauncy die?
Chauncy, the elephant died.   Chauncy, the elephant, died.

Note the difference in the use of terminals in the two sentences. The second *elephant* obviously modifies *Chauncy,* while the first is an elephant who is not Chauncy. The commas correspond to the intonation patterns in each sentence.

Since we've often come to associate commas with vocal pauses (falling terminals, rising terminals, level terminals), we're sometimes guilty of giving students an unhelpful "rule." How many times have you heard "When you hear a pause in a sentence, put in a comma?" It works for "Chauncy, the elephant, died." But many times we pause between the noun phrase and verb phrase of a sentence. Try saying:

Riki-Tiki-Tavi who is my favorite mongoose
successfully killed the huge cobra.

Notice the terminal contour on *mongoose.* And some students will put a comma after *mongoose.* We then have to tell them that's not correct, but they were only following the rule about commas and pauses.

Both intonation and structure combine to help students learn some punctuation. But some of it is still convention and very little related to either intonation or structure. Look at periods after abbreviations and the use of underlining for some foreign words such as *etcetera* to indicate italics. It seems reasonable, however, to initially approach punctuation as having at least some correlation with intonation patterns and syntactic structure. Perhaps intonation is the most useful starting point from the standpoint of connecting the written to the spoken language. As teachers, you can help students sensitize themselves to the intonation contours they use in speech and learn how to mark them on paper.

Final Comments on Writing

There are several shortcomings in most of the work done so far by linguists and educators applying linguistics to the areas of grammar and composition. First, the sentence is overwhelmingly the largest unit dealt with. But we know that writing is far more than an aggregate of sentences. Problems with individual sentences are often relatively trivial in the face of problems involving paragraphing, thematic development, and other factors going into what we call "good writing." Also syntax within a sentence being "acceptable" or "mature" may have relatively little to do with the function of the writing. It is, it seems to me, the functions for various kinds of written expression that are of great importance for students. And these have been largely ignored.

Also the problem of style has largely been ignored in much of this work. A "good" sentence is a "grammatical" sentence, a syntactically

186

acceptable sentence. Or a "good" sentence is one that is longer and has more embedding in it. It seems to me that such criteria apply mainly to expository prose, which is sometimes called "public writing," but certainly are not that useful in dealing with poetry or stories, in other words, with creative writing. And after a point, length can no longer be a positive criteria. We still have to deal with intuition and concepts such as *clarity.* Length can help cause clarity problems. And style problems cannot be dealt with simply in terms of syntax.

But a beginning has been made in this major curricular area. Most of the shortcomings of applied research reflect the state of much theoretical linguistics which, by and large, has not moved past the sentence, at least for the written language. As teachers, we recognize the need to go farther than that but also can use the aid given so far by applied studies.

Bibliography

Bateman, Donald, and Frank Zidonis. *The Effect of a Study of Transformational Grammar on the Writing of Ninth and Tenth Graders.* Research Report #6. Urbana: NCTE, 1966.

Bolinger, Dwight. *Aspects of Language.* Second Edition. New York: Harcourt, Brace, Jovanovich, 1975.

Braddock, Richard, Richard Lloyd-Jones, and Lowell Shoer. *Research in Written Composition.* Champaign, Ill.: NCTE, 1963, 37-8.

Combs, Warren E., "Further Effects of Sentence-Combining Practice on Writing Ability," *Research in the Teaching of English, 10* (1976), 137-149.

DeStefano, Johanna, and Sharon E. Fox, "Children's Oral Language Development: The Literature and Its Implications for Teachers," in *Language and the Language Arts,* edited by Johanna S. DeStefano and Sharon E. Fox. Boston: Little, Brown and Co., 1974, pp. 48–58.

Elley, W.B., Barham, J.J., Lamb, H., and Wylie, M., "The Role of Grammar in the Secondary School English Curriculum," *Research in the Teaching of English, 10,* No. 1 (Spring 1976), 5-21.

Hunt, Kellogg W. *Grammatical Structures Written at Three Grade Levels.* Champaign, Ill.: NCTE, 1965.

———, "Teaching Syntactic Maturity," in *Language and the Language Arts,* edited by J.S. DeStefano and S.E. Fox. Boston: Little, Brown, 1974, pp. 363-376.

Mellon, John. *Transformational Sentence-Combining: A Method for Enhancing the Development of Syntactic Fluency in English Composition.* Urbana, Ill.: NCTE, 1969.

Miller, B.D., and J.W. Ney, "The Effect of Systematic Oral Exercises on the Writing of Fourth Grade Students," *Research in English, 2* (1968), 44-61.

Moffett, James. *Teaching the Universe of Discourse.* Boston: Houghton Mifflin Co., 1968, pp. 344-351.

O'Donnell, Roy C., William J. Griffin, and Raymond C. Norris. *Syntax of Kindergarten and Elementary School Children: A Transformational Analysis.* Champaign, Ill.: NCTE, 1967.

O'Hare, Frank. *Sentence Combining: Improving Student Writing Without Formal Grammar Instruction.* Urbana, Ill.: NCTE, 1973.

————, Presentation and accompanying mimeo, October 6, 1976, Ohio State University.

Palmer, Frank. *Grammar.* Harmondsworth, England: Penguin Books, Ltd., 1971.

Rutherford, William, no title, transcription of comments in *Discourse Analysis as an Extension of Linguistics: A Colloquy.* Professional Paper 37, October, 1976, SWRL Educational Research & Development.

Scully, Malcolm G., " 'Writing Crisis' Spurs Big Corrective Effort," *The Chronicle of Higher Education,* Vol. XV, No. 7 (October 18, 1976), 1 ff.

Thurber, Samuel, "Suggestions of English Study for Teachers of English," *The Academy* (January, 1891).

Verma, S.K., "Towards A Linguistic Analysis of Registral Features," *Acta Linguistica Academiae Scientarium Hungaricae, 19* (1969), 293-303.

For Further Reading

Hunt, Kellogg W., "Teaching Syntactic Maturity," in *Language and the Language Arts,* edited by J.S. DeStefano and S.E. Fox. Boston: Little, Brown, 1974, 363-376.

This is a very readable article encapsulating his important research, explaining the T-unit and making applications to the classroom.

O'Hare, Frank. *Sentence Combining: Improving Student Writing Without Formal Grammar Instruction.* Urbana, Ill.: NCTE, 1973.

This NCTE Research Report #15 is full of writing suggestions for teachers at a variety of grade levels. A reading must for helping students improve their "sentence sense."

7

Language and Spelling

Spelling is another aspect of literacy, another aspect of the written language (Chapter 6), and an important extension of communicative competence in our society. The ability to spell is taken as a mark of being educated as well as being a major tool used in writing. In a sense, we acknowledge its societal importance by the attention devoted to it during school days. It's looked at carefully in written work and is taught as a specific part of the language arts curriculum in elementary schools. In fact, there is still a national spelling contest held yearly, and spelling games are diversions both at home (Scrabble) and in the school. But, as teachers, we're also aware that some students become good spellers and some don't. Hence the question—how can we help more of our students become "good spellers", help them add this major aspect of communicative competence to their language repertoire? A corollary question is how and in what ways can linguistic findings about spelling help us in this crucial task?

What could be proposed as being the major contributions of linguistic studies to the language arts/English education curriculum area of spelling? Let me begin by describing the areas in which they have *not* been; not yet in comprehensive instructional strategies for teaching spelling. There is no one or even several "linguistic methods" of teaching spelling, even though you may find this claimed by a spelling series. Certainly instructional strategies need careful reassessment, since we're only too aware of how many times the "good spellers" remain the good spellers, and "poor spellers" remain the poor spellers after years of instruction. Yet at present, we can't look to linguistics for a well-conceived set of strategies.

What does linguistics tell us about the process of spelling, about what a "mature" speller does when he or she spells? This is very necessary information for teachers, but unfortunately we are told very little again. Little is known about how a mature writer spells. However, there is some speculation that a mature speller of English takes the morphological system into account to a greater degree than the sound system. As in reading, there seems to be cutting out of some of the more obvious relationships between language systems—spoken and written. And also there is the same greater reliance on the eye than on the ear. How frequently do you need to see a word written down before you're sure of its spelling? There is definitely a strong visual component in the spelling process of a mature writer, partly because there is no simple one-to-one correspondence between the phonemic system and the graphemic[1] system in American English.

Perhaps we could benefit from the concept of *miscue* as applied to spelling. If we can profitably analyze oral reading "errors" or changes from the printed page, we might be able to analyze spelling "errors" and find developmental patterns that would reveal some of the orthographic features students attend to. But these are largely unresearched areas at present, except for beginning spellers' strategies discussed below.

So where is the contribution? It's primarily in the area of describing the spelling system, or orthographic system,[2] of American English and of specifying the relationship between the sound system and the orthographic system—that is, various types of sound-symbol correspondences. We know already a fair amount about the sound system. And because of work on reading patterns, we know something about the orthographic system. However, a reading pattern is not necessarily a spelling pattern and vice versa; the former is recognition and an oral cue to reading aloud while the latter is production. Cues we need in spelling, such as when to double letters as in *pill* and *address,* are not operative in oral reading in that the letters *ll, dd* and *ss* do not cue pronunciation. Whether double or single letters, we pronounce them /l/, /d/ and /s/.[3]

It is perhaps this concept of spelling patterns that is the most important contribution linguistic studies have made so far, since we now know about regularities that were not clear before. In fact, the irregularity of our spelling system is a common theme. Much ado is made that English spelling is "chaotic" and "unsystematic." Or as put by Bolinger (1975, p. 480):

> *No other spelling system in the world has been the occasion of so much amazement, frustration, irritation, sarcasm, and cold fury as that of English—a reflection as much of the large numbers of*

[1] *Grapheme* is the term used for the letter or letter combination symbolizing (or "standing for") a phoneme in a language. It is used in alphabetic systems to represent a spoken sound. /ši/ is represented by the graphemes *sh* for /š/ and *e* for /i/.

[2] *Orthography* means a system for spelling in a language.

[3] In Finnish, the doubled letters do signal corresponding pronunciation differences, as vowel and consonant length are distinctive differences in spoken Finnish.

192

non-English speaking people who have tried to learn it as of its own inherent refractoriness.

But we are dealing with a system of which the outlines are becoming more clear.

Different sets of orthographic patterns have been suggested, largely based on more surface or deeper level regularities. These will be discussed in some detail later, and their implications for the teaching of spelling explored. Certainly they do have implications for diagnostic procedures, which are so important in any type of classroom, for instructional strategies and for materials that can be used to help students become mature spellers. For example, these patterns may be highly effective in helping students learn to generalize, an important ability utilized widely by mature spellers. Carl Personke (1973) suggests this ability to generalize in spelling is one of the most valuable we learn. What is it? If you were asked to spell /net/, you'd probably spell it *nate;*; or if given /zot/, *zote.* We are familiar with the common pattern *CVCE* (the so-called silent *e*), which is used to symbolize the "long" vowel sound, and we have little difficulty generalizing the pattern to "non-English" and nonsense words. Patterns are the components of generalizations.

The Spelling Process

Very little work has been done on developing a psycholinguistic model of the mature spelling process and on delineating the parameters of acquisition of that process. However, the concept of visual distinctive features described in Chapter 5 can also be applied to spelling, especially in explaining the rapid checking of accuracy in spelling. Undoubtedly there are also generative spelling rules, just as there are phonological rules for generating the utterances of a language. (Remember the rules for specifying which plural phoneme—/s/, /z/ or /əz/—appears in which sound environment.) But they do not take the shape of the time-honored "*i* before *e except* after *c*" and other such familiar rules.

Ability to exploit redundancy in the orthographic system is another part of the mature speller's competence. We know, for example, that the *u* following *q* is totally redundant. It adds no new information about the use of *q* but is part of the American English system of orthography—completely predictable. Doubling a final *l* as in *bill, pill,* and *rill* is also redundant. It adds no new information, is not a cue in reading, but is a convention in our orthographic system. As a matter of fact, some students have a great deal of difficulty doubling that final *l* when they're learning

193

to spell, many spelling *will* as *wil.* They have not yet learned that particular redundancy to produce the more adult spelling.

Much more needs to be learned about redundancies in the orthographic system, about what the distinctive features are in that system, and about the rules used to generate mature spellings. We also need to learn about the eye-ear, the visual-auditory correspondences used by mature spellers. We have hunches that spelling may be largely visual for adult spellers, but how the two interact is important because you can hear mature spellers "sounding out" words sometimes when spelling them. A glimpse into several eye-ear "mature" strategies is afforded by Chomsky's work presented later in this chapter.

Is there a progression from the auditory to the visual in learning how to spell? There is some indication that this may be the case. Charles Read (1975) notes that children (ages 3 to 6) who have taught themselves to write work at what he calls the phonetic level, in other words below the phoneme and at the level of the phone. He notes that these children develop their own orthographies based partially on the letter names of vowels and on the letter names for consonants minus the vowel sound in the name (such as "tee" for *t*). So you find *fin* for *fine, rit* for *write, fel* for *feel, at* for *ate, lik* for *like,* and *bot* for *boat.* Of course, they eventually run out of letter names. Then they turn to using letter names that contain the sound they are after. Thus you see *feh* or *fes* for *fish* (*h* or *s* is used for /š/). And some of these self-taught spellers pay such close attention to phonology that they symbolize the /t/ and /d/ before /r/ with an *h* or *j,* as in *hra* for *tray* and *jragn* for *dragon.* (Say those two words and listen carefully to the first sounds.) The phonetic correspondence would probably be even closer if the children were not restricted to letter names.

Other findings: the *phonetic* resemblances and differences of English are obviously attended to by self-taught spellers. Read states, " . . . the children were capable of grouping one speech sound with another in order to devise *relationships* [italics mine], and that the groupings all reflect genuine phonetic relationships...." (1975, p. 72). For example, he found the two midfront vowels, /e/ as in *laid* and /ε/ as in *bet* (very similar in articulation), tend to be spelled alike, often with an *A* letter. So he found *shalf* for *shelf, davl* for *devil, ane* for *any* (Read, 1976), *fas* for *face, kam* for *came,* and *tabil* for *table* (Read, 1975). He also found *truck* frequently spelled as *chrok,* the children cueing into the phonetic similarity between the initial sounds in *truck* and *chicken.* He says, "A child who wants to spell *truck* with a *ch* will not be enlightened by being told that *ch* spells 'chuh," as in *chicken.* The child already knows that; in fact, the relation between the first segments of *truck* and *chicken* is exactly what he or she wants to represent" (1975, p. 78).

194

These children also tend to drop out certain redundancies in the adult orthographic system, such as the unstressed /ə/ in final syllables, to get *bitn* for *button* and *bitm* for *bottom*. O'Neil suggests that for children, phonology seems to be quite separate from the morphological system, since their spelling largely reflects phonology. He notes a child who wrote past tense markers as *t, d,* and vowel *+d,* which reflects the past tense phonemes used in English. Later she simply wrote *d* for past tense. Thus she began with phonology and worked her way to a morphological rendition later. On the other hand, some research indicates that the American English orthographic system relates phonology and morphology rather closely for adults. Evidently children's emerging phonological system is different from adults', with a resulting difference in the ability to exploit the relationships in traditional orthography. However, we must remember that this emergence is systematic in itself. Zutell notes, "This line of research [using the Chomsky model presented later in this chapter] has produced some significant evidence indicating that children's spelling attempts are not random, but that they seem to follow an orderly sequential progression dependent upon the sophistication of the child's abstract phonological system and his ability to integrate other sources of information into an understanding of English orthography" (1975, p. 25). Again we find a systematic movement toward the acquisition of another language system. Chomsky (1975) also notes that " . . . created spellings are surprisingly uniform from child to child." For fun, you have no trouble reading the following, do you? If these early spellings were unsystematic, I don't think we'd be able to decipher them.

MY WISL IS BROKUN

DOT MAK NOYS

MY DADAAY WRX HER

> *5 year old child*

> *(Read in presentation, 1976)*

WUNS A LITL BUNE HOPT A CROS MI LON
AND THAT BUNE HOPT
RUYT IN MI HAWS AND I GAV THT
BUNE SUM MILK

> *5:2 year old child*

> *(Chomsky, 1976)*

195

How about this one?

> *This is a rockit the looner mojrai is on the therd deck. It's a peas av siyintific equipment the next peas av siyintifit equipment is the cmand mojrai.*
>
> *(This is a rocket. The lunar module is on the third deck. It's a piece of scientific equipment. The next piece of scientific equipment is the command module.)*
>
> > *6 year old child in*
> >
> > *Franklin School, Lexington, Mass.*
> >
> > *(Chomsky, 1975)*

Unfortunately we know relatively little about the stages of acquisition of a "mature" spelling process or about the "mature" spelling process itself. It may be that some children use more visual cues initially than do other children. From what we know about the variability in human development, this would not be at all surprising. Such variability in learning to spell needs to be diagnosed, and teaching strategies adapted. But much more research into the spelling process is needed before diagnosis and strategies can proceed effectively at the "learning to spell" level. Except, Read (1975) suggests that at this level, children need to be encouraged that their phonological judgments are reasonable and that their attempts to categorize are positive, even though they are not adult judgments or categories. Remember, from Chapter 2, that a phoneme is an abstraction from actual sounds. So we must expect some children will hear these allophonic differences and attend to them. Then they can be encouraged to "hear" phonemic similarities, which will presumably let them better match sound to symbol.

Fortunately, though, since we now know more about spelling patterns in American English, we have at least a beginning description of the "*what* is learned" (content), even though we lag behind on the "*how* it is learned" (process).

American English Spelling Patterns

Linguists have been currently describing spelling patterns in the orthographic system. These patterns have been looked at in essentially two ways, though they prove to be complementary: a relatively "surface" look at sound-symbol correspondences (phoneme-grapheme relationships), and a "deeper" level (or below speech) approach with emphasis on morphology rather than on phonology.

As noted above, *grapheme* is the term used for the letter or letter combination symbolizing a phoneme in a language. Graphemes are part of an alphabetic writing system in which letters stand for speech sounds. [4] Single letters or more than one letter may be graphemes. For example, *ey* in *key* is the grapheme for the vowel phoneme /i/. *Tch* as in *hatch* is the grapheme for the consonant phoneme /č/.

As mentioned previously, there may be at least several graphemes representing one phoneme in English. For example, /v/ is usually symbolized by the letter *v*. But it's *ph* in *Stephen* and an *f* in *of*. Some alphabetic systems have a closer grapheme-phoneme correspondence than English; Finnish is one for which there is a closer approach to a grapheme for each phoneme. Spanish also has a closer match of graphemes to phonemes. Actually, in English we have a modified alphabetic system. We have over 40 phonemes in the language but only 26 letters; obviously there is no one-to-one match. And it turns out we have many more graphemes than phonemes because of the letter combinations we use as graphemes.

Whichever descriptive approach is used, the emphasis in linguistics is definitely on the patterns in spelling. But for a long time, many people have despaired over the inconsistencies in American English spelling. They have cited *rough, bough,* and *through* as only one example of the irregularities that plague children and adults alike. In this above case, one grapheme set—*ough*—symbolizes three different phonemes or phoneme combinations—/f/, /æw/ and /u/. Fromkin and Rodman (1974, p. 297) give these examples of different sounds with the same spelling.

Consonant: Vowel:

/Θ/ *th*ought   /e/ *a*te

/ð/ *th*ough   /æ/ *a*t

/t/ *Th*omas   /ʊ/ f*a*ther

                   /ɛ/ m*a*ny

[4] It is generally accepted that the ancient Greeks created the alphabet by devising symbols to stand for sound segments, both vowels and consonants. For an excellent overview of the history of writing and the development of the alphabet, see *A Study of Writing* by I.J. Gelb, Chicago: University of Chicago Press, 1965.

The reverse has been mentioned above—where one phoneme, often a vowel sound, is symbolized by a variety of graphemes, as in the /i/ in *Caesar, amoeba, bead, heed, quay, people,* and *machine.* Note the "irregularities" pointed out in the following poem:

OUR QUEER LANGUAGE

When the English tongue we speak,
Why is "break" not rhymed with "freak"?
Will you tell me why it's true
We say "sew" but likewise "few";
And the maker of a verse
Cannot cap his "horse" with "worse"?
"Beard" sounds not the same as "heard";
"Cord" is different from "word";
Cow is "cow", but low is "low";
"Shoe" is never rhymed with "foe."
Think of "hose" and "dose" and "lose":
And think of "goose" and yet of "choose."
Think of "comb" and "tomb" and "bomb";
"Doll" and "roll" and "home" and "some,"
And since "pay" is rhymed with "say,"
Why not "paid" with "said", I pray?
We have "blood" and "food" and "good";
"Mould" is not pronounced like "could."
Wherefore "done" but "gone" and "lone"?
Is there any reason known?
And, in short, it seems to me
Sounds and letters disagree.

Lord Cromer[5]

Certainly these "irregularities" exist in American English—and many more. Why? One reason is that we have borrowed many words from different languages without necessarily modifying the spelling. According to Fromkin and Rodman, ". . . of the 20,000 or so words in common use [in English], about three-fifths are borrowed" (1974, p. 204). We have *tortilla* from Spanish where the *ll* represents /y/ as in *yellow,* definitely

[5] Lord Cromer, "Our Queer Language," undated. Reprinted by permission of the current Lord Cromer.

not a pattern in American English orthography. We have *parfait* from the French; the *ait* ending is atypical in our spelling system for the /e/ phoneme. Note *Vinci* is pronounced "Vinchy," the *c* grapheme for /č/ being an Italian orthographic pattern we have not modified. We can add borrowings from Latin, Greek, German, and so on.

We can also find historical sources for what we now perceive to be irregularities in the spelling system. For example, the graphemes *k* and *c* can both represent /k/, and *c* and *s* can both represent /s/. Students have to deal with *cell* and *sell*, which are homophones. Fred Brengelman notes that in Old English all /k/ phonemes were represented by *c* and all /s/ phonemes by *s*. However, under the influence of the French language over a long period of time—from even before 1066 and The Battle of Hastings—some /s/ phonemes began to be represented by *c* as well as *c* being used for /k/ phonemes. So we can trace the history of *c* being used for both /k/ and /s/ (1970, p. 87).

Fromkin and Rodman (1974) note other historical forces shaping our modern English spelling. They assert that modern spellings reflect Late Middle English pronunciation (Chaucer's era) and early forms of Modern English (Shakespeare's English). Example: today *knight* and *night* are homophones; at one time the *k* grapheme and *gh* grapheme both represented phonemes. The sound spelled by *gh* has dropped out of English entirely, and somewhere along the way, /k/ no longer preceeds /n/ as in *knight, knife, know, knit* and *knot.* (All of these are Old English in origin, except for *know,* which comes from Greek and Latin.) Another force was the printing press invention; when we began to print English, its spelling became more "frozen." And etymology is yet another factor. During the 15th and 16th centuries, scholars changed Middle English spelling to conform to "original" Latin and Greek spellings to give:

Middle English	"Reformed"
indite	indi*c*t
dette	de*b*t
receit	recei*p*t
oure	*h*our

(Fromkin and Rodman, 1974, p. 298).

199

But the important question to ask is what part of the spelling system do these irregularities represent? Are there more irregularities than regularities? You will see that there are not. When looking at the overall spelling system, the patterns far outweigh the spellings which don't seem to fit patterns. For example, *choir* is held to be a unique spelling for the phonemes in the word, in other words, an exception to American English orthographic patterns. As such, it probably has to be visually memorized. However, it's not a frequently appearing word, and therefore its lack of pattern shouldn't disrupt the learning of patterns. Patterns are obvious as in the following: initial /kw/ is usually spelled with a *qu* as in *quiet, quick,* and *queen.*

In English, phoneme-grapheme correspondences definitely are patterned, with many of the most common or frequent words included in those patterns. To spell *fish* as *ghoti,* as George Bernard Shaw did, is to ignore many of these patterns. According to the Hannas (DeStefano and Fox, 1974), to spell /f/ as *gh* as in *cough* is to ignore the usual patterned spelling of that phoneme. The /I/ is spelled *o* as the first vowel sound in *women.* That spelling is extremely rare—obviously atypical. The *ti* spelling for /š/ as in *nation* doesn't occur initially or finally in English but is found in medial position in multisyllabic words and only when followed by a vowel. In the initial and final positions, the *sh* spelling is far more common. Thus *fish* represents common spelling patterns; it's an extremely regular spelling, while *ghoti* is not. To quote the Hannas:

> *Most consonants and short-vowel phonenes [/I/, /ε/, etc.] are nearly always represented in a specific position by the same grapheme. The majority of variances are found in the representation of vowel phonemes other than the "short ones" [as /i/ in amoeba, bead, etc.], and even these are ordinarily [emphasis added] represented in one of only two or three ways. Most of the assumed irregularities are not genuine irregularities but are governed by rather consistent patterns that the good speller follows, often without being conscious of doing so (DeStefano and Fox, 1974, p. 276).*

The vowel phonemes mentioned above can further be patterned within other sets of patterns presented later in this chapter.

The point is that American English spelling is largely systematic and patterned. The system of patterns can be demonstrated and used by teachers to help students learn to spell. It is unfortunate when irregularities are stressed to them, because the powerful patterns that exist then may not be able to be exploited in learning to spell. In other areas of the language arts curriculum regularity is stressed. But for some reason, just the opposite is often true in spelling. Students are often given frequency word lists to learn to spell, and they definitely rupture patterns. Yet many spelling series are based on those lists. It's time to present regularities to students to allow them to discern patterns and to match them to their own emerging system. What sorts of patterns do we know about?

Phoneme-Grapheme Patterns

The first type of pattern description is based on phoneme-grapheme correspondences, including stress patterns. A helpful way to approach these patterns is through the idea, also used in reading, that writing is talk written down. The oral language and the written language thus connect in a "surface" way; reading aloud is the spoken language mapped into the written language. Spelling, in some ways, is the reverse of that. Most of the information about these patterns comes from a study by computer analysis of 17,000 words representing a core vocabulary for educated speakers and writers, conducted by Paul and Jean Hanna, Richard Hodges, E. Hugh Rudorf, and others (Hanna, Hodges, and Hanna, 1971). They looked at three major factors that they felt had a great deal to do with determining the "productive patterns" of the American English spelling system.

One factor was the incidence of phonemes that fairly strictly adhere to the alphabetic principle—in other words, those phonemes that are symbolized by the same grapheme regardless of the position of the phoneme in a word. For example, /d/ is usually spelled with a letter *d* as in *dog* (initial), *faded* (medial), and *fad* (final). The consonant phonemes tend to be more alphabetic in nature than do the vowel phonemes—that is, they are more invariantly represented by the same grapheme. Vowels are spelled in more different ways than consonants.

A second factor Hanna et al, considered in spelling was how the *position* of a phoneme in a word or syllable affects its spelling. To use a Hanna and Hodges example, /f/ is usually spelled with an *f* at the beginning of a syllable or word as in *fat* or *afar.* It may be spelled *ph* as the second element in a consonant cluster (*sphere*) and *ff* when it is in final position as in *stuff. Gh* is another word final and syllable final spelling as in *cough* and *tough.*

Finally, *stress* as a factor in spelling must be taken into account in this approach, since the phonemes in a word alone may not give clues to the spelling of some of them. The schwa phoneme /ə/ is a major example of this, being the prevalent vowel sound in lightly stressed syllables but spelled in a variety of ways. For example, /ə/ is the second vowel in *democratic* but not in *democracy* where the stress pattern is different. Or take the /ən/ sequence—note its spelling in *happen, bobbin,* and *organ* (Brengelman, 1970).

Thus, position in a syllable or word and stress may have an influence on spelling certain phonemes, while others tend to be spelled more invariantly in spite of stress and position.

Therefore, how much invariant spelling—one-to-one, phoneme-grapheme correspondence—was found in the 17,000 common words studied? It is this invariance that can elucidate some of the most important teaching patterns, especially if beginning spellers tend to be more orally than visually oriented. (Remember the self-taught spellers studied by Read.) Thus when children pronounce a word, they can write it in traditional orthography (regular spelling) if there is the invariant correspondence. It was found that "the greatest majority of consonants had single spellings which were used 80 percent or more of the time" in the words investigated (Hanna, Hodges, and Hanna, 1971, p. 81). But this was not true of the vowel phonemes. Only a small number had single spellings, those being /æ/ as in *hat, can;* /ɛ/ as in *set,* pen; and /a/ as in *on* and *top.*

Some of the consonant phonemes found to have at least a 90 percent consistency in spelling in the 17,000 words studied were: /t/ spelled with a letter *t,* /b/ spelled with a letter *b,* /d/ with a letter *d,* /l/ with the letter *l,* /m/ with the letter *m,* /n/ with the letter *n,* /p/ with the letter *p,* and /r/ with the letter *r.*

A second finding was that position of a phoneme in a word could affect its spelling. For example, /e/ is commonly spelled (81 percent of the time) as *a* when the phoneme is in a final position in a syllable in a multisyllabic word, as in *table.* But it's spelled *ay* in *say,* a single syllable word.

Finally, stress was also found to be a factor in spelling, but in a less clear way than position. For example, /č/ is spelled *ch* 97 percent of the time when it is the initial phoneme in a primary stressed syllable. So we have *charcoal,* but *tch* in *fletcher,* which is /č / in a weaker stressed position.

All these factors play a part in determining the patterns of American English spelling. The Hannas, Hodges, and Rudorf then programmed a computer with the phoneme-grapheme correspondence "rules" they had found for the 17,000 words and had it spell the words according to that system of rules, or *algorithm,* as they call it. Although all the information was phonological, the computer spelled 49.8 percent of the 17,000 words correctly. Certainly 50 percent spelling accuracy isn't enough for a speller, but it does show that simply phonological information will yield that high a regularity. There definitely is pattern in the spelling system, despite what is often thought.

Finally, an additional 37% of the words were spelled with only *one* error, for a total of 86.8 percent of the 17,000 words spelled either correctly or with one error. Spellings with two errors occured in 11.4 percent of the words, and only 2.3 percent of the spellings contained three or more errors.

According to the study, several recurrent errors made by the computer accounted for many of the misspellings: misspellings of compound words such as *plaground,* double letter problems as in *adress,* problems with borrowed words—of which there are many in English—whose spelling reflect phoneme-grapheme relationships from different languages, and spelling errors based on morphological rules rather than on phonological ones (which the computer wasn't programmed to handle). Then, of course, there was a small residue of words that are simply irregular: *one, acre, colonel, of.* We recognize that *one* and *of* are usually taught as "sight words" in reading. And there are also *homophones,* those words that sound alike but often have a different spelling. As we know, students sometimes have trouble with *bare* and *bear;* with *aisle, isle,* and *I'll;* with *they're* and *their;* with *its* and *it's;* and with *two, too,* and *to.* Here context and meaning are important. The particular spelling must be correlated with what the word means, since each above homophone does have a different meaning or function from the others.

Many of the misspellings produced by the computer programmed only with phonological rules are of the same sort as those made by beginning spellers. Certainly doubling letters, which is not phonologically marked in English, is a common one. The self-taught spellers Charles Read studied paid no attention to that characteristic of traditional orthography. And how many children have you found spelling *bill* as *bil* or *tanner* as *taner?*

The highly irregular words the computer had trouble with are often called "spelling demons." Although many of them yield to pattern analysis, *to, two,* and *too* are truly demons that still bother some adults. Of course this is a relatively small category of words, representing only about 3 percent of the 17,000 word core vocabulary the study analyzed, but these words may also appear *frequently* in the written language. However, the regularities far outweigh the irregularities in the American English spelling system.

What are some of the regularities in phoneme-grapheme relationships that were found in the study? The chart shows the phonemes with the corresponding graphemes achieving a relatively high degree of

203

regularity in the word positions indicated. For many of the phonemes, the grapheme is invariant in all positions.

Table 6

Phoneme or Phoneme Combination	Spelled	Condition in Which Phoneme Occurred	Example	Percentage of Predictability
		Consonants		
/b/	b	All other cases[a]	rob	
			boy	98.00
/č/	t	In initial position of unaccented syllable and followed by /ə/	posture	100.00
			nature	
	ch	All other cases	church	97.9
			chart	
/d/	d	All other cases	dog, pad	93.3
/f/	f	All other cases	fish, elf	80.4[b]
/g/	g	All other cases	go, agog	92.0[c]
/h/	h	All cases	here, hello	97.9
/hw/ (in some varieties; in others, *what* is pronounced /wət/)	wh	All cases	what, which, when	100.00
/k/	c	All other cases	cow, come	86.1[d]
/ks/	x	All other cases	mix, box, axe	100.0
/kw/	qu	All cases	queen, quick	97.4
/l/	l	All other cases	lamp, label	92.7
/əl/	le	All cases	table, fable, able	95.3[e]
/m/	m	All cases	man, rim, humor	94.3[f]
/əm/	m	All cases	chasm, prism	100.0
/n/	n	All cases	new, fan	97.3[g]
/ŋ/	n	In medial position	sink, pink	98.5
	ng	In word-final position	sing, ring	99.4
/p/	p	All other cases	push, stop	95.8
/r/	r	All cases	run, bar	97.1
/s/	s	All other cases	say, cats	81.00
/š/	t	Initial position of unaccented syllables	fiction, nation	85.7

Table 6 (CONT'D.)

Phoneme or Phoneme Combination	Spelled	Condition in Which Phoneme Occurred	Example	Percentage of Predictability
	sh	All other cases	ship, wash, rasher	81.5
/t/	t	All other cases	toe, rat	97.0
/θ/	th	All cases	thing, both	100.00
/ð/	th	All cases	this, them	100.00
/v/	ve	In word-final position	have, drive	100.00
	v	All other cases	vet, liver	100.00
/w/	w	All other cases	wet, power, plow	98.3
/y/	i	In unaccented syllables	junior	86.3
/ž/	s	In all cases when followed by /ə/	fusion, derision	98.00
		Vowels		
/e/	a	In syllable-final, but not word-final, position	placate, ratable	92.5
/æ/	a	All cases	cat, mat	99.7
/a/	a	All cases	arm, father	92.4
/i/	e	In syllable-final, but not word-final, position	legal, regal, behold (in some varieties)	96.6
/ɛ/	e	In initial position	etch, edge	98.9
	e	In medial position	bet, fetch	92.0[h]
/ay/	i–e	In medial position when next phoneme is word-final	dime, betimes	90.7
/I/	i	All other cases	tip, flippant	94.2
/o/	o	All other cases	told, behold	94.4
/ɔy/	oy	In word-final position	toy, boy	100.00
/æw/	ou	In initial position	out, outer	97.2
	ow	All other cases	how, now	90.0
/ɔ/	o	In all cases	boss, moss	96.8
/U/	u	All other cases	pull, put	81.9
/yu/	u	In syllable-final, but not word-final, position	cupid	93.8 (**Note** stupid)
	u—e	In medial position	cube	81.2
/ə/	u	All other cases	cup, pup	91.6

Source: Adapted from Paul Hanna, Richard Hodges, and Jean Hanna, *Spelling: Structure and Strategies.* Boston: Houghton Mifflin Co., 1971. Used by permission of the publisher.

[a]"All other cases" indicates that other "rules" were included for spelling the phoneme in question, in addition to the rule shown. Rule means "Spelled" column.
[b]Spelled *ph* in a few borrowed words: phone; spelled *gh* after *ou* in five words: laugh.
[c]Spelled *gh* in a few common words: ghost.
[d]Note chi*c*ken and other words with /k/ in the medial position.
[e]Note labe*l* and a few other words that end with *-el*.
[f]spelled *mb* in a few words: bomb, lamb.
[g]Spelled *gn, pn,* and *kn* in a short list: gnat, pneumatic, knight.
[h]Note head and said.

Note the high incidence of regularity in the phoneme-grapheme correspondences on the chart. These correspondences can be especially useful to beginning spellers because of their phonological basis. A student attempting to match sound and letters, especially at the phonemic level, can learn to exploit the patterns of correspondence shown by the Hanna et al study. With less energy expended in this task, the student can turn more attention to learning spellings that do not demonstrate this particular kind of regularity, this so-called surface regularity. I say "so-called" because actually phonemes are abstractions from the actual speech stream as well. Remember the children who spelled *dragon* as *jragn;* they were not responding to phonemic differences.

Fred Brengleman (1970, p. 96) has succinctly summarized this knowledge about the sound-letter relationships in the spelling system of American English. He, too, stresses the regularity and patterns in the system:

1. English consonant sounds have generally predictable spellings. For example, in such homophonous suffixes as -el and -al, -ous, and -ess, the consonant spellings can be predicted from the pronounciation. The vowels must, of course, be identified on the basis of grammatical information.

2. English vowel spellings are predictable (but less so than consonants) in stressed monosyllabic words and in the stressed syllables of polysyllables.

3. In polysyllables vowels whose stress has shifted from strong to weak are spelled as though their stress was strong. Cf. "reform" and "reformation."

4. Affixes often have arbitrary spellings. Cf. "shun" and "-tion," "friendless" and "marvelous."

Because of the fact that English spelling is in general related to larger rules of English structure which the child already masters (e.g., phonological and grammatical rules), spelling can be taught most efficiently by relating orthographical rules to the rules the child already knows.

Implications for Instruction

As teachers of beginning spellers especially, you can first diagnose the initial spelling attempts of a student from the basis of phoneme-grapheme correspondences. Is the student making the connection between sounds and letters? If not, there could be a real problem developing. In my experience with older students, those who couldn't spell were the ones who couldn't make many phoneme-grapheme correspondences. For them, spelling was a laborious process of visual memorization, often with virtually no transfer of the traditional spelling of the word to contexts other than the one in which it was learned. These students seemed unable to exploit phoneme-grapheme correspondences, in reading as well as spelling. Somehow they do not seem to have grasped the connection between the oral and written language. The latter evidently was not related to their speech, but was taught as a strange system with a life of its own. If this can be diagnosed early—when the child is learning to read and write initially—then the correspondence patterns can be stressed. Certainly the spelling process should progress further than this, but the student who spells *action* as *akshun* is far ahead of the student who spells it *tach* (as I have seen some students do).

For the student who doesn't seem to be making phoneme-grapheme correspondences in spelling, you can devise strategies stressing the patterns in American English. For some students, minimal pairs could be a useful strategy. For example, you can have the student contrast:

pit
pat
pot
put
pet

since the "short" vowels are more regularly spelled than are the complex vowel nuclei or "long" vowels. Some reading patterns can also be applied to spelling if they are "reversed" for the production process; a student reading *rate* is usually taught that in single syllable words, the letter *e* indicates that orally the vowel should be "long." Often the pattern is taught by contrast:

fat—fate
rat—rate
mop—mope

In order to help with spelling, it can be pointed out that the so-called long vowel in that medial position often indicates the grapheme needed is the vowel letter + *e* separated by a consonant. The grapheme for many so-called long vowels in single syllable words is actually an *a-e* or *o-e* or whatever. The *e* letter is part of it.

In an even simpler way phoneme-grapheme relationships can be a help to spellers. We know that students will often put in extra letters and make reversals of letters, as well as making substitutions of the *nashun* —*nation* type. Many insertions can be handled by having the student *pronounce* the word as it is written to hear if it "sounds right." For example, let's say *being* is spelled *bienging,* or *minute* as *minutute* or *minutre.* Asking the student to compare the pronunciation of the word he or she has written to the word in traditional orthography can help the student learn to compare phonemes and graphemes. Are there too many, as in the case of *bienging*? (That spelling looks as though predominately visual clues were somehow short-circuited.)

Reversals of letters are also common. Possibly they are due partly to an emphasis on visual cues. For example, if you find *derset* for *desert,* *stearm* for *stream,* or *unerdneath* for *underneath* on a student's paper, you have them read the word aloud to see if they can catch the reversal in spelling. The student will become a more powerful speller by such checking and by becoming more attuned to sound-letter relationships through it.

However, we must remember the type of student Savin found in Philadelphia schools (see Chapter 5). These students evidently could not exploit minimal pairs, since they worked on a syllabic level rather than on a phonemic level. Definitely different spelling strategies must be used with them, ones that are not derived from phoneme-grapheme correspondences. It is likely that stressing the visual component would help, although it's difficult to specify exactly how to accomplish this. Hopefully research with deaf children who obviously cannot exploit phoneme-grapheme correspondences but who do learn to read and spell will provide teachers with useful strategies for students who work on a syllabic level. Certainly we have much to learn about visual features from study of the ways in which the deaf learn to read and write.

After you've diagnosed that a student is able to exploit and use phoneme-grapheme relationships, you can work with some spelling strategies based on the regular patterns of correspondence found in the American English orthographic system. Materials stressing the patterns can be devised for use by your students. But a few words of caution: students learn in different ways. To stress *only* phoneme-grapheme correspondences can still produce spellers who are inadequate. How many times have you heard adults say, "I don't spell very well. I was taught to sound everything out." Obviously, the Hanna, Hodges and Hanna study shows that phoneme-grapheme correspondences can take us only so far. Some of the most commonly used words are "exceptions to the rules." Pronouns are notorious for this: *I, he,* and *she* are irregular. *Of* is irregular. And we could add to this list.

Still, there are important correspondences. At the sound-letter correspondence level, there are patterns students can exploit in learning to spell, which will make their task far easier than will the idea that a word is a unitary part of the written language to be learned as a whole element. (For a more intensive discussion of these patterns and suggested teaching strategies, the reader is referred to the Hanna and Hanna and Lamb references at the end of this Chapter.)

Lexical Spelling Patterns

Words pattern in different ways on different levels. One is the phoneme-grapheme correspondence level discussed previously. There is another level that other researchers' work is making more and more clear. This level that is stressed by researchers such as Carol Chomsky is "below" or more abstract than the sound-letter correspondences dealt with in the research of Hanna et al. Chomsky characterizes the phonemic level as dealing with the surface phonetic form which, as we have seen, does not have a one-to-one correspondence with graphemes in American English. In other words, pronunciation of words will not always clarify their spelling.

The more abstract level used by Chomsky in explaining even more spelling patterns is called the *lexical* spelling level. It underlies the phonological realization of words and represents the abstract forms to which phonological rules are applied to arrive at a pronunciation. Chomsky diagrams this level:

209

$$\text{LETTERS} = \text{segments in } \underset{\text{lexical spelling}}{\overset{\text{phonological rules}}{\longleftrightarrow}} \text{PRONUNCIATION}$$

In other words, letters and letter combinations represent a level below actual pronunciation and do not hook up as directly to sounds as they do in the phoneme-grapheme model. Some researchers call the lexical level the morphemic level, again in an effort to get at a level "deeper" than actual sounds.

One reason such an explanation has validity for many words is that English speakers may vary their phonological system somewhat depending on the variety they speak but, if literate, are generally able to spell the same as any other speaker of English. In other words, the orthographic system is the same for all varieties of English and is usable by literate adults. It does not admit many dialect or sociolect differences. Obviously then there are patterns "below the surface" that adults are able to exploit, irrespective of their phonological system. This can be explained partly by the fact that the phonological differences vary *systematically,* not randomly, and therefore can still pattern with orthographic patterns in turn. For example, for the "*r*-less" speaker of English, there is little difficulty in associating "cah" with *car* or "Cubar" with *Cuba,* since the /r/ phoneme is not realized or realized elsewhere systematically. Also, the theoretical construct indicates that the lexical level is the one with which spellings are correlated: in the "*r*-less" case, the phoneme is realized or not at the level of pronounciation, not at the lexical level. In other words, at this "lower" level, *car* is *car,* although the notation may be different. It's at the phonological level that we hear either /kar/ or /ka/.

The theory of language from which this construct of spelling is derived is transformational-generative grammar, which was used partially as a description of American English in Chapter 2. Much of the information for this construct comes from *The Sound Patterns of English* by Noam Chomsky and Morris Halle,[6] in which many of the phonological rules of American English are described. Again we can think of the generative nature of language, this time in relation to the spelling system.

One of the major principles of orthography found by Chomsky and Halle was that when phonetic variation is predictable by a general rule (by phonological or morphophonemic rules), this variation is not indicated by the spelling system—for example, in the use of /t/, /d/, and /əd/ for the past tense morpheme. In other words, spellings remain invariant even though sounds shift. Another example is a shift from the /e/ phoneme to

---

[6]New York: Harper and Row, 1968.

/æ/ in certain word changes such as *nation* to *national, nature* to *natural,* and *sane* to *sanity*. The grapheme *a* is not shifted to indicate the phonemic (or phonetic as Chomsky calls it) shift. As speakers of American English, we unconsciously know this rule and use it widely—it is called *vowel shifting*. We also use it for:

/i/ to /ɛ/ as in *convene—convention*

/ay/ to /I/ as in *wide—width*

/o/ to /a/ as in *phone—phonic*
           compose—composite

These word pairs are also related because they have the same roots. So what we call traditional orthography better captures the link among the words in a family than does phonetic spelling.

Another example of the regularity in the lexical spelling level that shows the relationship among words is shown in the following word set:

photograph
photography
photographic
photographer

First, say the words aloud and notice the phonological differences—have you ever even noticed them before? Don't be surprised if you haven't, since the spelling of the words captures so well the relationship among them. The phonological differences are not important to adults, and they are not preserved in the spelling. Certainly when we *read* the words silently, they *look* alike. And we know they all belong to the same family, with the same roots: *photo* and *graph*.

In American English, we also have consonant alternations as well as the obligatory vowel alternations mentioned above. Note the following:

/k/ to /s/ as in *medicate—medicine*
           critic—criticize
/g/ to /ǰ/ as in *sagacity—sage*
           prodigal—prodigious
/d/ to /ǰ/ as in *grade—gradual*
           mode—modular[7]

---

[7] Note the vowel alternation rules also apply in these words: from /e/ to /æ/ and /o/ to /a/.

/t/ to /č/ as in *resident—residential*
expedite—expeditious
/z/ to /ž/ as in *revise—revision*

Again, how many of us have noticed those changes? We are used to the printed words and to the automatic phonological shift rules when we speak. Certainly it doesn't seem wise to propose that we spell *residential* as *residenchal,* as it would obscure the relationship between the two words *resident* and *residential.* They are in the same family, come from the same root, and have much the same meaning, one being a noun and the other the adjective form of the noun. These are patterns with sematic links that the pattern *mat-mate* does not have at all. And because semantics plays a role in these patterns, it can be used by students learning to spell as a further cue. If a word means the same as another word or part of a word, they are probably spelled in the same way. As Carol Chomsky (1970) puts it: " . . . on the lexical level and in the orthography, words that *are* the same *look* the same."

There are at least two other common phonetic variations in English that are not recorded in the spelling system: stress placement and vowel reduction. Vowel reduction means that the vowel /ə/ appears in uns-tressed positions in certain words, but another vowel appears when that position is stressed, as in *composition* and *compose* and *celebrate* and *celebrity.* In *composition,* the second *o* grapheme symbolizes the /ə/ vowel sound, while in *compose,* the *o* grapheme stands for /o/. Stress placement appears in speech in some situations to differentiate between a noun and a verb, as in récord (noun) and recórd (verb). (Refer back to Chapter 2 for a fuller discussion of English stress patterns.) Neither stress placement nor vowel reduction, as you can see, are noted in the spelling of the words. But both are prevalent in word families where the /ə/ invariably appears as the vowel sound in an unstressed syllable.

Implications for Instruction

What meaning do these patterns, different from the phoneme-grapheme patterns of the Hanna, Hodges and Rudorf work, have for students learning to spell and for teachers teaching spelling? First, they represent a stage beyond beginning spelling (if what we know about the spelling process is accurate). If children, at first, depend more on phonological information to specify the graphemes they use, as we currently believe, lexical spelling may not be as useful to them. In other words, beginning spellers seem to respond to the surface structure of the phonology of the language and not to the semantic relationship between words, which is clarified in the "deeper" structure of the language. However, we must be aware that some students may be able to exploit the lexical spellings far earlier than others. Also, the *visual* similarity among such families as *photograph, photography,* and *photographic* may be a set of cues that students respond to relatively early. We know there is a strong visual component in mature spelling.

As teachers we can also help develop lexical spelling through studies of word families, prefixes and suffixes, and roots—technically a part of morphology (see Chapter 2). For example, many of the words are of Latin and Romance language origin. And "the full phonological system of English depends heavily on a *learned stratum* [emphasis added] of vocabulary including Latinate forms and a network of affixes [prefixes and suffixes] which account for a large portion of surface phonetic variations" (Carol Chomsky, 1970). Vocabulary study seems in order to accompany spelling development. You can point out to students and help them discover that related words are spelled alike even though they sound different. The visual cues we have mentioned help to reinforce that relatedness. This type of generalization can be begun early in spelling, developed from the words the student is learning to spell, irrespective of the source of those words. And it can be an invaluable aid to older spellers who have moved from vocabulary with easily applied phoneme-grapheme correspondences (as in *cvc* patterns such as *can, fan, man,* and *pan*) to more Latinate vocabulary. Often it is with more mature spellers that we have the most difficulty in helping to develop precision in spelling, because the dictum "sound it out" leads to spellings that aren't "correct."

One of the biggest spelling "problems" is the spelling of /ə/, the reduced vowel, in unstressed syllables in multisyllabic words. Evidently most adult spelling errors involve the spelling of /ə/ and the doubling of letters, a problem of another sort. What sorts of exercises could be used to clarify the spelling of /ə/ in these environments? Carol Chomsky suggests that the student find a related word that phonologically would clarify the vowel letter, giving a list that could look something like:

Words with /ə/ misspelled	Words found to clarify /ə/ spelling
pres_dent	pres*i*de
prec_dent	precede

comp_sition	compose
maj_r	majority
imm_grate	migrate
cons_lation	console
comp_tent	compete

I've had adults tell me that an exercise of this sort is the most useful tactic they have found to help with spelling the reduced vowel /ə/.

Using some of the other patterns for consonant shifts we have mentioned, related words can again be used to clarify the spelling of a consonant. A student might spell *gradual* with a *j* to get *grajul*. Have the student compare *grade* with *gradual* or *native* with *nation* if he or she spells the latter *t* with an *sh* to get *nashun*. Or if you find *richus* for *righteous,* the beginning of the word including the consonant grapheme can be clarified by a comparison with *right*.

Another spelling problem area is that of the so-called silent consonants, which are really graphemes that don't correspond to a phoneme in a given word. *Sign* and *bomb* are good examples. In fact, Carol Chomsky has produced a list of these that again can be clarified by finding a related word in which there is a closer phoneme-grapheme correspondence.

Word with grapheme often omitted (italicized)	Related word
mus*c*le	mus*c*ular
si*g*n	si*g*nature
bom*b*	bom*b*adier
condem*n*	condem*n*ation
mali*g*n	mali*g*nant

One caution: this will work with many Latinate words but may not work with words of Middle or Old English origin. Take *lamb,* for example. It's Old English in origin and has no related word that will clarify the *b* grapheme phonologically. The *b* in *doubt* cannot be recovered in the surface phonology of a related word. According to Albert Baugh (1951), the *b* in that word was introduced to bring it into accordance with its Latin equivalent *dubitare.* This is called *false etymology* and evidently was practiced fairly widely in the sixteenth century and earlier in order to make English more like Latin, which was considered a more prestigous language. It consisted of making a word look more like a Latin word and thus assigning it, in a sense, a false or wrong etymology. People were to think the word was Latin in origin, not Old English. The *b* on *lamb* may have had the same false etymotogical origin, whereas *bomb* comes from the French *bombe* and Italian *bomba*, both languages signaling the *b* grapheme with a corresponding phoneme. Unfortunately English has a certain number of these spellings resulting not from the patterns of the words themselves but from patterns imposed from elsewhere.

Two final notes on the lexical spelling patterns described by Chomsky and Halle: first, many of the lexical patterns can be clarified phonologically. You often can find a word related to the troublesome word in which graphemes correspond more closely to the phonemes. You can suggest *signal* to clarify the spelling of *sign.* Such correspondences can help students make the connection between relatively simply spelled words (those having a more nearly one-to-one, phoneme-grapheme relationship) and multisyllabic words belonging to families making extensive use of prefixes and suffixes as well. Thus these more "mature" patterns can begin to emerge.

Second, we can see that there are patterns in English orthography and that we can help spellers find those patterns. They seem to exist on at least two levels—the phonemic and the lexical—and display the invariance associated with patterns. With a firm grasp of patterns, a developing speller is certainly far more able to deal with the remaining irregularities (which may have to be committed to visual memory). This is far easier than perceiving a vast part of the orthography as irregular, thereby necessitating letter-by-letter memorization. If students do spell phonemically or phonetically at first—or at least rely heavily on the sounds in words—this strategy should be exploited by the teacher. Also to be exploited is the visual similarity among related words. Both can be used if you are aware of these various spelling patterns.

Final Words About Spelling

The patterns of American English spelling described here do not necessarily imply *how* spelling can be most effectively taught. But communicative competence includes both *how* and *what.* A content is learned in some way and then applied to facilitate more effective communication. The information on spelling patterns is the *what,* or content, of spelling, which plays its role in communicative competence in a literate society. One not only reads; one also writes. A student learns to do both—we hope. We certainly see teaching the student to read and write and spell as part of our roles as teachers. Knowledge of the spelling process and of the patterns of American English orthography at least gives us the *what,* the content. And this knowledge may lead us to useful diagnostic and teaching strategies. For example, a student having difficulty spelling the reduced vowel, /ə/, can be helped through the use of word families as we have described. Diagnosis can also be done according to spelling patterns— which ones do the misspellings fit? And an individualized approach can be facilitated by teacher knowledge of the patterns, which represent a content framework for the student's spelling instruction. Thus more instructional options are open because of a greater knowledge of the content of spelling—the patterns in American English orthography.

Bibliography

Brengelman, Fred. *The English Language, An Introduction for Teachers.* Englewood Cliffs, N.J.: Prentice-Hall, Inc., 1970.

Chomsky, Carol, "Reading, Writing, and Phonology," *Harvard Educational Review, 40* (May 1970), 287–309. Also in *Language and the Language Arts,* by Johanna S. DeStefano and Sharon E. Fox. Boston: Little, Brown and Co., 1974, 297–312.

————, "How Sister Got Into the Grog," *Early Years,* Nov. 1975, 36–39ff.

————, "Invented Spelling in the Open Classroom," *Child Language— 1975,* special edition of *WORD,* edited by Walburga von Raffler-Engel. International Linguistic Association, 1976, 499–518.

Chomsky, Noam, and Morris Halle. *The Sound Patterns of English.* New York: Harper and Row, 1968.

Fromkin, Victoria, and Robert Rodman. *An Introduction to Language.* New York: Holt, Rinehart and Winston, 1974.

Hanna, Paul R., and Hanna, Jean S., "The Teaching of Spelling," *The National Elementary Principal,* (November 1965), 19–28. Also in *Language and the Language Arts,* 272–287.

Hanna, Paul R., Richard E. Hodges, and Jean S. Hanna. *Spelling: Structure and Strategies.* Boston: Houghton Mifflin, 1971.

Lamb, Pose, "Linguistics and the Teaching of Spelling" in *Language and the Language Arts,* by Johanna S. DeStefano and Sharon E. Fox. Boston: Little, Brown and Co., 1974, 288–296.

O'Neil, Wayne, "Our Collective Phonological Illusions: Young and Old" in

Language by Ear and by Eye, by James F. Kavanaugh and Ignatius G. Mattingly. Cambridge, Mass.: The M.I.T. Press, 1972.

Personke, Carl, "Generalization and Spelling: Boon or Bust?" in *A Forum for Focus,* by Martha L. King, Robert Emans, and Patricia J. Cianciolo. Urbana, Illinois: The National Council of Teachers of English, 1973.

Read, Charles. *Children's Categorization of Speech Sounds in English.* NCTE Research Report #17. Urbana: National Council of Teachers of English, 1975.

————, untitled mimeo, June 30, 1976.

————, presentation at language arts conference, June 30, 1976, Ohio State University.

Zutell, Jerome B., "Spelling Strategies of Primary School Children and Their Relationship to the Piagetian Concept of Decentration," unpublished Ph.D. dissertation, University of Virginia, 1975.

For Further Reading

Chomsky, Carol, "Reading, Writing, and Phonology," *Harvard Educational Review, 40* (May 1970), 298–309. Also in *Language and the Language Arts* by Johanna S. DeStefano and Sharon E. Fox. Boston, Little, Brown and Co., 1974. pp. 297–312.

This article clearly explicates the notion of lexical level spelling as well as suggests instructional strategies for certain kinds of spelling problems.

Hanna, Paul R., Richard E. Hodges, and Jean S. Hanna. *Spelling: Structure and Strategies.* Boston: Houghton, Mifflin, 1971.

This is a readable book covering a great deal of the area of spelling with special emphasis on phoneme-grapheme relationships and their implications for learning and teaching spelling.

Personke, Carl. "Generalization and Spelling: Boon or Bust?" in *A Forum for Focus* by Martha L. King, Robert Emans, and Patricia J. Cianciolo. Urbana, Illinois: The National Council of Teachers of English, 1973.

A close look at information about the process of spelling as well as much of the most recent work.

Read, Charles. *Children's Categorization of Speech Sounds in English.* NCTE Research Report #17, 1975.

217

This report is a highly detailed analysis of the spelling of self-taught spellers. It's of particular interest in its description of the patterns children use and of the basis of these patterns. It can be an aid in diagnosing certain "misspellings."

Index

Index